JOHN HENRY NEWMAN

ANGLICAN MINISTER, CATHOLIC PRIEST
ROMAN CARDINAL

John Henry Newman

BY J·ELLIOT ROSS

JOHN HENRY NEWMAN

ANGLICAN MINISTER
CATHOLIC PRIEST
ROMAN CARDINAL

W·W·NORTON & COMPANY·INC·
NEW YORK

𝔑𝔦𝔥𝔦𝔩 𝔒𝔟𝔰𝔱𝔞𝔱:

ARTHUR J. SCANLON, S.T.D.
Censor Librorum

𝔍𝔪𝔭𝔯𝔦𝔪𝔞𝔱𝔲𝔯:

✠ PATRICK CARDINAL HAYES
Archbishop, New York

ARCHDIOCESE OF NEW YORK, APRIL 10, 1933

"He was a scholar, and a ripe and good one;
Exceeding wise, fair-spoken and persuasive;
Lofty and sour to them that loved him not,
But to those men that sought him sweet as summer."

HENRY VIII, ACT IV, SC. 2.

CONTENTS

INTRODUCTION

" 'Viderit Deus.' I have lodged my cause with him."
NEWMAN'S JOURNAL, OCTOBER 30, 1867

JOHN HENRY NEWMAN was one of those men whose significance persists beyond their immediate age. The Victorian Era is dead, and many other eminent Victorians have only a sort of archeological interest for us. But Newman was a type and symbol of a most challenging and important development of the nineteenth century, whose challenge and importance have increased, rather than diminished, in the twentieth century. For Newman's birth coincided with one of the lowest depths of indifference to historical Christianity, and he lived to see—and himself largely to influence—a remarkable revival of interest which has not yet exhausted its strength.

The unity of Western Christendom was broken in the sixteenth century by the Protestant Revolt, with remote consequences for religion in our day not at all foreseen by the Reformers. Throughout a large part of Europe, the infallible teaching authority of the Church was discarded in favor of the infallibility of a Book. And an emphasis on private judgment in interpreting this Book led to still further disintegration. Sects multiplied, and bitter controversies as to dogma and usage developed among the Reformers themselves and their descendants.

Out of these conflicts which characterized the sixteenth and seventeenth centuries, there arose in the eighteenth century, among innumerable intellectuals, an indifference and often an opposition to Christianity in almost every form, whether Protestant or Catholic. In very large numbers the intelligentsia turned from the "supernatural" to the "natural," and from Church to State. Christianity ceased to exercise any intellectual control over scientific development. Religion was reduced to an innocuous "Deism," with a "God" who had no interest in mankind and no control over natural forces.

Moreover, as the authority of a Book had been substituted for the teaching authority of Rome, so the authority of the State came to be substituted for the governing authority of a central, supra-national Church. Under a nationalism run wild, organized religion in Protestant Europe was emancipated from the Pope, but it became the subject of King or Parliament. A divided Church could offer no effectual check upon the encroachments of politicians.

Rome's international prestige was diminished, not only by the defection of the northern nations, but also by untoward political and economic events in the so-called Catholic countries. Italy was no longer the inspiration of civilization, as she had been during the Renaissance, but had become the football of surrounding States; Spain had ceased to exist as a world power, in spite of the shell of a colonial empire; the French Revolution disestablished and disendowed the Catholic Church, while Napoleon expelled the Pope from Rome, and made him a prisoner on French soil. Likewise the Industrial Revolution served to put Protestant England in the lead materially.

However, Rome's loss, absolutely and relatively, was not pure gain for Protestantism. For opposed to this shadow of a former Roman Catholic Church was no united Protestant Church, but a series of State Churches, with subordinate non-conformists. When Newman was born at the dawn of the nineteenth century, Rome was everywhere on the defensive, with all the psychological disadvantages of such a position; but the Protestant Churches had become more and more mere departments of the civil government, and they were no longer national in the sense of embracing all who were not Roman Catholics.

And although the serious consequences of this situation for religion were to some extent cloaked in the Protestant countries by the prestige attaching to union with the State, the germs of disease were really present. Instead of an "integral" Catholicism giving a religious orientation to the whole of life, there was a divided Protestantism forced to concern itself with only one segment of living. As intellectual activity had been freed from any religious teaching authority other than a Book, so the political field and then the commercial or industrial became essentially non-religious under the mercantilist and *laissez faire* theories of the economists and statesmen.

In England, the Anglican Church succeeded in escaping disestablishment and poverty, but only at the cost of identifying itself with the ruling aristocracy. And it no longer stood for "historic Christianity." Outside of a very small and rapidly decreasing "High Church" group, "Apostolic Succession," a governing hierarchy, a sacramental system had really ceased to function even as theological theories. The Anglican Church was so "broad" that it could embrace the most latitudinarian viewpoints.

The nineteenth century bade fair to see historic Christianity sink into greater and greater insignificance. And then things began to happen. There was a popular reaction against the horrors of the French Revolution and the tyranny of the Napoleonic régime. It was realized that an omnipotent State, emancipated from all religious influence and control, could be a danger instead of a blessing. French émigrés were received in England, and exercised an influence in breaking down British prejudices against the historical Church as a purely continental institution.

Then, too, the Romantic Movement, literary and artistic in its origins but with inevitable religious connotations, swept through the intellectuals of France and Germany and England. Among other things, the romanticists tried to get into imaginative touch with far distant times, and particularly there was a strain of medievalism running through many of them. Moreover, there was a recognition that cold rationalism could never completely pierce the surrounding world of darkness and mystery, and men were not afraid to believe that there was a transcendental world of beauty and truth. All these aspects of Romanticism had an influence in reviving a consciousness of historic continuity, which had seemed almost universally dead in the Protestant countries. This revival of historical consciousness had important bearings upon religion, for Catholicism emerged as a massive historical fact. In England, Scott's novels especially tended to put Catholicism in a new and favorable light. There was a widespread popular and intellectual interest developed in the religious attitudes of bygone generations of Englishmen when Western Christendom was one.

Just at the moment when the Anglican Church seemed most subservient to the State, and when its Protestant character was most in evidence, a few Oxford scholars raised their voices in stirring protest against these tendencies. Because the first men engaged in such protests were Oxford men, their activities came to be called the "Oxford Movement." And foremost among these men was John Henry Newman. His remarkable intellectual acumen, his profound sincerity and unselfishness, his literary and dialectical ability, united with a vehement enthusiasm, gave Newman a leadership comparable to that of an ancient Hebrew prophet. The perspective of time has but served to clinch his outstanding position in the Movement.

In its wider aspects, the Oxford Movement emphasized a universal and Catholic, as opposed to an individualist, insular and Protestant, conception of Christianity. And it was in opposition to that "liberal" tendency which would eliminate all supernatural religion.

A century's flight has shown that this Oxford revival of interest in "historic Christianity" and supernatural religion was not a mere ephemeral and academic episode. It has continued unabated and vigorous to the present day. Although it has not led to a wholesale return of intellectuals to Catholicism or to any "supernatural" or sacramental religion, still less to the restoration of Christian unity, the Movement has served to increase the number of conversions of individual intellectuals to the Catholic Church, and to strengthen the position of Catholic Christianity in the contemporary world.

Newman's importance lies in the fact that he is a type of this modern tendency, and one of the noteworthy contributors to it. In the sixteenth century, the struggle had been primarily between one idea of religious authority and another, a living teaching organization or a Book. Both sides believed in divine Revelation and in the existence of sacraments. Controversy was principally a matter of quoting Scriptural texts. But it was clear to Newman that in this modern age a defense of Christianity must begin with a defense of supernatural religion itself, rather than with some particular interpretation of a Revelation no longer universally admitted to be divine. Newman was thoroughly alive to the fundamental character of modern doubt, and also to the complete sincerity of many doubters.

As a consequence, Newman did not approach the religious question as a medievalist, nor as a scholastic, nor as one who assumes the basic fact of biblical inspiration. Newman knew that it was futile to quote Scripture against a misconstrued Darwinism or a mechanistic science that refuses any special authority to the Bible. The corrosive influence of "liberalism" had to be met on its own ground. And so Newman grappled in a curiously contemporaneous manner with the problem of reconciling faith with reason, and science with religion. In this respect, Newman has builded for the present and the future, as well as for his own age, and he has contributed important elements to the best thought of our own day.

But beyond this intellectual and religious aspect, Newman's life has a poignantly human interest. It was filled with failures, yet crowned with some stirringly dramatic successes. Newman as a man is of perennial interest, because it was only his upstanding courage under crushing reverses that finally led to victory. In fact, the story of his life might be described as the triumph of failure.

Every schoolboy knows the words Shakespeare puts into the mouth of Cardinal Wolsey in the winter of that courtier's discontent:

"Had I but served my God with half the zeal
I served my king, he would not in mine age
Have left me naked to mine enemies."
(HENRY VIII, ACT III, SC. 2.)

But John Henry Newman served his God with every bit
as much zeal as Wolsey ever showed towards the uxorious
Henry; yet for forty years he was left naked to his enemies. And Newman found his enemies to be those of his
own household, even after changing households. Had
Wolsey been as good a churchman as he was a courtier,
he might have remembered those words, "whom the Lord
loveth He chastiseth"; or that famous exclamation of
Hildebrand, "I have loved justice and hated iniquity,
therefore I die in exile."

Newman had five great failures in his career, any one
of which would have wrecked a man of less determination.
And these failures were all the harder to bear, because his
early success had demonstrated his exceptional powers.

At thirty-three, Newman was the acknowledged head
of the Catholicizing group in the Church of England. As
Gladstone said, Newman's *Tract 90* shook the kingdom.
But in the event, that Tract proved as fatal to Newman
as Anne Boleyn did to Wolsey. The Anglican authorities
disowned Newman as completely and effectually as Henry
did his courtly cardinal.

Whereupon Newman despaired of the possibility of
reconciling the Anglican position with ancient Catholicism,
and made his submission to Rome. This was Newman's
first great failure. But his real farsightedness is demonstrated by the fact that the Catholicizing movement persisted without its leader. And to-day the Anglo-Catholics
are stronger than ever before. They are not only tolerated,
but they have been able to put through Parliament a

Catholic-tending revision of the Book of Common Prayer. Newman's *Tract 90* interpretations of the Thirty-Nine Articles have long ago been admitted as possible.

Shortly after he became a Catholic priest, Newman was asked to head the establishment of a Catholic University in Dublin. Newman failed in this because the Irish Bishops would not or could not give him the necessary support. But to-day the Irish Free State has in Dublin a National University that is practically Catholic.

Then at Cardinal Wiseman's request, Newman undertook a new English translation of the Scriptures. Almost immediately the idea had to be abandoned because the Bishops gave no effective support. But again, Newman was simply ahead of his times. For the Westminster Version has completed the New Testament and is going steadily on.

Newman accepted the editorship of *The Rambler*, a sort of liberal Catholic magazine in contrast with the conservative *Dublin Review*. In two months he was compelled to resign. But under the son of the ultra-conservative William George Ward, *The Dublin* became to a large extent what Newman had dreamt of for *The Rambler*. There really was, as Newman felt, a place in English Catholic life for such an organ.

Finally, Newman had visions of a Catholic intellectual center at Oxford, and bought ground there for the establishment of an Oratory. At the instigation of Manning, Rome blocked the plan. But Manning's successor reversed this policy, and to-day the Jesuits, Benedictines, Dominicans, and other religious communities are in Oxford with the full approval of Rome. Mass is said daily in nearly two dozen places, and Oxford is more of a Catholic center than Newman could have hoped for in his wildest expectations.

It is a strange coincidence that in his Anglican days Newman had selected with Froude, as a kind of motto, those words of Achilles, "They shall know the difference now that I am back." The opposition, if not the jealousy, of one or another Agamemnon in the Catholic ranks had made this incomparable religious warrior keep rather closely to his tent. He was not sulking, like Achilles, but rather sad and heavy at heart to realize his powers, and yet feel helpless to use them in the cause he loved. That intellect, to use Gladstone's phrase, "sharp enough to cut the diamond, and bright as the diamond which it cuts," had to remain largely idle.

But the time came at last when Newman was to be called forth by the supreme authority of his Church. Leo XIII indicated his desire to confer the cardinalatial dignity upon the octogenarian Newman. In his modesty, Newman hinted at the great cross it would be for him at his age to leave his brother Oratorians in England and settle down in Rome. His hint was taken for a refusal, and the matter was dropped. Then friends explained, Leo understood, the honor was conferred. As Newman wrote, "the shadow has been lifted forever"; or as some one else phrased it, "his life went down in a blaze of scarlet."

Out of all these wrecked hopes of Newman, three significant results, lasting to our own day, stand out in clear relief.

First, there is the Anglo-Catholic movement in the English Church. Anyone who wishes to grasp the importance of this religious stirring should read Thureau-Dangin's *The English Catholic Revival in the Nineteenth Century*. The Oxford Movement was a leaven that has leavened to some extent the whole Anglican Church, and we may say even the whole of English life. For the impulse, variously translated, has been felt far beyond the ranks of the Church of England. But for Newman and the ripple he started in 1833, there would not be to-day the free Catholic movement of Walter Orchard, the Congregationalist,[1] nor the similar movements of others too numerous to name.

Secondly, Newman started a flow of conversions to the Catholic Church in England. There has been a steady stream of converts ever since Newman's own conversion in 1845. That stream is not large enough to mean the near conversion of the whole of England, no; but it is large enough to be important. And some of the individual converts in that stream are large enough to give significance to the whole. If Newman had not blazed the way, perhaps Chesterton, different as he is in character and mental outlook, might still be an Anglican.

And thirdly, Newman started in the Catholic Church in England a movement that has revivified it, and, to a large extent, transformed it. Let anyone who wishes to realize the change wrought, read over Newman's description of the condition of Catholics in England during his own boyhood, and contrast this with the present position of Catholics. The Catholics are not by any means the largest religious body in the Kingdom. But Catholics are certainly among the most influential religious groups. And while many other persons participated in this development of the Catholic Church, more is due to Newman than to anyone else. But for his influence, Catholics would not have come out of their shell to the same extent, they

---

[1] Dr. Orchard in 1932 came to the same conclusion as Newman did—submission to Rome.

would not have won the intellectual position they have; while Catholics would have been so much more intransigent that their influence would have been cruelly crippled. Newman gave a set to the Catholic mind that would have been impossible without his conversion.

In all he did, both as an Anglican and as a Catholic, Newman was struggling to put religion on a solid basis to withstand the attacks of modern unbelief. Newman knew the worth and sincerity of many of those who were affected by the trends of modern thought. And he knew, too, the uselessness of mere intransigence, of the "take it or leave it" attitude on the part of those who had no sympathetic understanding of this wrestling with spirits. The Oxford convert finally triumphed, in the sense that he won recognition on all sides for the wisdom of the lines which he laid down for the conflict.

And Newman triumphed because throughout he had been true to himself and to his God. At any one of these critical points in his history, a more politic course might have won a seeming victory. By being disingenuous, the newcomer to Catholicism might have placated the ultra-conservative forces of religion, and thereby have increased his temporary influence with them. But if Newman had been a politician, his ultimate achievement would have been negligible. To-day his soul goes marching on, gathering stature with the years. Newman is more read than any one of his contemporaries in the Oxford Movement. Cardinal Cullen, who was largely responsible for the Dublin failure, is forgotten; Manning is a name; William George Ward, the thorn in his side on the question of papal authority, is hardly even a name. But Newman persists. And Newman persists because he is a symbol of a conflict persisting until to-day.

Since Newman's death in 1890, one monograph on him has followed another. No series of great religious leaders is complete without its biography of Newman. In the United States, as modern and up-to-date a Protestant as Dr. S. Parkes Cadman has given us a study of the great cardinal, while his influence continues to grow outside the English-speaking world. Some of his works and biographical studies have been published in France, Holland, Italy, Germany, and Poland. In fact, a complete edition of Newman's writings—some forty volumes—has been published in Germany under the editorship of Father Daniel Feuling, a Benedictine, and Father Erich Przywara, a Jesuit. In the printed catalogue of the British Museum, thirteen and a half columns are devoted to Newman.

Probably no man of the Victorian Era has influenced modern thought more profoundly than Charles Darwin. And when *The National Dictionary of Biography*, that standard reference work on British celebrities, gives Newman twenty columns as compared with Darwin's twenty-four, we may well conclude that Newman's place in the hall of fame is permanently secured. Disraeli, largely responsible for England's imperialism, gets twenty-seven columns. Comparison with religious leaders of Newman's day is even more illuminating. Pusey, sufficiently prominent in the Oxford Movement to give it for a while the alternative name of "Puseyism," receives sixteen columns; and Charles Kingsley, occasion of the *Apologia*, twelve. Of the Catholics who thwarted some of Newman's dearest projects, Manning has thirteen and a half columns, William George Ward five and a half, and Cardinal Cullen fares worst with three and a half.

Newman's reputation as a religious thinker of perennial interest seems as secure as Pascal's. "Between those two great names," says Professor Sarolea,[1] "—the greatest perhaps in the religious literature of the modern world —a comparison therefore naturally suggests itself. . . Both have turned religious thought into new and deeper channels; they have raised the moral temperature of those who have come under their spell. Consciously they have no doubt worked in the cause of Roman Catholicism in the strict sense of the word, but their influence has exceeded the influence of their Church; for they have been, and continue to be, the delight alike of Catholics and Protestants, of believers and skeptics—and thus unconsciously and above all they have worked in the cause of that wider catholicism which includes all those who believe in the 'Kingdom of God' and who strive to realize it in their lives and hearts."

But no one has summed up Newman's influence better than his friend Richard Holt Hutton: [2] "In a century in which physical discovery and material well-being have usurped and almost absorbed the admiration of mankind, such a life as that of Cardinal Newman stands out in strange and almost majestic, though singularly unpretending, contrast to the eager and agitated turmoil of confused passions, hesitating ideals, tentative virtues, and groping philanthropies, amidst which it has been lived."

[1] *Cardinal Newman,* pp. 125, 135.
[2] *Cardinal Newman,* p. 251.

JOHN HENRY
NEWMAN

CHAPTER I

THE OXFORD DON

"Lead, kindly Light, amid the encircling gloom,
Lead Thou me on!
The night is dark, and I am far from home—
Lead Thou me on!
Keep Thou my feet; I do not ask to see
The distant scene,—one step enough for me."

I F THE battles of England have been won on the cricket fields of Eton, much truer is it that England's religious thinking—and more especially the thinking of the Established Church—has been formed in the common rooms of Oxford. There is an old Latin couplet which aptly expresses this:

Chronica si penses, cum pugnant Oxonienses
Post paucos menses volet ira Angligenenses.[1]

And the names of John Wycliffe, John Wesley, and John Newman, all Oxford products, bear this out.

And so it is not surprising that a religious development in the Anglican Church in the nineteenth century should receive the name of the "Oxford Movement." What is surprising, however, under the circumstances, is the

[1] "When Oxford dons do fight, so history doth say,
Fierce hatred speeds through England's heart without delay."

I

Catholic nature of this movement and the measure of its success. To understand how extraordinary was the Oxford Movement, of which John Henry Newman was the originator and for ten years the dominant spirit, it is necessary to sketch briefly the religious history of modern England.

For the first few years after Luther's revolt, England was practically untouched by Protestant ideas. Henry VIII actually wrote a book *In Defense of the Seven Sacraments,* and was rewarded by the Pope with the title "Defender of the Faith"—a title, curiously enough, kept to this day by the English sovereigns. But when Henry tired of his first wife, Catherine, and, as Shakespeare puts it, his "conscience crept too close to another woman," he repudiated all papal authority because the Pope did not sanction a divorce. The first effect of this schism was merely a sort of "headless Catholicism," for, barring the supremacy of the Pope, the theology and liturgy and sacramental system of the Catholic Church were retained. And had Queen Mary, Henry's daughter, lived longer or been more tactful, the breach with Rome might have been permanently healed.

But the effect of Mary's ill-advised policy, seemingly more Spanish than English, was to arouse an intense nationalism, which the more Protestant party was not slow to utilize. Willingly or not, Elizabeth fell in with the Protestant tendency, and she accentuated the Protestantism of her Church. Under the Stuarts, it is true, Bishop Andrewes and Archbishop Laud attempted to stem the tide, and the term "High Church," as representing Catholic principles (minus the Pope), came into use. But the Calvinistic Puritans were too strong, and they swept away both king and hierarchy. The Anglican or Episcopal Church was supplanted and proscribed.

With the return of the Stuarts, the episcopate was restored and the High Church party attempted a Catholic revival. The Edwardine Book of Common Prayer was revised, and the sacramental and sacerdotal character of the English Church was brought into clearer relief. But the High-Churchmen suffered eclipse in the misfortunes of the Stuarts, and the accession of the Calvinistic William III (1689) made their rout complete.

So many changes in doctrine and practice through a change in political fortune had accustomed men's minds to a religious indifferentism. Thenceforth latitudinarianism prevailed, disdaining all religious enthusiasm, and priding itself on a rational religion broad enough to embrace quite disparate viewpoints. By one of those curious English compromises, the episcopate was retained in name, but it was an episcopate without authority, regarding its creed as a piece of conventional phraseology, and having for its expression a cold and empty form of worship in striking contrast with the richness of the Catholic liturgy. Religious pictures, statues, symbols were taboo; a table replaced the altar, for the Lord's Supper was no longer a sacrifice.

Not all men, however, were satisfied with this indifferentism and coldness, and in the eighteenth century two movements arose to counteract it. In the 1730's, Charles Wesley began an emotional and enthusiastic preaching, emphasizing personal conversion and justification by faith alone, love of Christ, sorrow for sin, fear of hell. Wesley's movement was disowned by the Church of England and became known as Methodism. The general tendency of Methodism was towards a more thoroughgoing Protestantism, and it discarded even the anemically Catholic Book of Common Prayer.

Following in the wake of Methodism, and emphasizing about the same doctrines and practices, the Evangelical movement somehow managed to remain with the Established Church. Like Methodism, Evangelicalism was largely a class movement. Its followers busied themselves with philanthropic measures for the betterment of the working classes. But by the beginning of the nineteenth century, the Evangelicals had to a large extent triumphed over the original contempt accorded them, and had secured an influential following in the English Church. Both Manning and Newman early came under Evangelical influences. The Evangelicals, however, even more than the Methodists, tended to sink the English Church deeper in Protestantism, for they remained in the Church. They had no conception of an episcopate as a depository of "Apostolic Succession," nor of a priesthood as ministers of sacraments. They considered the doctrine of the Real Presence of Christ in the Eucharist as a gross superstition, and auricular confession was anathema.

This, then, was the religious situation in the first quarter of the nineteenth century, when Newman began his career. The English Church was largely dead spiritually, and what religious fervor there happened to be, was non-Catholic or anti-Catholic. Men were dominated by the Protestant prejudice, which Newman was to describe so vividly in his *Lectures on the Present Position of Catholics in England*. They looked upon the Pope as Anti-Christ, the Mass as idolatrous, the veneration of the Virgin Mary and the Saints as blasphemous. Guy Fawkes' Day, commemorating an alleged popish plot, was celebrated with patriotic fervor and with oratory denouncing everything Catholic. With rare exceptions, High-Churchmen no longer stood for the Catholic tendencies of Andrewes and Laud. They were called "High and Dry"—not in the Volstead sense, as the sobriquet "two-bottle orthodox" was common—but to indicate their dullness. "Looking at the ordinary run of the High Church professors and lecturers in both Universities," writes Abbott in *The Anglican Career of Cardinal Newman,* "young men of active minds and religious dispositions could hardly be reproached for using the language of the prophet Ezekiel concerning the vision of the valley of bones: 'There were very many, and lo, they were very dry.' " [1] Oxford was in a rut intellectually and religiously.

Theologically, the Church of England was thoroughly Protestant; politically, it was completely subservient to the State, and exercised little or no influence for social justice. Union with the State meant dominance by the State—a condition technically called Erastian. Her bishops were appointed by the Queen, her laws and her doctrines were determined by Parliament, her internal disputes were judged by lay courts. There were numerous flagrant social injustices in the English laws, but the English Church, apart from a few Evangelicals, did nothing about them. As long as the bishops had plenty to live on, they did not care that debtors might be imprisoned for life, that men did not get a living wage, and that children of five or six had to work. The sees of Canterbury and Durham had incomes respectively of $150,000 and $100,000; the deaneries of Westminster, Windsor and St. Paul's netted from $35,000 to $60,000; and a number of rectories from $25,000 to $50,000 a year.

Anglican historians quite generally admit that al-

[1] I, 47.

though her house still stood, thanks to union with the
State, the religious life of the Establishment was dead.
"For the most part," says Abbott, "the Church sat with
folded hands, unmoved until something occurred touching
its temporalities; or, if it moved at all, it was first to push
itself forward as the opponent of national progress, and
then to slink backward when frightened out of opposition."[1]

When John Henry Newman came up to Oxford in
1817, no observer would have predicted that within a few
years the dry bones of the Church of England, like the
dry bones in Ezekiel's vision, would have new life infused
into them. Still less would anyone have picked the somewhat shy and awkward youth, John Henry Newman, as
the prophet in the case, as the moving spirit of a Catholic
revival in the moribund Establishment. To infuse any
sort of religious vigor into the Church of England seemed
a highly improbable undertaking; but to infuse a Catholic
spirit was to go so much against the tide of Protestant
prejudice and liberal indifference, that, as Manning later
said, it was like making the rivers of England which had
flowed south change their course and flow north.

John Henry Newman was born in Old Broad Street
in the City of London on February 21, 1801. His father,
also John, was a banker. His mother, Jemima Four-
driniers, was of a French Protestant family which left its
native land on the revocation of the Edict of Nantes.
There is no foundation for the suggestion that Newman
was of Jewish descent.

As a boy, the young John was serious-minded, but he
tells us in the *Apologia* that although he had been brought
up to delight in reading the Bible, and knew the catechism

[1] I, 52.

perfectly, he had no definite religious convictions till he was fifteen. Newman's father does not seem to have been particularly religious, but his mother was Evangelical, and at fifteen Newman apparently had the experience of personal conversion, with a conviction that he was predestined to be saved. The reverse of this doctrine, however, that others were predestined to be lost, did not enter his consciousness. Newman rested "in the thought of two, and two only, absolute and luminously self-evident beings— myself and my Creator."

In that phrase we have the key to Newman's later influence, and also to the notable defects in his sympathies. Absorbed in the problem of the relations of the individual soul—his soul—to God, Newman thought and wrote and preached about this subject. Newman's sermons at St. Mary's were largely communings between himself and God. And for those who were going through the same stage of thought, they exercised a marvellous fascination.

But this absorption kept Newman from concerning himself with the practical applications of religion to everyday life, or at least with the social applications of the Gospel. Newman's famous opponent of the *Apologia,* Charles Kingsley, wrote novels and tracts dealing with the industrial problems of the 1830's and 1840's, but Newman's writings show no reflection whatever of these matters. Newman's two novels are religious, not social, and one cannot imagine him writing such a book as Abbé Lugan's *L'Enseignement social de Jésus.*

Much of Newman's earliest childhood was spent at a country home called Grey's Court, near Richmond. The quiet and peace of country life made such an impression on him that he was always haunted by the desire to have a living in the country. And nearly eighty years after leaving that home, he wrote, "I dreamed about it when a schoolboy as if it were paradise. It would be here where angel faces appeared 'loved long since but lost awhile.' "

On May 1, 1808, when he was just a little over seven, Newman was sent to a private school at Ealing, conducted by Dr. Nicholas, of Wadham College, Oxford. Newman himself begged not to be sent to Winchester, and his mother backed him up in this. As Newman never took part in any physical games, was shy, serious, sensitive, he would probably have been most unhappy at a great public school.

When Newman's father was about to make the necessary arrangements for the transfer of his son to a University, he was actually in doubt between Oxford and Cambridge. And the doubt was only resolved when the carriage was at the door. Was it the "kindly Light" which turned that first step of Newman towards the spires of Oxford? At any rate, Newman was entered as a commoner of Trinity College, Oxford, on December 14, 1816, and came into residence the following June.

In spite of his deeply religious youth, Newman's first idea was to study for the law. But his failure in the examinations for a double first led his father to think that he was unsuited for the bar, and his own profound religious tendencies decided his career for Holy Orders.

It was characteristic of Newman that his failure in the examinations did not break him. Newman readily adjusted himself, and went out after a fellowship at Oriel. On April 12, 1822, he received the news of his election to the fellowship while playing the violin, and kept on fiddling until the messenger had gone. Then he flung down the instrument and rushed downstairs with all speed to Oriel.

At this time the Oriel fellows were largely men with liberal tendencies, who afterwards came to be known as the "Noëtics." Chief among them was Whately, later Anglican Archbishop of Dublin. Whately was a brilliant thinker, a logician, a determined realist. From the first, Whately took Newman under his wing, and tried to develop the latent powers he recognized. And it is due to Whately, more than to anyone else, that the shy, diffident, somewhat awkward John Henry Newman of the examination failure became the confident, clear-thinking, brilliant Newman of 1825. In that year, Newman wrote to Whately: "Much as I owe to Oriel in the way of mental improvement, to none, as I think, do I owe as much as to you. I know who it was that first gave me the heart to look about even after my election, and taught me to think correctly, and (strange office in my instructor) to rely on myself."[1]

Among others of the Noëtic school with whom Newman came in contact, and by whom he was influenced, were Copleston, Davison, Hawkins, and Arnold. As Newman says, they called everything in question, and disallowed authority as a judge in matters intellectual. The natural result of such influence was that Newman drew away from the Evangelicals, and that he came to see the impossibility of his reaching religious certitude on Evangelical principles. In a note to the *Apologia* on "Liberalism," Newman says, "the party called Evangelical never has been able to breathe freely in the atmosphere of Oxford, and at no time has been conspicuous, as a party, for talent or learning."

[1] *Letters,* I, 105.

A man of different temperament from Newman, losing his Evangelical moorings, would have become a liberal
in theology. And Newman seems to think that for a time
there was grave danger of this. "The truth is," he wrote
nearly forty years later in his *Apologia,* "I was beginning
to prefer intellectual excellence to moral; I was drifting
in the direction of the Liberalism of the day." [1]

But we may well look upon this statement as the
exaggeration of an over-sensitive conscience. For as far
as one can learn from Newman's own account of his religious opinions in the *Apologia,* his drifting does not
seem to have gone much farther than a very keen and
sympathetic understanding of the liberal objections to
divine faith. Newman chronicles quite clearly the additions to his religious beliefs received during this period
from these very men of Oriel. From Hawkins he took the
idea that Tradition is necessary as well as the Bible, and
from reading suggested by Hawkins the idea of baptismal
regeneration; from William James, about 1823, the doctrine of Apostolic Succession; and from Whately, the idea
of the Church as a substantive organization independent
of the State.

From this it can be seen that Newman was instinctively making a selection from his environment of the
Catholic-tending principles held by one or another of the
otherwise liberal group. It was no accident, therefore,
that Newman gradually grew away from the Noëtics,
and came to be influenced by, and in his turn to influence,

---

[1] P. 14. Newman defines Liberalism as "the mistake of subjecting to human judgment those revealed doctrines which are in their
nature beyond and independent of it, and of claiming to determine
on intrinsic grounds the truth and value of propositions which rest
for their reception simply on the external authority of the divine
word."

such men as Pusey and Hurrell Froude. It was Pusey
who had the curacy of St. Clement's offered to Newman
in May, 1824. Newman accepted, and took Orders in that
same year.

In 1826, Newman resigned his curacy to accept the
position of public tutor of Oriel. Two years later he was
made Vicar of St. Mary's, a church which will always be
associated with his name.

Almost coincident with Newman's appointment as
tutor, came an acquaintance with Hurrell Froude. By
1828 the acquaintance had ripened into friendship. "It is
difficult," wrote Newman years later, "to enumerate the
precise additions to my theological creed which I derived
from a friend to whom I owe so much. He taught me to
look with admiration towards the Church of Rome, and
in the same degree to dislike the Reformation. He fixed
deep in me the ideal of devotion to the Blessed Virgin, and
he led me gradually to believe in the Real Presence." [1]

In proportion as Newman "moved out of the shadow
of that liberalism which had hung over" his course, his
"early devotion to the Fathers returned; and in the Long
Vacation of 1828" he "set about to read them chronologi-
cally." One result of Newman's reading was *The Arians
of the Fourth Century*. The subject was interesting to
Newman because he thought he saw a parallel between
the condition of the true Church at that time, and the
Anglican Church of his own day. It was when the parallel
broke down that he became a Catholic. But that was not
to be for a dozen years.

In some ways things had not been going very well
for Newman at Oriel. He was not a success as an ex-
aminer, and the Provost had decided not to give him any

[1] *Apologia* (Oxford University Press), p. 127.

more pupils. No doubt this failure was a cross to Newman, but he was freed for more important work than tutoring undergraduates. Newman's influence as a preacher increased, and he gradually became the religious leader of a group.

Partly because of the situation at Oxford, partly because his work on the Arians had exhausted him, Newman welcomed the chance of a voyage with Hurrell Froude in December, 1832. They visited Italy, northern Africa, and Greece. Naturally the Christian associations connected with all these places profoundly affected Newman. Rome, particularly, made a deep impression. Yet Newman's deliberate verdict was:

"As to the *Roman* Catholic system, I have ever detested it so much that I cannot detest it more by seeing it; but to the Catholic system I am more attached than ever, and quite love the little monks [seminarians] of Rome; they look so innocent and bright, poor boys! And we have fallen in, more or less, with a number of interesting Irish and English priests. I regret that we could form no intimate acquaintance with them. I fear there are very grave and far-spreading scandals among the Italian priesthood, and there is mummery in abundance; yet there is a deep substratum of true Christianity; and I think they may be as near truth at the least as that Mr. B., whom I like less and less every day." [1]

From Rome, Newman went to Sicily, and was ill there alone for three weeks with a dangerous fever. On his homeward voyage to Marseilles, when becalmed in the straits of Bonifacio, Newman wrote on June 16, 1833, his famous hymn,

[1] *Letters*, I, 378.

LEAD, KINDLY LIGHT

"Lead, kindly Light, amid the encircling gloom,
  Lead Thou me on!
The night is dark, and I am far from home—
  Lead Thou me on!
Keep Thou my feet; I do not ask to see
The distant scene,—one step enough for me.

"I was not ever thus, nor prayed that Thou
  Shouldst lead me on.
I loved to choose and see my path; but now
  Lead Thou me on!
I loved the garish day, and spite of fears,
Pride ruled my will: remember not past years.

"So long Thy power hath blest me, sure it still
  Will lead me on
O'er moor and fen, o'er crag and torrent, till
  The night is gone;
And with the morn those angel faces smile
Which I have loved long since, and lost awhile."

Newman came back to England full of health, and
eager to throw himself into the defence of the English
Church. The Government had introduced a bill to sup-
press a number of the Established Church's bishoprics in
Ireland, and Newman and his friends looked upon this
as the forerunner of similar steps in England. The action
of the Government seemed to imply a very dangerous
supremacy of the State over the Church. It was part of
what Newman called liberalism—in religion, he is careful
to say, not in politics. Newman was not concerned with
the question of whether or not the sees should be suppressed, but only with the usurpation of authority by the
State in suppressing them. Similarly, Newman in 1829
had opposed Catholic Emancipation, not because he advocated the persecution of Catholics, but because he

thought the supporters of the movement were dominated by religious liberalism or indifferentism.

Keble, Froude, and Palmer had already in the Oriel common room discussed the critical ecclesiastical situation, and had pledged themselves to write and associate in defence of the Church. Of course, the Church of England had really long been subservient to the State, but the consequences had been largely concealed while there was a Tory Government friendly to the Church. When the Government apparently turned against the Church, the real situation was revealed, and many friends of the Church were roused. On July 14, 1833, preaching the Assize Sermon before the University of Oxford, Keble delivered his famous discourse on *The National Apostacy*, and the Oxford Movement had begun.

The Tracts for the Times started to appear in September, 1833. Their first object was to defend the Apostolic Succession and the integrity of the Book of Common Prayer. In this, the Tractarians could claim to be merely reviving the teaching of the great Anglican divines of the sixteenth and seventeenth centuries. The fundamental principle, however, for which the Tractarians fought, was the spiritual independence of the Church and the defeat of Erastianism. With the exception of Pusey's contributions, the *Tracts* were not signed. They were independent, however, and the authors differed in details.

With the *Tracts*, Newman entered upon the last phase of his Anglican career. And although the immediate occasion of the *Tracts* was a defence of the Establishment against the encroachments of the State, Newman all along was concerned with a deeper problem. The tendencies of the Noëtic school had shown him that the fundamental question was the relation of all religion to rationalism.

And he felt instinctively that unless a firmer foundation could be found for religion than the current theology of the Anglican Church, the victory must rest with negation. Newman thought that he could find this basis in the Catholic tradition latent in Anglicanism. The frills of ritualism never interested him, and the services he conducted at St. Mary's were austere in their simplicity.

Newman's sermons preached before the University at this time are a better index of his mind than his contributions to the *Tracts*. All of these University sermons deal with the relations between reason and faith. The preacher was trying to show the reasonableness of faith. He started with the fact that men hold to revealed religion with as much certitude as they hold to innumerable other propositions. And he undertakes to answer the question, Can such certitude be intellectually justified?

It was not Newman's purpose to attempt a metaphysical demonstration, nor a theological disquisition, but rather a psychological study of the process by which the ordinary Christian gives assent to his creed. If anything in Newman's work is original, it is his contribution to this problem. For he did not set out to follow previous theologians, whether Catholic or Protestant, much less to seek help from the Fathers he was so assiduously reading. His main source of information was his own heart, and no one was ever keener at introspection.

Newman's argument, influenced somewhat by Keble and Bishop Butler's *Analogy*, is summed up in the *Apologia:* "That that absolute certitude which we were able to possess, whether as to the truths of natural theology, or as to the fact of a revelation, was the result of an *assemblage* of concurring and converging probabilities, and that, both according to the constitution of the human mind and the will of its Maker; that certitude was a habit of mind, that certainty was a quality of propositions; that probabilities which did not reach to a logical certainty, might create a mental certitude; that the certitude thus created might equal in measure and strength the certitude that was created by the strictest scientific demonstration; and that to have such certitude might in given cases and to given individuals be a plain duty, though not to others in other circumstances." [1]

But Newman knew as well as anyone else that he had not exhausted the subject. In 1843 he wrote to Archdeacon Manning: "My *University Sermons* were a course begun; I did not finish them." [2] Thirty years later he was to return to the task in his *Grammar of Assent,* and to treat the question at more length. Nevertheless, these *University Sermons* are still profitable reading for anyone interested in the perennial problem of reason and faith.

During these same years, Newman was also preaching his *Parochial and Plain Sermons* in St. Mary's. And it was through these sermons, principally, that Newman became the great religious leader of the day. For fifteen years, his intellectual reputation had been high; he now became a religious prophet. "These sermons belong," says Dean Stanley, "not to provincial dogma, but to the literature of all time." "The influence of his singular combination of genius and devotion," writes Dean Lake, "has had no parallel before or since." On their publication in book form, Newman's sermons drove out all other sermons, as Scott's novels had superseded all other attempts in their field.

[1] *Apologia* (Oxford University Press), p. 122.
[2] *Correspondence of J. H. Newman with Keble & Others,* p. 276.

J. A. Froude, who took the other turning from Newman and became an agnostic, was an undergraduate at Oxford during the height of Newman's influence, and he has left us a very vivid description of the preacher of St. Mary's. "His appearance was striking. He was above the middle height, slight and spare. His head was large, his face remarkably like that of Julius Caesar. The forehead, the shape of the ears and nose, were almost the same. The lines of the mouth were very peculiar, and I should say exactly the same. I have often thought of the resemblance, and believed that it extended to the temperament. In both there was an original force of character which refused to be molded by circumstances, which was to make its own way, and become a power in the world; a clearness of intellectual perception, a disdain for conventionalities, a temper imperious and wilful, but along with it a most attaching gentleness, sweetness, singleness of heart and purpose. Both were formed by nature to command others, both had the faculty of attracting to themselves the passionate devotion of their friends and followers." [1]

Aubrey De Vere in describing Newman said that his "slight form and gracious address might have belonged to a youthful ascetic of the middle ages or to a graceful high-bred lady of our own days." Lytton Strachey and J. L. May have fastened on this expression of De Vere to describe Newman's appearance as being effeminate. And they have repeated and reiterated the phrase until it is this particular point which stands out. But De Vere's words, if carefully noted, do not indicate that Newman's appearance was effeminate. And no matter what his appearance, Newman was not effeminate in the sense of being

[1] *Short Studies,* IV.

weak. The way he triumphed over failures that would have broken many a strong man is ample evidence of his vigorous character. If Newman was effeminate, it was with the effeminacy of an Elizabeth of England or a Catherine of Russia.

"This movement [of Newman's at Oxford], however, when at its height," writes another eye-witness, Principal Shairp, "extended its influence far beyond the circle of those who directly adopted these views. There was not, in Oxford at least, a reading man who was not more or less directly influenced by it. Only the very idle or the very frivolous were wholly proof against it. On the others it impressed a sobriety of conduct and a seriousness of mind not usually found among large bodies of young men. It raised the tone of average morality in Oxford to a level which perhaps it had never before reached. You may call it overwrought and too highly strung. Perhaps it was. It was better, however, for young men to be so, than to be doubters and cynics.

"If such was the general aspect of Oxford society at that time, where was the centre and soul from which so mighty a power emanated? It lay, and had for some years lain, mainly in one man—a man in many ways the most remarkable that England had seen during this century, perhaps the most remarkable whom the English Church has produced in any century—John Henry Newman."

A biographer paraphrasing the language of Newman's contemporaries to describe his influence and position might be thought to have fallen into the mistake so natural to biographers of exaggerating the importance of their subject. And so it is best to let the men who knew Newman speak for themselves.

"The influence he had gained, apparently without setting himself to seek it," continues Shairp, "was something altogether unlike anything else in our time. A mysterious veneration had by degrees gathered round him, till now it was almost as if some Ambrose or Augustine of elder ages had reappeared. He himself tells you one day, when he was an undergraduate, a friend with whom he was walking in the Oxford street, cried out eagerly, 'There's Keble!' and with what awe he looked at him. A few years, and the same took place with regard to himself. In Oriel Lane light-hearted undergraduates would drop their voices and whisper, 'There's Newman!' when with head thrust forward, and gaze fixed as though on some vision seen only by himself, with swift, noiseless step he glided by. Awe fell on them for a moment, almost as if it had been some apparition that had passed. For his inner circle of friends, many of them younger men, he was said to have a quite romantic affection, which was returned with the most ardent devotion and the intensest faith in him. But to the outer world he was a mystery."

"What were the qualities that inspired these feelings?" asks Shairp. And he puts his finger squarely upon the essential characteristic of Newman, his religiousness. "There was, of course, learning and refinement. There was genius, not indeed of a philosopher, but of a subtle, original thinker, and unequalled edge of dialectic, and these all glorified by the imagination of a poet. Then there was an utter unworldliness, the setting at naught of all things which men most prize, the tamelessness of soul, which was ready to essay the impossible. Men felt that here was

> 'One of that small transfigured band
> Which the world cannot tame.' "

"It was this mysteriousness which, beyond all his gifts of head and heart, so strangely fascinated and over-awed,—that something about him which made it impossible to reckon his course and take his bearings, that soul-hunger and quenchless yearning which nothing short of the eternal could satisfy. This deep and resolute ardor, this tenderness yet severity of soul, were no doubt an offence not to be forgiven by older men, especially by the wary and worldly-wise; but in this lay the very spell which drew to him the hearts of all the younger and more enthusiastic. Such was the impression he had made in Oxford just before he relinquished his hold on it. And if at that time it seemed to persons at a distance extravagant and absurd, they may have learnt since that there was in him who was the object of this reverence enough to justify it." [1]

If at the very time, as Principal Shairp says, the reverence paid to Newman seemed extravagant to those at a distance, who had not come under Newman's spell, to us at this late day it seems fantastic and untrue. And so it has been necessary to give this long quotation from an eye-witness to overcome a natural skepticism. Equally strange does it seem to us who never heard that matchless voice, that the style of Newman's preaching should ever have produced the results it did. There was nothing of the traditional orator about him, and he read his sermons. As one goes over these talks given at St. Mary's— "Plain" is certainly an appropriate adjective for them— one wonders how men like Froude and Gladstone and Shairp should ever have been so enamored of them. Would Newman have the same effect in Oxford to-day, with this blasé and disillusioned post-war generation? Or would he

[1] *Studies in Poetry,* essay on Keble.

be able to draw a crowd and hold it at some American university, or in a church in New York or Chicago?

Those who wished to hear Newman at St. Mary's had to miss a hot dinner. The Heads of Houses had changed the dinner hour for this very purpose—an illustration of the pettiness to which human beings will descend in a struggle to advance their cause. But the Heads of Houses were not only uncharitable, they were unwise, for such persecution always helps the persecuted. The attendance at St. Mary's was increased rather than diminished, although it is true that Newman rarely had a crowded church. Shairp says that St. Mary's was usually about half filled—a few hundred people.

"The service was very simple—no pomp, no ritualism," Shairp tells us. "When he began to preach a stranger was not likely to be much struck, especially if he had been used to pulpit oratory of the Boanerges sort. Here was no vehemence, no declamation, no show of elaborate argument, so that one who came prepared to hear a 'great intellectual effort' was almost sure to go away disappointed. Indeed, I believe that if he had preached one of his St. Mary's sermons before a Scotch town congregation, they would have thought the preacher a 'silly body.'

"The delivery had a peculiarity which it took a new hearer some time to get over. Each separate sentence, or at least each short paragraph, was spoken rapidly, but with great clearness of intonation; and then at its close there was a pause, lasting nearly half a minute; then another rapidly and clearly spoken sentence, followed by another pause. It took some time to get over this, but, that once done, the wonderful charm began to dawn on one. The look and bearing of the preacher were as of one who dwelt apart, who, though he knew his age well,

did not live in it. From the seclusion of study, and abstinence, and prayer, from habitual dwelling with the unseen, he seemed to come forth that one day of the week
to speak to others of the things he had seen and known.
Those who never heard him might fancy that his sermons
would generally be about apostolical succession or the
rights of the Church, or against Dissenters. Nothing of
the kind. You might hear him preach for weeks without
an allusion to these things. What there was of High
Church teaching was implied rather than enforced. The
local, the temporary, and the modern were ennobled by
the presence of the catholic truth belonging to all ages
that pervaded the whole. . .

"To call these sermons eloquent would be no word
for them; high poems they rather were, as of an inspired
singer, or the outpourings as of a prophet, rapt yet self-
possessed. And the tone of voice in which they were
spoken, once you grew accustomed to it, sounded like a
fine strain of unearthly music." [1]

"Modern English literature has nowhere any language
to compare with the style of these sermons, so simple
and transparent, yet so subtle withal; so strong yet so
tender; the grasp of a strong man's hand, combined with
the trembling tenderness of a woman's heart, expressing
in a few monosyllables truths which it would have cost
other men a page of philosophic verbiage, laying the most
gentle yet penetrating finger on the very core of things,
reading to men their most secret thoughts better than
they knew them themselves." [2]

In April, 1839, Newman began a systematic reading
of the Monophysite heresy. As the name implies, this

[1] *Ibid.,* 11-12.
[2] Shairp, *Aspects of Poetry,* p. 443.

heresy practically restricted Christ to one nature, in that the divine nature had absorbed the human. Eutyches had been the protagonist of the Monophysites, and Pope Leo I their great opponent. As Newman read the details of this ancient controversy, the fact dawned upon him that a living authority had decided the matter. The influence of Pope Leo forced itself upon his attention, and he recognized in a letter to Rogers, "the great power of the Pope, as great as he claims now, almost." For the first time a doubt of the validity of his *via media* for the Anglican Church insinuated itself into his mind.

"My stronghold," wrote Newman, "was Antiquity." But the Monophysites had appealed to antiquity, and the Church had disallowed the claim. "Now here in the middle of the fifth century, I found, as it seemed to me, Christendom of the sixteenth and nineteenth centuries reflected. I saw my face in that mirror, and I was a monophysite. The Church of the *Via Media* was in the position of the Oriental communion, Rome was, where she now is; and the Protestants were the Eutychians. . . It was difficult to make out how the Eutychians or Monophysites were heretics, unless Protestants and Anglicans were heretics also." [1]

On top of this jolt from Newman's reading on the Monophysite heresy, came Wiseman's article in *The Dublin Review* comparing the Anglicans with the Donatists. Originally only a schism in the African Church, the Donatists (so called from one of their leaders, Donatus) had drifted into heresy on baptism and other matters. St. Augustine of Hippo was their famous opponent. Like the Anglicans, the Donatists had appealed to antiquity and claimed to belong to the universal Church. Augustine re-

[1] *Apologia*, V.

plied, that for a religious group to belong to the Church, it was necessary for the Church to acknowledge the membership. And Augustine used about Rome, the center of unity, a phrase that kept ringing in Newman's mind, *securus judicat orbis terrarum*. "By those great words of the ancient Father (interpreting and summing up the long and varied course of ecclesiastical history), the theory of the *Via Media* was absolutely pulverized."

The extreme Protestant position in Newman's time was that of private judgment. The Bible and the Bible only, privately interpreted, was the cry. In contrast to this was the position of Rome, accepting Tradition as well as the Bible, and maintaining that both Scripture and Tradition needed a living interpreter. Realizing from his association with the Noëtics that private judgment really leads to rationalism, Newman had thought to find a middle ground for the Anglican Church in accepting Tradition as well as the Bible. But gradually the conclusion forced itself upon him that some living authority was necessary to determine what was and what was not Tradition. Otherwise, it was private judgment deciding. Newman's *via media* was merging with rationalism, and he shrank from that position.

While Newman was struggling with these doubts, some of the younger men in the Movement became restless. They saw more clearly than their leader the Romeward tendency of his thought, or at least they were willing to accept conclusions leading in Rome's direction. William George Ward, particularly, was rigorous in his logic. He pestered Newman with conclusions drawn from Newman's own premises. And then he quoted Newman as acknowledging the validity of the conclusions. Newman was annoyed. He hesitated. He delayed. He wished to work out his own conclusions quietly and calmly.

Newman began to see that some of those in the Oxford Movement might be carried on to Rome. He himself recognized that Roman Catholics in England really belonged to the Universal Church, and no longer spoke of them as being in schism. Presumptions shifted. Rome was in a stronger position than the Anglican Church. And it became increasingly necessary to interpret the Thirty-Nine Articles of the Anglican Church in a Catholic sense. Such an interpretation was the object of the famous *Tract 90* published in February, 1841.

In *Tract 90,* Newman undertook to interpret the Articles in a way that would be consistent with Catholic doctrine. He claimed that the framers of those Articles had intended to be obscure and ambiguous. They wanted to satisfy the Protestants at the same time that they made it possible for Catholics to subscribe. Whether Newman was right or wrong historically, his interpretation is accepted to-day as perfectly possible. Anglo-Catholics and Modernists alike find no difficulty in subscribing to the Articles, and their subscription arouses no storm of popular protest.

Abbott, a very unfriendly critic of Newman, says that "a school of thought in the English Church, widely differing from his, must admit a debt to the author of *Tract 90* for an elastic interpretation of the Articles which has led to a lightening of their heavy yoke, and to the greater freedom enjoyed by all the clergy." [1] And certainly Newman was putting no more artificial construction upon these Articles than good Protestants put on many

[1] *The Anglican Career of Cardinal Newman,* I, vi.

passages of Scripture in order to reconcile them with modern thought.

But at the time, *Tract 90,* as Gladstone said, shook the kingdom. And first of all, it shook Oxford. Tait, the future Archbishop of Canterbury, and three other tutors formally protested. A week later the Hebdomadal Board of the Heads of Houses censured the *Tract.* The Bishop of Oxford sent a formal message objecting to *Tract 90* and recommending a suspension of the whole series. Newman published a second edition with changes and additions intended to meet the criticisms, but they failed completely to fulfill this intention. At the same time he wrote to the Bishop expressing his willingness to discontinue the *Tracts.*

Bishop after Bishop issued official Charges against the *Tracts,* emphasizing the Protestant character of the Church of England. Then came the affair of the bishopric of Jerusalem. By an agreement with the Lutherans, the English primate consecrated a bishop to rule not only the Anglicans in Jerusalem, but the Lutherans and Calvinists. Nothing could show more clearly that the rulers of the English Church looked upon it as completely Protestant.

What Newman suffered when many of his friends began to waver and his own doubts to thicken, can be read between the lines of the last sermons he preached at St. Mary's.[1] Now he seems to see himself as Balaam, producing results he had never intended; now as Elijah fulfilling his mission in a world when the heaven above is dark and the stars are hidden; now as the exiled Israelite singing the song of the Lord in a strange land; and at last as Jacob, "parting with all that his heart

---

[1] The last five *Sermons on Subjects of the Day.*

loved," and setting out upon a dreary way over Jordan into a strange country.

Newman's position in Oxford grew more and more difficult. His visits to Littlemore, a tiny village near Oxford and within the parish of St. Mary's, where Newman had a cottage and chapel, became more and more frequent and lengthy. Finally, on April 19, 1842, Newman went to his cottage at Littlemore for good. Everyone else knew that the logic of events was irresistibly pushing him onwards to Rome, but Newman himself would not be hurried. He loved the Church of his childhood too much; the break with old traditions and with carefully thought out intellectual positions was too serious for him to move hastily. Newman gave himself three years for the problem.

During the Oxford Movement, Newman had been almost intimate with Henry Edward Manning, then Rector of Lavington, and connected by marriage with Bishop Wilberforce. Like Newman, Manning had been early under Evangelical influence. But in 1835 Manning offered his services to Newman as a translator for some of his series of the Fathers. The closeness of the two men can be gauged by the fact that "the only allusion to his [Manning's] wife's death, excepting the bare announcement of the fact in a letter to Mr. Gladstone, to be found in the whole of Manning's correspondence, was in a letter to Newman, dated October, 1837." [1]

But while intimate with Newman, Manning did not break entirely with the Evangelicals. In this, Manning need not have been insincere. Like any good political realist, Manning recognized that his advancement depended upon being trusted by the Protestant element. And perhaps Manning argued with himself, as so many

[1] Purcell, *Life of Cardinal Manning*, II, 225.

others have argued, "Get a reputation for dependability, and afterwards you can indulge your more personal and idealistic inclinations." But Manning's fundamental sincerity is evidenced by his later giving up a most promising career in the Church of England to become a Catholic.

At any rate, Manning accepted an invitation to preach the Guy Fawkes' Day sermon at Oxford, November 5, 1843. Manning lived up to the traditions of the day, and his sermon was ultra-Protestant, with plenty of vigorous attacks on the Church of Rome. There was not the slightest thing that could be held against him by the dominant party. And though Manning can be absolved from playing politics, even by such an observer as Arnold Lunn, it would seem to have been extremely bad taste for Manning to preach such a sermon in Newman's old pulpit of St. Mary's so shortly after the magic voice of the leader had ceased to be heard there.

This sermon was a bold stroke by the Archdeacon of Chichester. But the sermon was mild compared with the boldness of what followed. Newman's personal friends in Oxford were deeply hurt, and some of them refused to speak to Manning after the sermon. Manning, however, went to Littlemore to call on Newman. He received word that Newman was "not at home." Manning understood the meaning of the phrase, and so did all Oxford. For under the circumstances, Newman took Manning's sermon as a personal affront. In the eyes of sincere men of all parties, Newman came through the incident better than Manning.

Later Manning and Newman were to break irrevocably—although there was to be nothing unseemly in their public relations—but at this time, Newman with his usual magnanimity forgave Manning. Their relations were renewed through correspondence. In this Manning showed himself a superb judge of character, for his calculation that he could prove himself an ultra-Protestant and still keep Newman's friendship was correct. And the incident is a refutation of the assertion that Newman always demanded complete agreement as the price of his friendship.

In the meantime, left without the restraining hand of Newman after his retirement to Littlemore, William George Ward and his friends emphasized the Roman tendency of the Tractarian Movement. In the summer of 1844, Ward published his book, *Ideal of a Christian Church,* which gave him the nickname of "Ideal Ward." Convocation on February 13, 1845, condemned the book and deprived the author of his degrees. A vote of censure on *Tract 90* was proposed at the same meeting, but was defeated. The trek towards Rome commenced.

The Romeward movement was to include such names as W. G. Ward, Capes, Frederick Oakeley, Frederick Faber, Albany, Christie, J. B. Morris, G. Ryder, and David Lewis. Wiseman, the leader of the Roman Catholics in England, was eagerly watching, and had great hopes of actual reunion between Rome and England. He sent Bernard Smith, a recent convert, to Littlemore for a report on Newman. Smith's visit took place on June 26, 1845, and although he could not break through Newman's reserve, he reported that the end was near—because Newman had worn gray trousers.

Newman was living a life of ascetic seclusion at Littlemore, his days devoted to prayer and study. Divine office was recited daily. There were but two meals—breakfast, consisting of tea, bread, and butter, and dinner. In Lent no meat was eaten. Silence was maintained for half the day. In the afternoon Newman took his companions for a walk.

Living with Newman were his dear friends Richard Stanton, J. B. Dalgairns, and Ambrose St. John. St. John became Newman's great help and consolation in later years, and it was to him Newman wrote that beautiful tribute, worthy of a place with Ruth's declaration to Naomi, in the closing paragraphs of his *Apologia:* "And to you especially, dear AMBROSE ST. JOHN; whom God gave me, when he took everything else away; who are the link between my old life and my new; who have now for twenty-one years been so devoted to me, so patient, so zealous, so tender; who have let me lean so hard upon you; who have watched me so narrowly; who have never thought of yourself when I was in question."

Occasionally Newman went to Oxford to visit Pusey. Oakeley, Church, Pattison, Palmer, and other Oxford friends called or dined at intervals. It was during this time that Newman went up to London now and then to sit for his portrait by Richmond.

During these last months of his Anglican life at Littlemore, Newman wrote his *Essay on the Development of Christian Doctrine*. Without doubt, this is Newman's greatest and most original contribution to religious thinking. It is a remarkable case of intuition. Fifteen years before Darwin's formulation of the theory of evolution, Newman was applying this idea of evolution—or development—to religious dogma. It would have been a significant feat for Newman to have done this after Huxley and Spencer had popularized evolution and the theory was being applied to everything under the sun. It was still more significant for Newman to anticipate any such theory of evolution. If Newman had called his book *An Essay on the Evolution of Christian Doctrine,* the title would have been equally appropriate and the philosophical insight of its author would have been clearer to the man in the street.

As a Protestant, Newman had grown up in an atmosphere that emphasized the divergencies between the apparent teachings of the New Testament and those of Catholicism. At first he had thought that these divergencies presented a strong case against the historical continuity of Roman doctrine. But the farther Newman delved into patristic lore, the more his easy Protestant assumptions were shaken. And in the quiet of Littlemore Newman set himself seriously to answer the question whether or not these Roman variations could be reconciled as actual necessary parts of a homogeneous whole.

The thesis of Newman's book, in brief, is that a Church is a living organism, and as a living organism it must grow. The growth of a Church, however, concerns not merely an increase in adherents, but a growth of doctrine. What has first been merely implicit in the beliefs of the Church becomes explicit. The Anglican creed accepted the additions made by the Councils of the first four centuries. But these Councils added to the primitive explicit doctrines, just as really as ever Trent added to them. And historically, those bodies of Christians which had refused to accept these explicit additions had been sloughed off from the main body. In many instances they had ceased to exist at all.

On the other hand, it is perfectly obvious that there may be corrupting additions. Heresy may easily be adding doctrines that are not really implicit in the original deposit of faith. A development may in one sense be natural, as a disease may be "natural," and yet untrue to its original; what Roman Catholics claim as legitimate "developments" might be what Protestants call "corruptions." And so criteria are demanded to distinguish between faithful and unfaithful developments.

These criteria Newman derives partly from the analogy of an organic body, and he enumerates seven notes of a true development. In relation to its earliest form, the new idea must, if the development be genuine, exhibit preservation of type, continuity of principles, power of assimilation, and logical sequence; similarly, throughout its history, the development must show anticipation of its future, conservative action on its past, and finally chronic vigor. Throughout the book, these notes are fully illustrated and applied in detail to the facts of Christian history, and the thesis is enforced that the distinctive doctrines of the Roman Catholic Church are genuine developments of original Christian teaching. For one writing after Darwin, the example of the homoidal apes suggests itself. Here we have a development as contrasted with more primitive forms, but a development which branched off into a barren side issue, instead of anticipating the future in Homo Sapiens.

Newman's reading of Christian history convinced him that for practical purposes a living authority is needed to determine development from corruption. And that living authority, found in the early Councils, must have persisted to the present day. Every age presents its conflict of thought, and it is purely arbitrary to say that nothing later than the Councils of the first four centuries is accepted as a test of true developments. Whereas, if the individual is to be made the judge of true and false developments, then one is thrown back once more on private judgment. To appeal to antiquity alone is to be static and moribund.

As Newman looked around him, he could see only one claimant to this living teaching authority—Rome. Newman's own Church of England repudiated his theory. The Anglican Church denounced belief in a living teaching authority on an equality with the early Councils. That idea was anathema.

Newman's whole book was an argument from analogy. And there is an analogy to his theory of development with persisting identity which is of particular interest to Americans, and which may even clarify, for some, Newman's line of thought as applied to religion. This analogy is the Constitution of the United States. In the original Constitution, we had something perfectly definite and to the point, written by men speaking our own language, living our culture. But John Marshall, as justice of the Supreme Court, found a great deal more to be implied in the Constitution than some of its original contemporaries had dreamed of. Undoubtedly, Marshall achieved for the Supreme Court a place in the life of the nation that was a natural, perhaps an inevitable development—nevertheless a development, and therefore not explicitly in the original.

The Civil War is another analogy. The South was technically correct in maintaining that any State had the right to secede from the Union. However, the South was mistaken in leaving out of the reckoning the development of political doctrine that had gone on during the decades since the adoption of the Constitution. It was not only the arbitrament of war which decided that States might not secede; it was also the logical growth or development of the organism. And to-day the South admits that her success in seceding would have been a calamity.

Ambrose St. John and Dalgairns were received into the Roman Catholic Church while on a holiday from Littlemore. On October 3, 1845, Newman resigned his fellowship. On the same day he wrote a letter to Pusey informing him of this step, and adding, "anything can happen to me now any day." St. John returned to Littlemore on October 7, and Newman disclosed to him his intention of joining the Church of Rome. The other members of the Littlemore household were kept in ignorance of Newman's determination until the very end.

On the evening of October 8, 1845, Father Dominic, a Passionist, was met in Oxford by Dalgairns and St. John. They accompanied him to Littlemore in a pouring rain. That night Newman made a general confession. Next day he and Stanton and Bowles made their profession of faith, were baptized conditionally, and received Holy Communion.

Some cynical historian has said, "if it's dramatic, it isn't true." But here was real drama in actual life. Father Dominic was a foreigner who could not speak English correctly, and a man of no particular intellectual reputation. Kneeling before him was one of the greatest Victorian masters of English prose, the intellectual peer of any man in England, a religious leader whose moves were watched with anxiety and hope by Anglicans and Catholics alike. For this conversion was to wound sorely the Church of his fathers, and to regain for Rome an influence she had not known in England for centuries. Twenty-five years later Disraeli was to speak of Newman's conversion as "a blow to the Church of England under which she still reels." [1]

And the drama of souls was heightened by the fact that in this same October, Ernest Renan, the famous French rationalist with a literary style to rival Newman's, put off his cassock, bade farewell to the seminary of St. Sulpice, and curiously enough went to a college for laymen conducted by the Oratorians, Newman's future brothers in the religious life. A few weeks later Renan severed all connection with the Catholic Church. It was a strange historical coincidence of "Loss and Gain" which is still registering its consequences.

For Newman to leave the Church of his youth, to sever the ties of friendship with such men as Pusey and Keble, to face he knew not what, must have been a great wrench. In spite of some harsh things he said later, Newman always retained his love for the Anglican Church and for his Anglican friends. Twenty-two years after his conversion, when Newman's life in the Catholic Church was so full of crosses, Canon Irvine was to observe a man, very poorly dressed, leaning over the gate of Littlemore crying. It was Newman, whose affection for the scenes of his Anglican life never diminished.

After his *Apologia* had reinstated him in Protestant eyes, Newman renewed his friendship with Keble, Pusey, Church, and others who had not followed him to Rome. And in the summer of 1872, Church, then Dean of St. Paul's, writes to Newman to ask if the newspaper report he encloses is correct: "A few weeks since one of the vergers of the Cathedral accosted a poorly clad, threadbare individual who stood scanning the alterations of the sacred edifice with 'Now then, move on, we don't want

[1] *Lothaire,* preface.

any of your sort here!' It was Dr. Newman!" Playfully pleading guilty, Newman replied: "I stood just inside the door listening to the chanting of the Psalms, of which I am so fond... Did not St. Augustine, while still a Manichee, stand and watch St. Ambrose? No verger turned him out." [1]

Newman's example undoubtedly led to the conversion of many other Anglicans, and perhaps of some non-conformists. Wiseman was elated. With his characteristic optimism, Wiseman confidently expected the whole Church of England to unite bodily with Rome. Looking back on the situation from the vantage point of nearly a century, one can see that there was never any likelihood of such corporate reunion. It is true that comparatively few of the English Catholics of that time shared Wiseman's optimism or his generous attitude towards the Anglicans. Mistakes were made, opportunities were neglected, the cold shoulder was shown. But even if all the Catholics had been as zealous and generous as Wiseman, the most that could have been accomplished would have been the conversion of more individuals.

Newman's accession, together with that of so many other university men, profoundly affected the Catholic Church in England. There was friction between the new-comers and the "old" Catholics. Those who had kept the faith during two centuries of persecution felt somewhat towards the recent converts as the laborers who had borne the heat and brunt of the day felt towards those employed at the eleventh hour. In some instances the newcomers— Newman always excepted—rather looked down upon the "old" Catholics. They thought that the Catholics were un-educated, as compared with Oxford and Cambridge stand-

[1] Ward, *Life of Newman*, II, 385.

ards, although men like Lingard and Wiseman certainly could hold their own in any university. Also, they looked upon the "old" Catholics as provincial from a religious standpoint, as having been out of the current of real Catholic life for too long. Men like Faber were indiscreet in introducing Italian devotions into England, and parading the streets in their cassocks as if they were in a Catholic country.

But the outcome of this accession of converts was the infusion of new blood into the Catholic body, the taking on of new life, the gradual acquiring of courage to assume their rightful place in the life around them. The Catholic Church in England to-day is immensely stronger because of the group of men who joined her at this time of Newman's accession.

Thus closed the Anglican career of Newman. But the movement that Newman started in the Anglican Church went on in spite of his defection. The carrying of a certain number of Anglicans with him to Rome is only one of the results of Newman's activity as an Anglican. Pusey and Keble and many others remained in the Church of their fathers. They did not have their great leader's doubts as to the validity of their position. For the most part, those influenced by the Oxford Movement still believed that the Church of England was part of the Church Catholic, and that their duty was to work as Anglicans to bring that Church back to Catholic teaching and Catholic practice.

Those who are interested can read the subsequent history of this Catholicizing movement in Thureau-Dangin's admirable volumes, *The English Catholic Revival in the Nineteenth Century*. Thureau-Dangin brings his story down to the opening of the twentieth century, and shows how the things Newman fought for gradually obtained a recognized place in Anglican life. To-day the Anglo-Catholic party is stronger than ever. And while there is no prospect of corporate reunion, there is prospect of this party infiltrating more and more of Newman's ideas into the consciousness of the Church of England.

We can say, then, that two results stand out from what at the time seemed the wasted efforts of this middle-aged, disappointed, disowned man of Littlemore. First, there was the conversion to Rome of numbers of brilliant men, who afterwards made their mark in the Church of their adoption, and profoundly influenced the spirit and temper of that Catholic Church in England. Secondly, there was the founding in the Anglican Church of a party with Catholic tendencies that has gone on increasing in strength and influence to the present day, adopting more and more Catholic principles, until now the only difference between this party and Rome is the question of the supremacy of the Pope.

CHAPTER II

STARTING ANEW AT FORTY-FIVE

> "We mourn over the blossoms of May, because
> they are to wither; but we know, withal, that
> May is one day to have its revenge upon No-
> vember, by the revolution of that solemn circle
> which never stops,—which teaches us in our
> height of hope, ever to be sober, and in our
> depth of desolation never to despair." (FROM
> NEWMAN'S SERMON CALLED "THE SECOND
> SPRING," PREACHED AT THE SYNOD OF WEST-
> MINSTER, 1852.)

NEWMAN'S outlook, from a human standpoint, was
blank, indeed, when he took the fateful step of becoming
a Catholic. In reality, he was beginning life over again in
full maturity. All his old friends and associations and
skills were abandoned. Oxford, with its cultural and intellectual advantages, the Establishment with its comfortable
wealth and security and social prestige, Newman was ex-
changing for membership in a despised religious group
whose utter desolation was little less than that which he
himself was to describe so vividly in his famous sermon
of 1852 called "The Second Spring."

Men still living could just recall the days when all
public exercise of their religion was forbidden to Catholics,
and Mass was allowed only under the protection of foreign

embassies. Catholic chapels were not legalized until 1791.
For years after that the chief "Mass houses" in London
had been a backyard in Warwick Street, the Neapolitan
chapel located in a stable yard, and a room in Moorfields,
with a "spy window," so that those seeking admission
could be carefully scrutinized and foes excluded.

Before Catholic Emancipation in 1829—due, ironically enough, to those Liberals whom Newman spent his
life in opposing—Catholics in England were not allowed
to vote, to be officers of the army or navy, to practice law,
or to hold any post of profit and prestige under the Crown.
In effect, Catholics were excluded from the national life,
even from attendance at the old universities. An Act of
Parliament could not change over night the habits ac-
quired through generations of persecution, and in 1845
Catholics still retained many characteristics of that *gens
lucifuga,* as Newman called them.

Speaking of conditions prevailing during his boyhood,
Newman said: "No longer the Catholic Church in the
country; nay, no longer, I may say, a Catholic community;—but a few adherents of the Old Religion, moving
silently and sorrowfully about, as memorials of what had
been. 'The Roman Catholics';—not a sect, not even an
interest, as men conceived of it,—not a body, however
small, representative of the Great Communion abroad, but
a mere handful of individuals. . . Here a set of poor Irishmen coming and going at harvest time, or a colony of
them lodged in a miserable quarter of the vast metropolis.
There, perhaps, an elderly person walking in the streets,
grave and solitary, and strange, though noble in bearing,
and said to be of good family, and a 'Roman Catholic.'
An old-fashioned house of gloomy appearance, closed in
with high walls, with an iron gate, and yews, and the re-

port attaching to it that 'Roman Catholics' lived there; but who they were, or what they did, or what they meant by calling them Roman Catholics, no one could tell."

"The revolution of that solemn circle," as Newman called it, was one day to bring Newman a "second spring," to restore the joy of life, to give a position greater than the one he had abandoned in leaving Anglicanism. But in the interval was to be a depth of desolation requiring all his strength of will, his courage of heart, his trust in God to keep him from despair.

When Newman became a Catholic, the leader of his new co-religionists in England was Nicholas Wiseman, at that time president of Oscott College. Prior to that, Wiseman had been rector of the English College, in Rome, and had made a reputation as a scholar through his publication of *Horae Syriacae*. On visits to England, he had shown himself capable of meeting non-Catholics on their own ground, and he carried back to Rome optimistic accounts of the future of Catholicism. The Vatican authorities had now sent Wiseman to England permanently, and undoubtedly he was a rising man in the ecclesiastical world.

It was natural that shortly after Newman's conversion he should visit Wiseman, and that Wiseman should wish to keep the great convert near him. So Newman settled with several companions at Old Oscott, the name of which they changed to Maryvale. It is interesting to speculate on what might have been Newman's future if at this time Wiseman had been Archbishop of Westminster, and Newman to be near him had taken up his residence in the London district. For Wiseman was to be succeeded in Westminster by the redoubtable Henry Edward Manning, and Newman and Manning were to be at

cross purposes for years. The situation was disagreeable
enough for Newman as it was, but it would have been a
great deal worse if Manning had been Newman's ecclesiastical superior.

Newman remained in the ecclesiastical district of
Oscott. Consequently he came under the famous Bishop
Ullathorne of Birmingham, a man capable of appreciating
Newman, and of sympathizing with him even when they
differed. Ullathorne was a born Catholic, coming from
an old Yorkshire family. In his early days he had run
away to sea, and was always a man's man. Later he had
become a Benedictine, doing yeoman missionary service
in Australia during the penal-colony days. In the English
hierarchy, Ullathorne was an outstanding figure that was
not eclipsed even by the brilliance of Cardinal Manning.
It is related that at some ecclesiastical gathering Ullathorne bluntly told Manning, in the Yorkshire accent he
never lost, "I was a Bishop with a mitre on my 'ead when
you were still a 'eretic!"

Inevitable as it probably was that Newman should
become a priest, nevertheless he hesitated. But on October
26, 1846, Newman and Ambrose St. John reached Rome
with the intention of prosecuting their studies for the
priesthood. For a few days they stayed at the same hotel
with George Talbot, afterwards the confidant of Manning at the Vatican, and who as a papal chamberlain was
to prejudice Pius IX and influential Roman officials
against Newman. At this time, however, the two recent
converts were friends. On November 9, Newman and St.
John took up their residence at the Collegio di Propaganda. In spite of the kindness of Cardinal Franzoni, and
of Monsignor Brunelli, the secretary of Propaganda, these

days with a group of young boys were very trying to the
middle-aged scholar.

No very strict attendance at classes was required,
and Newman was principally interested in getting some
sort of approval for the principles of his recent book on
the development of doctrine. As far as the doctrine of
the Immaculate Conception (defined in 1854) was concerned, and the infallibility of the Pope (already crystal-
lized for its definition in 1870), Roman theologians
admitted the idea of development. They could not well do
otherwise, else there would have been no need for definition. Yet they did not come out explicitly for the principle
of development as expounded by Newman.

One thing that influenced the theologians was the
uproar over Newman's thesis in the United States. Apparently the first ones to notice the book in this country
were the Unitarians, who claimed that Newman said the
idea of the Trinity was not explicit in the first age of the
Church. Orestes A. Brownson, a Catholic convert from
Unitarianism, who was the William George Ward of
America, condemned the book in round terms, saying that
it was half Christian and half pagan.

Newman arrived at a *modus vivendi* with Fr. Per-
rone, the famous Jesuit theologian of the time, but he
did not secure any sort of general or formal approval.
On the whole, his experience in Rome was a presage of
what his life as a Catholic was to be for thirty years.
"Philosophising in general," says Ward, "was suspect."
And Newman feared that if he pressed his point, his
theory of the development of doctrine might meet the
fate of Rosmini's attempt to reconcile Catholic theology
and modern philosophy. How parlous were the times is
indicated by Ward's statement that Newman "found to

his surprise that both St. Thomas and Aristotle were now out of favor in Rome." [1]

Even after being settled at Propaganda, what to do after ordination presented a problem to Newman. His life at Littlemore had been monastic, and Newman naturally turned over in his mind the possibility of joining one of the established religious orders. Fr. Dominic, who received Newman into the Church, was a Passionist. The Benedictines and Jesuits were well established in England, and the Dominicans and Redemptorists also were there.

One thing or another, however, was against each of the religious communities mentioned. And the final outcome of the matter was that Newman had a novitiate under an Oratorian specially appointed for this purpose by Pius IX. Newman and St. John were ordained subdeacons by Cardinal Franzoni in his private chapel on May 26, 1847. The diaconate and priesthood followed on the 29th and 30th. On Christmas Eve, 1847, Newman and St. John reached England, and said their first Mass on English soil the following day.

Undoubtedly, this founding of an English Oratory was a happy solution for Newman. Each Oratory is independent of the others and forms a closed corporation. Because of his sensitiveness, Newman never could have been happy in a provincial community, such as the Redemptorists, with a constantly shifting personnel in the houses, sent around from one place to another, never sure of his abode or of his occupation for more than a year or two at a time.

As an Oratorian, Newman was preserved from all this because he was his own superior. It is true that the Oratorians are secular priests living in community, but

---

[1] *Life of Newman*, I, 165.

practically they are as independent of the bishops as are any of the exempt orders. And while Newman might have founded a provincial congregation of his own, it is fortunate that he did not do so. For Newman's talent lay in preaching and writing, not in managing a number of men, or in collecting the large funds that would have been needed for a provincial organization.

Manning was the executive, the manager of other men, the born ruler, sure of himself, dominating everyone around him by the force of his personality. Newman was even still somewhat shy and retiring, seeing so many sides to an intellectual problem that he proceeded slowly, cautiously, with an economy that led some who could not understand him to say that he was insincere, playing a game, careless of the truth.

It was fortunate for Newman, fortunate for the cause of Catholicism in England, and fortunate for religious thinking generally that Newman chose as he did in regard to religious communities. And after ordination, Newman settled down to the quiet life of an Oratorian in Birmingham, albeit a life in striking contrast with his beloved Oxford. For Birmingham was a large manufacturing city, and the section in which the Oratory was first situated was partly a slum.

Newman was never a parish priest in the sense of going on sick calls, hearing confessions regularly, looking after the spiritual interests of a particular geographical area. Nevertheless, Newman's life as an Oratorian in Birmingham brought him into sufficiently close contact with the conditions of life of the Catholic people in this district to make it remarkable that he never adverted to them. At Oxford, he had stayed through one epidemic without flinching, when other ministers fled to safer quarters. In Birmingham, he volunteered during the cholera, and showed heroic fearlessness. Yet Newman does not seem to have been interested in the practical social problems of his day. Contemporary with Newman in Birmingham was George Cadbury, who amassed a fortune in the chocolate business and then devoted it to undertakings of social welfare. But the example failed to touch Newman, absorbed as he was in other problems.

During his seclusion at Littlemore, Newman was entirely unaffected by Henry Broadhurst, afterwards parliamentary secretary of the Trades Union Congress, whose stirring speeches were resounding through the village streets. The 1830's and 1840's were replete with "reform" legislation and agitation—parliamentary reform, local government reform, educational reform, factory reports and legislation, repeal of the corn laws, the Chartist agitation for thoroughgoing democracy. During the decades of Newman's prime, Carlyle and his disciple Ruskin, Kingsley and Disraeli, Michael Sadler and the Earl of Shaftesbury, were arousing the English social conscience with books that have found a permanent place in English literature. Newman moved through it all like a ghost, showing not the slightest indication that he ever knew of such a thing as social injustice.

One will vainly search the index to Newman's works prepared by Rickaby for any references to "social question," "intemperance," "drink," "sexual immorality," "prostitution." Newman was living in the realm of theological speculation, rather than in the practical world of applied Christian justice and charity. And this blindness in Newman may have been the real secret of the antagonism between him and Manning. Newman was the speculative thinker, realizing the intellectual difficulties in the

way of faith, and having a profound sympathy for anyone bitten by religious doubts. Theoretically, Newman
knew that men were tempted to sexual sins, to intemperance, to dishonesty, but he himself was not troubled
in that way, and apparently he did not care much about
the men who were.

Manning, on the other hand, was the practical man
of affairs, of action, whose forte was governing. He was
concerned chiefly with the application of Christianity to
living, and became a violent temperance advocate, a foe
of prostitution, a "Christian Socialist," as Cardinal Capecelatro called him. In the great London dock strike, the
workers bore Manning's picture, as well as that of Karl
Marx, on a banner. No flight of imagination could ever
conceive of these rough strikers carrying the picture of
the speculative theologian, Newman. Manning had the
greatest possible sympathy for those who were the vic-
tims of social injustice, and he felt deeply for those who
were tempted to drink or to sexual immorality. But Manning did not sympathize at all with those who were
troubled by intellectual doubts of religion—nor with those
who even considered such doubts. Manning never understood Newman, and always suspected that because Newman tried to help these men afflicted with doubt, Newman
himself must be a doubter. But it would have been just
as reasonable for Newman to have retorted that because
Manning tried to help drunkards, therefore Manning must
himself be a drunkard.

The parallel between Pascal and Newman has often
been worked out. And the essence of the parallel is in
this very point. Pascal was a speculative thinker. He
could not understand the casuistry of men of action who
developed an elaborate system regarding such sins as

drunkenness and sexual immorality, and who seemed to have an evident sympathy for men given to such sins. Pascal's sympathy was for the man who found faith of any sort difficult, who was tortured by intellectual doubts. And there was the inevitable *impasse* between Pascal and the Jesuits, as there was between Newman and Manning.

Men of action seldom understand the thinkers. Manning could as little tolerate sympathy with unbelievers as a general fighting a war can tolerate sympathy with the enemy. Newman was about as popular at York House as a man who questioned the advisability of democracy would have been at the White House during the World War. Men of action take principles for granted, and then go ahead to perform their deeds. They do not understand the need of establishing principles in the face of adverse criticism. Wilson could not stop in 1917 to demonstrate that democracy was safe and the best thing for the world. He merely coined the slogan, "Make the world safe for democracy."

The Oratory of Birmingham was formally inaugurated on February 2, 1848, the Feast of the Purification. Newman was novice master and lecturer in theology, while as superior the full weight of details incident to a new establishment fell upon him. Newman felt the irksomeness of it all very keenly, and was depressed by a sense of failing powers. At forty-seven, Newman should have been in the full vigor of his manhood, but he writes to Henry Wilberforce: "It is an awful thing, beginning life in the end of my days. How I wish I had in me the energy which I had when I began the *Tracts for the times!* Now I am scarce more, to my own feelings, than an *inutile lignum;* so stiff, so wooden."

Shortly after the establishment of the Oratory by

Newman, Frederick Faber, also an Oxford convert, proposed that the group he had founded under the name of Wilfridians, at St. Wilfrid's, Cotton Hall, Cheadle, should unite with the Oratorians. But the Wilfridians were hardly settled with Newman before differences developed. Faber had all the zeal of a new convert. He and his companions took delight in shocking the "old" Catholics as well as the Protestants by introducing the most exaggerated devotions from southern Italy.

Difficulties developed, too, in regard to a series of lives of the English Saints projected and begun by Faber. These lives were translations from the Romance languages, and they abounded in the miraculous and wonderful. "Old" Catholics, used to the austerity of Butler and *The Garden of the Soul,* were astounded. Protestants mocked. And these tales were to form ammunition for Kingsley in his famous controversy with Newman. The fact that Newman himself seems to have sanctioned such material throws a curious light on the credulous side of Newman's character. That credulity is one of the counts in Brémond's *Mystery of Newman.* And it is surely a mystery how a man of Newman's acute mind, with his tendency to skepticism, his hearty appreciation of intellectual difficulties, could nevertheless have been so easily led to believe in fantastic medieval legends.

Edwin A. Abbott, in his book called *The Anglican Career of Cardinal Newman,* illustrating Newman's credulity quotes from one of his sermons preached during this period—about 1850—describing the condition of religion in England during the century after its conversion. "The fair form of Christianity," said Newman, "rose up and grew and expanded like a beautiful pageant from north to south; it was majestic, it was solemn, it was bright, it was beautiful and pleasant, it was soothing to the griefs, it was indulgent to the hopes of man; it was at once a teaching and a worship; it had a dogma, a mystery, a ritual of its own; it had an hierarchical form. A brotherhood of holy pastors, with mitre and crosier and uplifted hand, walked forth and blessed and ruled the joyful people. The crucifix headed the procession, and simple monks were there with hearts in prayer, and sweet chants resounded, and the Holy Latin tongue was heard, and boys came forth in white, swinging censers, and the fragrant cloud arose, and Mass was sung, and the saints were invoked, and day after day, in the still night, and over the woody hills and in the quiet plains, as constantly as the sun and moon and stars go forth in heaven, so regular and solemn was the stately march of blessed services on earth, high festival, and gorgeous procession, and soothing dirge, and passing bell, and the familiar call to evening prayer: till he who recollected the old pagan time, would think it all unreal that he beheld and heard, and would conclude he did but see a vision, so marvellously was heaven let down upon earth, so triumphantly chased away the fiends of darkness to their prison below." [1]

Abbott makes the comment: "The man who in an advanced period of life could write down such a description of the 'brotherhood of holy pastors' blessing and 'ruling the joyful people,' and apply it to the times of the 'battles of the kites and crows' before the Heptarchy, is obviously capable of being led on a long way by dreams, and of confronting with audacity the obstacles of intervening facts." [2]

[1] *Sermons Preached on Various Occasions,* 127.
[2] I, 317.

Anyone who reads Abbott will recognize that he starts with a thesis and collects everything he can to prove it. Obviously Abbott is biased. But in spite of Döllinger's statement that Newman was the greatest living authority on the history of the first three centuries of the Christian era,[1] the best friend of Newman must admit that to-day his standing as an historian is not very high. Newman has, indeed, written extensively in the field of history—a history of the Arians in the fourth century, some studies in the Church Fathers, three volumes of historical sketches, and two volumes called *Essays Historical and Critical*. But Newman was not a "scientific" historian in the present-day sense. His chief claim as an historian was not any particular research in original sources, but a power of description, a psychological insight into character, with now and then a touch of genius in guessing and in criticism. He was a poet in feeling and sensitiveness, and although the description invidiously cited by Abbott may not be historically sound, it is certainly ideally beautiful.

The criticism of Faber's *Lives of the Saints* led to a discontinuance of the series, and shortly thereafter Newman and Faber separated. It was better so. Faber betook himself with his followers to London to establish a new Oratory. In the light of subsequent events, it is interesting to note that Newman thought at the time he was giving Faber the better part, although he himself had no desire to leave Birmingham. Wiseman was now in Westminster, and the thought of being in his diocese might easily have made Newman prefer London for his own residence. But it is fortunate that Newman did not go to the Westminster diocese. For Wiseman was to be

[1] Ward, I, 444.

succeeded by Manning, and while Faber could fit in perfectly with Manning, Newman never could.

In summarizing the advantages on the side of the London Foundation, Newman mentioned "wealthy friends, and those, gentlemen, instead of a population exclusively of poor Catholics." This indicates clearly enough the character of the Catholic people with whom the Oratorians were dealing in Birmingham, and makes all the more remarkable the fact that Newman never took any interest in advancing their circumstances in this world. The social implications of the Gospel never struck him. Newman said the "Our Father," and prayed that daily bread might be given *us,* but he never did anything in a social way to help the poor people to get their daily bread. He was charitable, but his charity was individual, personal, remedial, not social and preventive.

Faber and his companions secured a building in London in King William Street. Later on, this building became Toole's Theatre, and William George Ward remarked after going to a very good play there: "Yesterday I visited Toole's Theatre. Two thoughts occurred to me. The first thought was, 'The last time I was here I heard Faber preach.' And the second thought was: 'How much more I am enjoying myself than when I was last here!'"

On May 9, 1850, Newman began his series of *Lectures on Anglican Difficulties* in the King William Street Oratory. It was Newman's first public appearance as a lecturer since his conversion, and numbers of Protestants came to hear him. R. H. Hutton writes of the lectures: "I shall never forget the impression which his voice and manner, which opened upon me for the first time, made on me. Never did such a voice seem better adapted to persuade without irritating. Singularly sweet, perfectly free from any dictatorial note, yet rich in all the cadences proper to the expression of pathos, of wonder, and of ridicule, there was still nothing in it that any one could properly describe as insinuating, for its simplicity, and frankness, and freedom from the half-smothered notes which express indirect purpose, was as remarkable as its sweetness, its freshness, and its gentle distinctness." [1]

These lectures are a good illustration of Newman's power and method as a controversialist. His exposition of the weakness of the Anglican position is devastating, and yet it arouses no unnecessary antagonism. There is no unfairness, no cheap sarcasm, no empty rhetoric. One senses that here is a man pleading with those who disagree with him, because he is convinced that their views are hurtful to them. He sees men of his former persuasion drifting comfortably in the Anglican boat, without realizing that they are approaching rapids in which they will inevitably be destroyed. And from the sure security of the bank, he cries to them to beware, to act while there is yet time.

In the lectures devoted to answering the difficulties felt by Anglicans concerning points of Catholic doctrine or practice, Newman disarms criticism by stating the objections more forcibly than the objectors. Consider, for instance, his summing up of the element of superstition among Catholics: "Hence, the strange stories of highwaymen and brigands devout to the Madonna. And their wishes leading to the belief, they begin to circulate stories of her much-coveted compassion towards impenitent offenders. . . Or men have thought, by means of some sacred relic, to be secured from death in their perilous and guilty expeditions. . . The troubadour offered tapers, and paid

[1] *Cardinal Newman*, p. 207.

for Masses, for his success in some lawless attachment. . .
The crusaders had faith sufficient to bind them to a perilous pilgrimage and warfare; they kept the Friday's abstinence, and planted the tents of their mistresses within
the shadow of the glorious St. Louis. . . You enter into one
of the churches close upon the scene of festivity. . . There
is a feeble old woman, who first genuflects before the
Blessed Sacrament, and then steals her neighbour's hand-
kerchief, or prayer book, who is intent on his devotions."

There were some conversions traceable to these lectures of Newman, and Rome conferred on him the degree
of Doctor of Theology. Wiseman was particularly delighted with the King William Street lectures. For the
time being, Newman seemed to have gained a permanent
place in the hearts of English Catholics. Wilfrid Ward
calls this period the "honeymoon" of Newman's Catholic
life. Rather it was, to borrow Newman's phrase, a "second
spring." Or perhaps we might better call it a deceptive
Indian summer, whose comfortable promise was soon to be
swallowed up in a cruel winter. Newman's proper second
spring was to come with the *Apologia*.

Scarcely had the echo of Newman's King William
Street lectures died out, when the storm against "papal
aggression" broke. Proceedings had been going on for
some time to put England on the same Catholic ecclesiastical basis as the rest of the world. For a time after
the Protestant Revolt, England had had no Catholic
bishops whatever. The religious care of the Catholics, in
so far as it was met at all, was in the hands of missionaries.
Then bishops were appointed as "vicars apostolic." They
had no ordinary jurisdiction, but were subject to the Pope
in much the same way as an auxiliary bishop is subject to
his ordinary. Now the hierarchy was to be restored, and

Wiseman from Vicar Apostolic of the London District was to become Archbishop of Westminster.

The historian Lingard's advice was not taken to avoid assuming episcopal titles from English cities. The titles for Anglican sees were not duplicated, it is true, for the Roman Catholic bishop of London took his title from Westminster. But this hardly mitigated the offense to Protestants. A Catholic bishop seemed to be assuming some authority over *all* who lived in a particular city. And at any rate, the assumption of territorial titles by Catholic bishops seemed to derogate from the dignity of Anglican bishops.

The restoration of the hierarchy had an extrinsic significance for Protestants because the Catholic body had recently grown so considerably in numbers and importance through conversions and a large Irish immigration. Such an important gesture from Rome was bound to be scrutinized through prejudiced eyes, and Wiseman started a veritable conflagration when with extraordinary lack of appreciation for the fitness of things he wrote his famous pastoral "from out the Flaminian gate" of Rome, October 7, 1850. To Protestant Englishmen, the whole setting, and the words themselves of the pastoral seemed like the exultant announcement of a Roman triumph—even a Roman conquest. A fury of opposition swept the country. Wiseman and the Pope were burned in effigy. The streets were placarded with such signs as "Down with Popery," "Down with Tyranny." Priests and congregations were booed and hooted.

But Wiseman redeemed himself by the courage and tact he showed on his return to England, November 11, 1850. He wrote a long letter to *The Times* that was reprinted and distributed by the scores of thousands. He was incessant in representations to the Government. He preached and lectured on every possible occasion. The reorganization of the Catholic Church was certainly advertised. And if it pays to advertise, the experience was worth the suffering entailed. On the whole, the Church emerged stronger than if there had been no hullabaloo. Numerous converts entered the Church at this time— among them Henry Edward Manning, Archdeacon of Chichester, afterwards Cardinal Archbishop of Westminster. Manning was received in London on April 6, 1851, and on April 23 he visited Newman at the Oratory in Birmingham.

On June 30, 1851, Newman began his series of *Lectures on the Present Position of Catholics in England*. The lectures were delivered once a week in the Corn Exchange of Birmingham. Manning was present at the first of the series. "The peals of laughter audible from outside," writes Ward, "showed something in the lectures unlike Newman's ordinary manner. In truth, as those who have read them are aware, they abounded in pungent satire, the more effective because it came not from a controversialist who delighted in strong words and startling statements, but from one who was notoriously reserved in language and self-restrained. In constructive argument, more especially, Newman, alive as he was to all the anomalies and scandals visible in Church history, could very rarely bring himself to employ the positive and confident tone, the strong expressions, the one-sided statements, the would-be demonstrative proofs of many popular Catholic controversialists. His fastidiousness and his sense of tact forbade it. The approach to a breach of this rule in the case of the King William Street lectures was probably one of the things which made their preparation distasteful to him. In the present case such objections to vehement language no longer held. He had satisfied himself that he was face to face not with serious convictions, but with a monstrous and preposterous phenomenon—the No-popery prejudice, which had for more than two centuries deformed and disgraced the national mind. He revelled in the strength of his case; and though never off his guard and never forgetting the reservations in his attack which truth required, he let himself go in occasional passages with complete unreserve and great effect."

The Corn Exchange lectures undoubtedly contain some of the finest specimens of irony in the English language. From that standpoint, they are as alive to-day as when they were first delivered. No man's education in English literature is entirely complete, who is not familiar with certain passages. I shall quote just one, where Newman introduces his hypothetical Russian denouncing the British Constitution. The passage is long, but its brilliance excuses its length.

"I will suppose, then," says Newman, "a speaker, and an audience too, who never saw England, never saw a member of parliament, a policeman, a queen, or a London mob; who never read the English history, nor studies any one of our philosophers, jurists, moralists, or poets; but who has dipped into Blackstone and several other English writers, and has picked up facts at third or fourth hand, and has got together a crude farrago of ideas, words, and instances, a little truth, a deal of falsehood, a deal of misrepresentation, a deal of nonsense, and a deal of invention."

And is it necessary to point out that in the speaker thus supposed, Newman is painting a picture of anti-Catholic lecturers, who know Catholicism only from the outside? The speaker, a Russian Count, goes on to address an audience in Moscow:

"The Count began by observing that the events of every day, as it came, called on his countrymen more and more importunately to choose their side, and to make a firm stand against a perfidious power, which arrogantly proclaims that there is nothing like the British Constitution in the whole world, and that no country can prosper without it; which is yearly aggrandizing itself in East, West, and South, which is engaged in one enormous conspiracy against all States, and which was even aiming at modifying the old institutions of the North, and at dressing up the army, navy, legislature and executive of his own country in the livery of Queen Victoria... He repeated that there were in that city educated men, who had openly professed a reverence of the atheistical tenets and fiendish maxims of John-Bullism."

All this is not a parody of anti-Catholic propaganda, it is a deadly parallel. And note the art with which Newman prepares his Protestant auditors for a sympathetic hearing of his side, by putting these grotesque misconceptions of the British Constitution and laws in the mouth of a Russian Count. For at this particular time, the world stage was being set for the Crimean War with Russia, and Englishmen were ready to believe almost any absurdity about Russians. Then by this rhetorical device having put his audience in the right frame of mind, Newman goes on with stroke after stroke of inimitably deft touch to fill in the details.

The Count said "he had used the words 'atheistical' and 'fiendish' most advisedly, and he would give his reasons for doing so. What was to be said to any political power which claimed the attribute of Divinity? Was any

term too strong for such a usurpation? Now, no one would
deny that Antichrist would be such a power; an Anti-
christ was contemplated, was predicted in Scripture, it
was to grow slowly, it was to manifest itself warily and
craftily, and then to have a mouth speaking great things
against the Divinity and against His attributes. This pre-
diction was most literally fulfilled in the British Constitution. Antichrist was not only to usurp, but to profess to
usurp the arms of heaven—he was to arrogate its titles.
This was the mark of the beast, and where was it fulfilled but in John-Bullism?

"I hold in my hand," continues the speaker, "a book
which I have obtained under very remarkable circumstances. It is not known to the British people, it is
circulated only among the lawyers, merchants, and aristocracy, and its restrictive use is secured only by the most
solemn oaths, the most fearful penalties, and the utmost
vigilance of the police. I procured it after many years
of anxious search by the activity of an agent, and the co-
operation of an English bookseller, and it cost me an
enormous sum to make it my own. It is called 'Blackstone's Commentaries on the Laws of England,' and I am
happy to make known to the universe its odious and
shocking mysteries, known to few Britons, and certainly
not known to the deluded persons whose vagaries have
been the occasion of this meeting. I am sanguine in thinking that when they come to know the real tenets of John
Bull, they will break off all connection with his adherents. . ."

It is no wonder that gales of laughter swept the audience. But Newman was not through. His effect depended
partly upon an accumulative argument, and he piled
illustration upon illustration in an artistic crescendo, slyly

throwing in the equivalent of the bigot's stock charge that the Pope is impeccable.

"I open the book, gentlemen, and what are the first words which meet my eyes? *'The King can do no wrong.'* I beg you to attend, gentlemen, to this most significant assertion; one was accustomed to think that no child or man had the gift of impeccability; one had imagined that, simply speaking, impeccability was a divine attribute; but this British Bible, as I may call it, distinctly ascribes an absolute sinlessness to the King of Great Britain and Ireland. Observe, I am using no words of my own, I am still but quoting what meets my eyes in this remarkable document. The words run thus: 'It is an axiom of the law of the land that the *King himself can do no wrong.'* Was I wrong, then, in speaking of the atheistical maxims of John Bullism? But this is far from all: the writer goes on actually to ascribe to the Sovereign (I tremble while I pronounce the words) absolute *perfection;* for he speaks thus: 'The law ascribes to the King in his political capacity ABSOLUTE PERFECTION; the *King can do no wrong!*—(groans). One had thought that no human power could thus be described; but the British legislature, judicature, and jurisprudence have had the unspeakable effrontery to impute to their crowned and sceptred idol, to their doll, . . . this puppet, whom they have dressed up with a lion and a unicorn, the attribute of ABSOLUTE PERFECTION! . . . As if this were not enough this Blackstone continues, 'The King, moreover, is not only incapable of *doing* wrong, but even of *thinking* wrong!! *he can never do an improper thing; in him is no* FOLLY *or* WEAKNESS!!!' "

After the Pope, I suppose the attitude of Catholics towards the Blessed Virgin Mary suffers more Protestant

misrepresentation than any other one doctrine or practice. And the fact that England then had a Queen makes
all the more telling Newman's subsequent point.

Next, then, he drew attention to the point that the
English Sovereign distinctly claimed to be the '*fount* of
justice'; and, that there might be no mistake in the matter, the author declared, 'that she *is never bound in justice
to do anything.*' What, then, is her method of acting?
Unwilling as he was to defile his lips with so profane a
statement, he must tell them that this abominable writer
coolly declared that the Queen, a woman, only did acts
of reparation and restitution as a matter of *grace!* He
was not a theologian, he had spent his life in the field,
but he knew enough of his religion to be able to say that
grace was a word especially proper to the appointments
and decrees of Divine Sovereignty. All his hearers knew
perfectly well that nature was one thing, grace another;
and yet here was a poor child of clay claiming to be the
fount, not only of justice, but of grace. She was making
herself a first cause of not merely natural, but spiritual
excellence, and doing nothing more or less than simply
emancipating herself from her Maker. The Queen, it
seemed, never obeyed the law on compulsion, according
to Blackstone; that is, her Maker could not compel
her..."

But Newman's fertility was not yet exhausted. Parliament must be brought in as an equivalent of Protestant
conceptions of a College of Cardinals or a Church Council.

"Let it be observed, the Apostle called the predicted
Antichrist 'the wicked one,' or, as it might be more correctly translated, 'the lawless,' because he was to be the
proud despiser of all law; now, wonderful to say, this was

the very assumption of the British Parliament. 'The Power of Parliament,' said Sir Edward Coke, 'is so transcendent and absolute, that it cannot be confined within any bounds!! It has sovereign and uncontrollable authority!!' Moreover, the Judges had declared that 'it is so high and mighty in its nature that it *may make law*, and THAT WHICH IS LAW IT MAY MAKE NO LAW!'... The gallant speaker then delivered the following passage from Blackstone's volume, in a very distinct and articulate whisper: 'Some have not scrupled to call its power—the OMNIPOTENCE of Parliament!'"

Then lest his hearers should have forgotten one or other of his points, Newman sums up for them:

"The speaker continued, evidently laboring under intense emotion:—'Have you not heard enough, my dear compatriots, of this hideous system of John-Bullism? Was I wrong in using the words fiendish and atheistical when I entered upon this subject? And need I proceed further with blasphemous details, which cannot really add to the monstrous bearing of the passages I have already read to you? If the Queen "cannot do wrong," if she "cannot even think wrong," if she is "absolute perfection," if she has "no folly, no weakness," if she is the "fount of justice," if she is the "fount of grace," if she is simply "above law," if she is "omnipotent," what wonder that the lawyers of John-Bullism should also call her "sacred"! what wonder that they should speak of her as "majesty"! what wonder that they should speak of her as a "superior being"! Here again I am using the words of the book I hold in my hand. "The people" (my blood runs cold when I repeat them) "are led to consider their Sovereign *in the light of a* SUPERIOR BEING." "Everyone is under him," says Bracton, "and he is under no one." Accordingly, the law-books call him "Vicarius Dei in terra," "the Vicar of God on earth"; a most astonishing fulfillment, you observe, of the prophecy, for Antichrist is a Greek word, which means "Vicar of Christ." What wonder, under these circumstances, that Queen Elizabeth, assuming the attribute of the Creator, once said to one of her Bishops: "Proud Prelate, *I made you, and I can unmake you!"* ' "

How obvious is the meaning of Elizabeth's words, that she had made them bishops and that she could depose them as bishops. In fact, the explanation is so simple that a careless reader might miss the real force of the Russian Count's interpretation—that he understood Elizabeth in an absolute sense, to be assuming God's creative power, just as in the question and answer of the catechism, "Who made you?" "God made me."

For the sake of space, I am omitting some of Newman's phrases, without, I hope, materially spoiling the effect. But I must quote the next paragraph because it took a genius to crowd into these few sentences so many absurd mistakes and confusions in imitation of a certain type of Exeter Hall controversialist.

"And my Lord Clarendon, the present Lord Lieutenant of Ireland [as of course he was not] in his celebrated *History of the Rebellion* declares that ... King James 'actually on one occasion called himself "a god" '"; and in his great legal digest, commonly called the *Constitutions of Clarendon* [which were not named after this Clarendon at all, and were not a legal digest prepared by any Clarendon], he gives us the whole account of the King's [not James by name nor by centuries in time] banishing the Archbishop, St. Thomas of Canterbury, for refusing to do him homage. Lord Bacon, too, went nearly as far when he called him 'Deaster quidem,' 'some sort of little god.' Alexander Pope, too, calls Queen Anne a goddess; and Addison, with a servility only equalled by his profaneness, cries out, 'Thee, goddess, thee Britannia's isle adores.' Nay, even at this very time, when public attention has been drawn to the subject, Queen Victoria causes herself to be represented on her coins as the goddess of the seas, with a pagan trident in her hand."

No typically Protestant tirade against the Pope would be complete without fixing upon him the number of the Beast. And so Newman makes the Count, in a way not a whit more foolish than that used by anti-Catholic bigots, show how Queen Victoria fulfills this mystic number.

"Gentlemen, can it surprise you to be told, after such an exposition of the blasphemies of England, that, astonishing to say, Queen Victoria is distinctly pointed out in the Book of Revelation as having the number of the beast! You may recollect that number is 666; now, she came to the throne in the year thirty-seven, at which date she was eighteen years old. Multiply 37 by 18, and you have the very number 666, which is the mystical emblem of the lawless King!!! ..."

To show how one can prove anything with a certain plausibility when one sets out to do so, Newman then adds an absurd claim for the Queen, that Protestants never in their wildest charges attached to the Pope—a claim to immortality in this world.

"Once more I appeal to the awful volume I hold in my hands... Listen, then, once again; it is a fact; Jezebel has declared her own *omnipresence*. 'A consequence of the royal prerogatives,' says this antichristian author, 'is the legal UBIQUITY of the King!' ... Gentlemen, the sun would set before I told you one hundredth part of the enormity of this child of Moloch and Belial... Like the

Roman emperor, she actually has declared herself immortal! she has declared her eternity! . . . 'In the law,' says Blackstone, 'the Sovereign is said *never to die!*' Again, with still more hideous expressiveness, 'The law ascribes to the Sovereign an ABSOLUTE IMMORTALITY. THE KING NEVER DIES.' "

Newman goes on in this strain for several more paragraphs, and then adds: "Now, my Brothers of the Oratory, I protest to you my full conviction that I have not caricatured this parallel at all. Were I, indeed, skilled in legal matters, I could have made it far more natural, plausible, and complete; but, as for its extravagance, I say deliberately, and have means of knowing what I say, having once been a Protestant, and being now a Catholic—knowing what is said and thought of Catholics, on the one hand, and, on the other, knowing what they really *are*— I deliberately assert that no absurdities contained in the above sketch can equal—nay, that no conceivable absurdities can surpass—the absurdities which are firmly believed of Catholics by sensible, kind-hearted, well-intentioned Protestants. Such is the consequence of having looked at things all on one side, and shutting the eyes to the other."

These Corn Exchange lectures of Newman are not simply specimens of literary form. They are still an important contribution to an understanding of the relations between Catholics and Protestants in the English-speaking world. The same prejudices, the same slanders that Newman dealt with in the England of 1851 are to be met with to-day in the United States. No student of contemporary religious conditions can afford to pass over Newman's study.

But likewise, Newman's fellow Catholics in the

United States would profit by studying the advice he gave to English Catholics eighty years ago.

"What I desiderate in Catholics," said Newman, "is the gift of bringing out what their religion is; it is one of those 'better gifts,' of which the Apostle bids you to be 'zealous.' You must not hide your talent in a napkin, or your light under a bushel. I want a laity, not arrogant, not rash in speech, not disputatious, but men who know their religion, who enter into it, who know just where they stand, who know what they hold, and what they do not, who know their creed so well that they can give an account of it, who know so much of history that they can defend it. I want an intelligent, well-instructed laity; I am not denying you are such already: but I mean to be severe, and, as some would say, exorbitant in my demands, I wish you to enlarge your knowledge, to cultivate your reason, to get an insight into the relation of truth to truth, to learn to view things as they are, to understand how faith and reason stand to each other, what are the bases and principles of Catholicism, and where lie the main inconsistencies and absurdities of the Protestant theory.

"I have no apprehension that you will be the worse Catholics for familiarity with these subjects, provided you cherish a vivid sense of God above, and keep in mind that you have souls to be judged and saved... You ought to be able to bring out what you feel and what you mean, as well as to feel and mean it; to expose to the comprehension of others the fictions and fallacies of your opponents; and to explain the charges brought against the Church, to the satisfaction, not, indeed, of bigots, but of men of sense, of whatever cast of opinion. And one immediate effect of your being able to do all this will be your gaining that proper confidence in self which is so necessary for you." [1]

But in spite of Newman's general fairness in these lectures, there is a certain one-sidedness. In his study of the causes of Protestant prejudice, one misses the frank acknowledgment of some fault among Catholics that Newman had already made in the King William Street lectures, and that he was to make again twenty years later in answer to Pusey's *Eirenicon* on devotion to the Blessed Virgin, as well as in his reply to Gladstone's strictures on papal authority. Superb as these lectures are, they would have been strengthened by a few paragraphs here and there pointing out the extravagances of some Catholics.

However, there is another element we miss in these lectures on *The Present Position of Catholics in England*. For they are concerned with merely a theoretical or abstract discussion of bigotry. It is true that Newman sometimes gives concrete details in illustrating prejudice or in accounting for its origin. But he never discusses the broader statistical questions that would be implied by the title, "The Present Position of Catholics in England."

For instance, one aspect of the position of Catholics would be their number, their geographical and racial distribution, their social and economic status, their influence, if any, in politics. This was just about the time of the Irish Famine, and the large influx of Irish resulting therefrom. Irish immigration was a very significant fact in the position of Catholics in England, but Newman does not mention it.

Of course, all such considerations were apart from Newman's purpose. They would simply have cluttered up his book. But the fact that he never adverted to them

[1] *Present Position of Catholics in England,* 390.

here, or elsewhere, shows significantly the trend of his thinking. Newman was a speculative thinker, rather than a statistician or a social historian. One cannot be everything, and this limitation is mentioned not as a criticism, but merely as a fact. It was a limitation. And we may regret that some one did not in 1850 give an account of the condition of Catholics along these lines, that could be compared with their present position eighty years later in order to note the changes.

One of the things that stung Newman into delivering his Corn Exchange lectures, was the fact that the Protestant public, which prided itself on its honesty and truthfulness as compared with the "Papists," should be willing to believe the most outrageous and unfounded accusations of any scoundrelly anti-Catholic lecturer. In fact, it seemed that the less accurate the charges, the more chance for a hearing. England was afflicted with a number of travelling "ex-nuns" and "ex-priests" who made a living by vilifying the Catholic Church. Notorious among the anti-Catholic lecturers at the moment was a certain Dr. Giacinto Achilli, formerly a Dominican friar, and therefore unlike many of the supposed "exes," really a priest.

This Dr. Achilli had been the subject of an article in *The Dublin Review* by Wiseman. Therein were detailed some of his immoral escapades, and references were made to official proofs. The article had afterwards been reprinted and circulated as a pamphlet. As Achilli had made no effort to refute the statements, and had brought no suit for libel, Newman felt safe in using this material. The passage in which he referred to Achilli is worth quoting— and the more so as it does not appear in the revised edition of his works—as showing Newman's power of

restrained invective. Newman's words veritably snap and
hiss like a blacksnake whip.

"Ah, Dr. Achilli, I might have spoken of him last
week, had time admitted of it. The Protestant world
flocks to hear him because he has something to tell it of
the Catholic Church. He has something to tell it, it is
true; he *has* a scandal to reveal, he *has* an argument to
exhibit. It is a simple one, and a powerful one, as far as
it goes—and it is *one*. That one argument is himself; it is
his presence which is the triumph of Protestants; it is the
sight of him which is a Catholic's confusion. It is indeed
our great confusion, that our Holy Mother could have
had a priest like him. He feels the force of the argument,
and he shows himself to the multitude that is gazing on
him.

" 'Mothers of families,' he seems to say, 'gentle
maidens, innocent children, look at me for I am worth
looking at. You do not see such a sight every day. Can
any church live over the imputation of such a production
as I am? I have been a Catholic and an infidel; I have
been a Roman priest and a hypocrite; I have been a
profligate under a cowl.

" 'I am that Father Achilli, who, as early as 1826,
was deprived of my faculty to lecture, for an offense
which my superiors did their best to conceal; and who
in 1827 had already earned the reputation of a scandalous
friar. I am that Achilli, who in the diocese of Viterbo in
February, 1831, robbed of her honour a young woman of
eighteen; who in September, 1833, was found guilty of
a second such crime, in the case of a person of twenty-
eight; and who perpetrated a third in July, 1834, in the
case of another aged twenty-four. I am he who was afterwards found guilty of sins, similar or worse, in other towns

of the neighborhood. I am that son of St. Dominic who is known to have repeated the offence at Capua, in 1834 and 1835; and at Naples again, in 1840, in the case of a child of fifteen. I am he who chose the sacristy for one of these crimes and Good Friday for another.

" 'Look on me, ye mothers of England, a confessor against Popery, for ye "ne'er may look upon my like again." I am that veritable priest, who, after all this, began to speak against, not only the Catholic faith, but the moral law, and perverted others by my teaching. I am that Cavaliere Achilli, who then went to Corfu, made the wife of a tailor faithless to her husband, and lived publicly and travelled about with the wife of a chorus-singer. I am that Professor in the Protestant College at Malta, who with two others was dismissed from my post for offences which the authorities cannot get themselves to describe. And now attend to me, such as I am, and you shall see what you shall see about the barbarity and profligacy of the Inquisitors of Rome.' "

Whether Newman angered Achilli to a greater extent than Wiseman, or was thought to be bigger game, Achilli sued for libel. Naturally, Newman appealed to Wiseman for the documents on which the original article in *The Dublin Review* was based. The appeal was vain. The proofs were not forthcoming. Newman thought, whether justly or not, that Wiseman never even looked for the documents—and it became incumbent on Newman to secure copies of the official records, or to produce the witnesses. Several of Newman's brother Oratorians went to Italy, but they could not secure the necessary copies. However, they did discover some witnesses.

The verdict, on June 25, 1852, was for Achilli. *The Times,* in a leading article, spoke of the proceedings as

"indecorous in their nature, unsatisfactory in their result, and little calculated to increase the respect of the
people for the administration of justice or the estimation
by foreign nations of the English name and character...
We consider that a great blow has been given to the administration of justice in this country, and that Roman
Catholics will henceforth have only too good reason for
asserting that there is no justice for them in cases tend-
ing to arouse the Protestant feelings of judges and juries."

Much against Newman's will, his attorneys moved
for a new trial. This was refused on technical grounds.
The final outcome was that Newman was sentenced to a
fine of one hundred pounds and to imprisonment until the
fine was paid. That meant no imprisonment at all. Newman's friends, Catholic and Protestant, considered the result a triumph. Achilli faded out of view, and while there
have been subsequent Achillis, it is doubtful if they have
ever had the same following among educated and intelligent Protestants that their famous predecessor enjoyed.

The expenses of the trial were very large—twelve
thousand pounds—but they were generously met by contributions from all over the world. Newman was deeply
touched. And he has commemorated the fact in the dedication of his volume of lectures which were being delivered
in Dublin during that trying time. These lectures—*On the
Idea of a University*—form one of the world's great books.
Few men while fighting feverishly against bitter religious
hatred, with bankruptcy and imprisonment as the stakes,
could have concentrated sufficiently to produce an endur-
ing volume on such a subject. The only reference to the
very disagreeable personal circumstances under which the
book was written is in the dedication:

Hospes eram et collegistis me.

.   .   .

In grateful never-dying remembrance
Of his many friends and benefactors,
Living and dead,
At home and abroad,
In Great Britain, Ireland, France,
In Belgium, Germany, Poland, Italy, and Malta,
In North America and other countries,
Who by their resolute prayers and penances,
And by their generous stubborn efforts
And by their munificent alms,
Have broken for him the stress
Of a great anxiety,
THESE DISCOURSES
Offered to Our Lady and St. Philip on its rise,
Composed under its pressure,
Finished on the eve of its termination,
Are respectfully and affectionately inscribed
BY THE AUTHOR

When it was too late to affect the issue, Wiseman
found the documents.

CHAPTER III

A CAMPAIGN IN IRELAND

"I want a laity, not arrogant, not rash in speech, not disputatious, but men who know their religion, who enter into it, who know just where they stand, who know what they hold, and what they do not, who know their creed so well that they can give an account of it, who know so much of history that they can defend it."

(PRESENT POSITION OF CATHOLICS IN ENGLAND)

WHILE Newman was delivering his lectures in the Corn Exchange of Birmingham on *The Present Position of Catholics in England,* Archbishop Cullen of Armagh— afterwards Cardinal Archbishop of Dublin—called upon him to ask if he would undertake the presidency of a Catholic university to be established in Ireland. The National Synod of Thurles, meeting in 1850, had decided (by a majority of one, be it noted) upon the advisability of a Catholic university in Ireland, and Pius IX had given his approval to the idea.

It is the traditional policy of the Catholic Church to have universities of her own, and in Ireland there were special reasons making a Catholic university desirable. For the education of the clergy there were seminaries, such as Maynooth, and other institutions—the Irish colleges in Rome, Salamanca, and Lisbon, for instance, besides the houses of study of the religious orders—but they lacked the breadth of view that might have come from a university as the apex of the educational system. And there was no institution acceptable to all the bishops for the higher education of the laity.

Trinity College, Dublin, enjoying almost as much prestige in Ireland as Oxford and Cambridge in England, was in some ways even more Protestant than the English universities, for it had no Catholic traditions back of it. It had been founded by Protestants for Protestants, and it reflected the bitter religious animosities under which it had originated. The Queen's Colleges recently established under Peel's influence, although nominally non-sectarian, were really Protestant in tone and management. Moreover, in so far as they were not Protestant they divorced religion from education, and so were almost as unsatisfactory to many Catholics as the out and out Protestant Trinity.

The educational situation in England afforded no relief to Irish Catholics. Oxford and Cambridge at this time required subscription to the Thirty-Nine Articles, and London and Manchester labored under about the same objections as the Queen's Colleges. The Catholic colleges, Oscott, Ushaw, St. Edmund's, Downside, Ampleforth, Stonyhurst, carried the laity little farther in a liberal education than the great public schools of England, such as Eton College and Winchester. None of the Catholic colleges had the right to grant degrees recognized by the State.

What Purcell says of English Catholics could probably have been said with equal truth of British Catholics generally: for want of a university education, "they were everywhere placed at a disadvantage in the race of life.

Their intellectual inferiority was a reproach to the Church. It was more and worse; it was a danger to the Faith; for in the higher walks of literature, in philosophy, in science, Catholics occupied a lower intellectual ground. In argument with adversaries of the Faith possessed of the advantages of a University education they were often worsted. In their controversial writings against unbelief and agnosticism Catholics were apt to fall into blunders, which exposed not only themselves but their Faith to ridicule. The result was that for the most part they held their peace; and for want of University training let the argument against Christianity go by default." [1]

When one remembers Challoner, Lingard, Milner and Wiseman—certainly adversaries worthy of any Oxford man—and the fact that during this period many Catholics had been educated on the Continent, one may be tempted to look upon this description of Purcell as somewhat overdrawn. But Wilfrid Ward, a far more reliable witness, is even more drastic, while he is more specific, in his condemnation of the intellectual training given at that time in the English Catholic schools. "Philosophical and theological tenets and arguments," he writes, "were imposed by professors as though they were certain, with insufficient recognition of facts that did not square with them. Moreover, in philosophy itself, what was theologically orthodox was in some quarter insisted upon as therefore necessarily convincing. On the evils consequent on this habit in the ecclesiastical seminaries W. G. Ward often spoke with characteristic vehemence from his personal experience at St. Edmund's. 'The whole philosophical fabric which occupies our colleges,' he wrote to Newman in 1860, 'is rotten from the floor to the roof. Nay, no

[1] *Life of Manning*, II, 288.

one who has not been mixed up practically in a seminary would imagine to how great an extent it *intellectually debauches the students' minds.'* "

In a letter to John Stuart Mill, W. G. Ward wrote: "Untenable propositions are so mixed up with tenable in all the religious books on the subject I happen to know, and there is such a spirit of declamatory exaggeration and the pressing of the theory of innate ideas to such preposterous lengths, that even I myself get quite tempted to turn Atheist while reading them. I should tell you, however (which you possibly may not know), that the modern language, as to the self-evidence of Theism, is quite at variance with the older Catholic writers." [1]

William George Ward was an Ultramontane of the Ultramontanes, and no one would accuse him of the least disloyalty to the Catholic Church. And although we may think his criticism somewhat harsh, as not allowing sufficiently for the handicaps financial and otherwise under which the Catholics of that day were laboring, any unbiased person familiar with the Catholic colleges of this country a generation ago will probably conclude that he was fairly accurate in his statement of the case.

Realizing this educational condition as keenly as W. G. Ward, Newman was naturally interested in Dr. Cullen's proposal. Newman hoped that the five millions or so of Catholics in Ireland might be able to establish a Catholic university without State help, and he thought that a university in Dublin could become for all British Catholics—English and Scottish, as well as Irish—what Louvain was for Belgian Catholics. Newman's main line was education, and so when Dr. Cullen succeeded in get-

[1] Wilfrid Ward, *William George Ward and the Catholic Revival*, p. 27.

ting the Irish Episcopate to invite Newman to head the institution already voted by the Synod of Thurles and approved by Pius IX, Newman decided, in spite of his misgivings, to throw himself into the experiment.

At Dr. Cullen's request, Newman agreed as a preliminary step to give some lectures in Dublin the following May (1852). In the very first lecture he showed an acute realization of the difficulties in the situation. He knew that many persons in Ireland looked upon the University as impracticable, and he admitted that from a worldly standpoint their arguments as to the intrinsic impossibility of the undertaking were perfectly cogent. "Why then," Newman goes on, "should I be so rash and perverse as to involve myself in trouble not properly mine? Why go out of my own place? Why so headstrong as to lay up for myself miscarriage and disappointment, as though I were not sure to have enough personal trial anyhow without going about to seek for it?"

Against the objections of the University's opponents, Newman places just one consideration—the decision of Pius IX. "In the midst of our difficulties," says Newman, "I have one ground of hope, just one stay, but, as I think, a sufficient one, which serves me in the stead of all other argument whatever, which hardens me against criticism, which supports me if I begin to despond, and to which I ever come round, when the question of the possible and the expedient is brought into the discussion. It is the decision of the Holy See; St. Peter has spoken, it is he who has enjoined that which seems to us so unpromising. He has spoken, and he has a claim on us to trust him... All who take part with the Apostle are on the winning side."

"These are not the words of rhetoric," said Newman,

"but of history." No one can doubt Newman's own sincerity in believing this. But he was soon to find that in this particular instance history was to pass a different verdict. Too few among the Irish hierarchy had Newman's implicit trust in Pius IX's wisdom. And in the light of events this introductory lecture, with its abounding loyalty to the Holy See, its almost blind obedience to a papal command, has a poignant pathos.

Hindsight is better than foresight, and in retrospect we can point out a number of difficulties which made failure almost inevitable from the start. First of all, there were the lack of adequate funds and the poverty of the Irish people. To years of political oppression, religious persecution, economic discrimination, and the abuses of absentee English landlordism, there had been added the still persisting effects of the terrible famine of 1846. Not only were no funds in hand, but it was not evident where they were to come from.

Moreover, there was no clear understanding of the funds that would be needed, because there was no clear understanding of what a university should be. Since penal laws had for generations cut them off from normal educational currents, there were very few Irish with any first hand knowledge of real universities. The bishops had been educated almost exclusively in clerical schools, and many of them had little conception of the educational needs of the laity trying to make their way in a hostile world dominated by antagonistic Protestants with all the advantages of wealth, education, and social position.

Nor were the Irish bishops a unit in desiring a Catholic university. Archbishop Murray of Dublin, in whose diocese the University was to be established, and Dr. Russell of Maynooth, two of the foremost leaders among the clergy, thought that some arrangement should be arrived at by which Catholics might use the Queen's Colleges. Prominent laymen had a similar attitude towards Trinity. Mr. Thomas O'Hagan, afterwards Lord Chancellor, may be taken as representing an influential group. Newman thus records O'Hagan's views: " 'A feeling,' he says, 'on the side of Trinity College against a Catholic University is the historical feeling. For years under Dr. Doyle [Bishop of Kildare] mixed schools, that is, equal rights in education, were the cry. A bishop said the other day: "Where is the line of demarcation to be drawn? When people are mixed and society is mixed, education must be mixed." ' This feeling," adds Newman, "I found to be in full possession of educated minds in 1854."

In addition to all this, the situation was further complicated by political differences between some of the bishops and some of the laity. The Young Ireland movement was developing, and it met opposition in certain ecclesiastical quarters. Newman was to find that he was expected to consider not only the educational qualifications of his prospective professors, but also their political affiliations. Archbishop Cullen was vigorously opposed to the appointment of Young Irelanders, no matter what their training and ability. To the natural jealousy against Englishmen dominating an Irish university there were added internal jealousies among the Irish.

Considering the various differences among the Irish bishops, it is not surprising that little help and coöperation could be expected from the English bishops. They were too busy with mountainous difficulties at home to give much financial, or even moral, support to what was frankly an experiment across the Irish Channel. And racial and nationalistic antagonisms were not sufficiently overcome by a common Catholicism to produce a whole-hearted unity in the face of an undertaking that was at best of doubtful promise.

A final element of weakness in the situation was Newman's own lack of executive ability and his ignorance of the administrative problems of a university. There were friends of Newman who realized from the beginning that he lacked the qualifications necessary to start a university *de novo*, even if he had had the full backing of the Irish hierarchy. Thus Ambrose Phillips de Lisle wrote at the time: "As to the Irish University, I wish it well, but I have scant hopes of its success... Newman, though a man of extraordinary ability and prodigious learning, never had anything to do with the management of a University; his position at Oxford was always a subordinate one, and his great reputation was rather that of a Preacher and a Theologian than of a scholar or teacher in the literary acceptation of the term." [1]

Newman might have succeeded as president of an already successful, well-established university. With a united hierarchy, an enthusiastic laity, and ample financial backing, he might have been successful in establishing a new university. But under the circumstances he was foredoomed to failure in the Dublin experiment. For although Newman possessed great tenacity of purpose, he lacked the driving force, the judgment of men, the flair for politics necessary to overcome the obstacles in the Irish situation. How poor a judge of character Newman was is illustrated by the fact that he asked Manning to be his vice-rector. Manning, it is true, had in abundance the executive ability, the knack of governing men, which Newman very decidedly lacked, and if anyone could have

[1] Purcell, *Life of Phillips de Lisle*, I, 3.

handled the Irish bishops that man was Manning. But
these two could never have worked together as rector and
vice-rector, and Manning was too astute to accept a task
in which he would have been butting his head against a
stone wall. He showed his practical wisdom by staying in
England, where he later became Cardinal Archbishop of
Westminster.

Dr. Cullen was the strongest opponent of any compromise with the Queen's Colleges, and he had succeeded
in getting the policy adopted, although with a bare majority of one, by the Synod of Thurles. The alternative
to using the Queen's Colleges was to establish a separate
Catholic University. So the Irish bishops formally passed
a resolution (November 12, 1851) inviting Newman to be
rector. After his acceptance of the rectorship, however,
Newman felt himself so completely ignored by the Irish
hierarchy that in the spring of 1852 he fixed a date on
which he would resign unless a letter of some sort came
to him from Ireland. That day came with no letter, and
Newman actually wrote his resignation. But before he
mailed it a communication, having nothing to do with the
University, arrived from Dr. Cullen, and Newman did not
resign.[1]

Meantime, Archbishop Cullen had been transferred
to Dublin, and thus one obstacle to the University had
been removed—the establishment of an institution in a
diocese where the Bishop, Dr. Murray, was opposed to
the whole undertaking. So in May, 1852, Newman began

[1] Newman gives a history of the University and of his relations
with the Irish Bishops in a volume printed privately in 1872, and
not included in his collected works. The title, *My Campaign in
Ireland*, reflects Newman's mature judgment on the whole affair.
The quotations in the following account are taken from this
volume.

his series of nine discourses, to be given one each week, on *The Idea of a University*. The lectures were a success in spite of Newman's anomalous position as a man who had been invited to head a paper University without ever having been confirmed in the appointment.

In an attempt to end this awkward position, Newman wrote to Archbishop Cullen in July asking for a formal confirmation as rector and insisting that he must have the appointment of the vice-rector, deans, and tutors; as to professors, Newman was willing to accept any the Archbishop might name, "so that they were good ones and creditable to the University." But Dr. Cullen never answered the letter, and, with the approval of the other Archbishop, Dr. Taylor was made secretary of the University and Dr. Leahy vice-rector. Newman looked upon these appointments as a move on the part of the Archbishops to protect themselves against a rector who was an Englishman and an outsider. He makes the comment: "The truth is that these Bishops are so accustomed to be absolute that they usurp the rights of others and rough-ride over their wishes and their plans quite innocently, without meaning it, and are astonished, not at finding out the fact, but at its being impossible to those others."

Early in January, 1853, before the meeting of the Bishops that month, Newman wrote again to Dr. Cullen, urging that he must have a formal appointment. The Bishops' meeting came and went with no word from Dr. Cullen. On February 3 Newman wrote again, and a third time in March. He received no answer, and no acknowledgment of his letters. "I suppose," says Newman, "it was what he had learned in Rome,—to act, not to speak,—to be peremptory in act, to keep his counsel, not to commit himself to paper; to treat me not as his equal, but as his subject."

Not until October, 1853, did the University Committee at last summon Newman to Ireland, putting two thousand pounds in his hands. Looking back on the whole affair, it seems absurd that Newman should have waited two years before getting a really official call to undertake his duties as rector. But that was only typical of the delay, the lack of interest, the almost obstructionary attitude of some of the Bishops—and it shows also Newman's unfitness for dealing with them. A more worldly-wise man than Newman, once he had realized the situation, would have found some excuse gracefully to withdraw from the position; a very pugnacious man might have brought the Bishops to terms. But Newman was too shy, too sensitive, too proud, and too submissive to apostolic authority to fight. He felt that the Bishops should appreciate for themselves the great favor he had done them in accepting the work. If the Bishops did not have this appreciation, then Newman was not going to urge his own claims. In the parlance of the day, Newman failed to "sell" himself to the Bishops.

"I was disappointed, desponding, and sore," records Newman. "The Committee, *magno hiatu,* had done very little. They had called me over to Ireland, but they had done nothing to set me off... The éclat of the Synod of Thurles in 1850 and of the Pope's Brief had passed away. My lectures in Dublin in May, 1852 ... had been a flash in the pan... If in the coming January I went over to Ireland as I proposed, I should seem to be acting on my own hook. I should be an Englishman taking upon himself to teach the Paddies what education was, what a University, and how it was their duty to have one with me as Rector; I should seem to be carrying out, not a great Council's resolve, but a hobby of my own,—to be a propagandist, not an authoritative superior, a convert, without means, looking out for a situation and feathering my own nest from the pockets of the Irish, with an outlay for me and my surroundings to the tune of 5,000 pounds per annum. That I intended to make a good thing of it was actually said."

These are harsh words, and evidently they were written in some pique. There is no excuse for Newman calling the Irish "Paddies"—and that twenty years after the event. But who can doubt that Newman was accurately expressing the situation as far as some of the Irish went? Of course suspicions of self-seeking on Newman's part were utterly unfounded. And instead of being a propagandist, Newman failed partly because he was not one. If he had been a hearty, handshaking, backslapping mixer, the story of his "Campaign in Ireland" might have been different.

It was not until January 4, 1854—two years and six months after the original invitation to Newman to be rector—that Archbishop Cullen wrote undertaking to have such a public summons to Ireland as Newman desired. During the same month, Cardinal Wiseman wrote from Rome saying that the Pope was ready to issue another brief in regard to the University. Newman's experiences had apparently impressed Wiseman with the need of giving him an ecclesiastical dignity equal to that of the Irish Bishops, and on Wiseman's suggestion Pius IX agreed to make Newman a bishop *in partibus infidelium.*[1]

---

[1] That is, bishop of some see in Asia or elsewhere which had been suppressed because there were no longer any Roman Catholics in its territory. Such sees are perpetuated by giving the title to some

Unfortunately, Wiseman had not taken into account the natural sensitiveness of the Irish Bishops against outside influence appointing to equal rank with themselves a man holding office under them. Perhaps, too, Newman was right in thinking that Dr. Cullen wanted to keep him as his subject, instead of wishing him to be a bishop just as much as himself, although without territorial jurisdiction. At any rate, some of the Irish Bishops made their opposition known in Rome, and as the University was in Archbishop Cullen's diocese, Wiseman could not gracefully urge the matter further. Leastwise, Wiseman dropped the idea, and Newman never became a bishop.

However, the knowledge of the proposed honor for Newman became known before the opposition quashed the plan, and congratulations were showered upon Newman. Bishop Ullathorne even addressed Newman as "Right Reverend"—the title of a bishop—at a public gathering in Birmingham. "Various friends," writes Newman, "made me costly presents in anticipation of the requirements of a Bishop. The Duke of Norfolk sent me a massive gold chain. Mrs. Bowden a cross and chain of Maltese filigree work. Mr. Hope-Scott, a morse for a cope, ornamented with his wife's jewels, and Mr. Monsell a cross. So matters remained for some months. When I went to Ireland I made it known at Limerick and elsewhere that the Holy Father had designated me a Bishop."

The whole incident was most embarrassing to a man of Newman's sensitiveness. He must have felt like a girl who had announced her approaching marriage to a gentleman of distinction, had received congratulations and pres-

one elsewhere who never resides in his bishopric, and who while having the rank of bishop has no subjects and no territorial jurisdiction.

ents, only to find that the wedding was called off by the supposed groom-to-be. A crueler joke could hardly have been imagined, and a bigger man than Archbishop Cullen would have pocketed his own pride rather than wound Newman like this.

Newman reached Dublin on February 7, 1854. In a papal brief, he had been designated rector; the bishopric still seemed assured, and things looked fairly bright. But Newman's interviews with Irish leaders soon put another complexion on the situation.

The day after his arrival, Newman called on Father Curtis, "the Provincial (I think) of the Jesuits . . . a man of great character and experience." Father Curtis said, "on the experience of thirty years, that the class of youths *did not exist* in Ireland who should come to the University; that the middle class was too poor; that the gentleman class wished a degree for their sons, and sent them to Trinity College; and the upper class, who were few, sent their sons to English Universities,[1] etc. . . Father Curtis ended by saying: 'My advice to you is this: go to the Archbishop and say: Don't attempt the University—give up the idea.' "

Dr. Keneham, the president of Maynooth, showed distinct coldness towards the project of a university; and the prospects made Dr. Russell, also of Maynooth, very despondent. The Bishop of Limerick, Dr. Ryan, was "very strong against the possibility of a University," allowing his name to be used in connection with it only on condi-

---

[1] What Father Curtis meant by English universities is not quite clear. At that time the only English universities without a religious test for attendance were the recently established and still small London and Manchester. They can hardly have attracted many Catholics from Ireland. Oxford and Cambridge did not remove the religious test until that very year, 1854.

tion "that he should not be supposed to prophesy anything but failure." Dr. Ryan was convinced that it would be impossible to induce students to attend a university without power from the State to grant degrees, and that the State would not grant this power after what had been done in the way of the Queen's Colleges.

Undoubtedly, Bishop Ryan here put his finger on one of the major causes of the ultimate failure of the University. For if the world outside would not recognize the education as of university grade, Catholics were not strong enough to ignore such an attitude. But if Newman's idea had been carried out, this obstacle could have been overcome. For Newman wished to send the graduates of the University to take examinations before the Queen's Colleges, and to receive degrees from them. It was the system followed at Louvain—except for theological degrees—and Newman hoped to establish a sort of British Louvain.

The laymen whom Newman consulted personally, or through friends, took about the same view as Father Curtis and Bishop Ryan. Lords Kenmare, Castlerosse, and Fingall objected to the use of their names as supporting the University. On every side there was doubt and discouragement.

"Here then," sums up Wilfrid Ward, "was the position gradually brought home to him. A Catholic University was wanted as a political and ecclesiastical weapon against mixed education. For this purpose his name was a valuable asset. In this sense all the Bishops favored the University. But as a practical project, in the interests of education, hardly anyone took it seriously.

"And, on the other hand, Cullen's ecclesiastical ideals had helped to estrange the laity from the University.

Newman in his notes quotes one influential lay correspondent as forecasting its probable character as that of a
'close borough of clergymen and a clerical village.' Another held its *object* to be the placing of Catholic education entirely in the hands of the clergy, and the exclusion
of the laity from all interference."

But while interviewing the Irish leaders, Newman
had his droll experiences as well as his sad ones, and he
narrates them with a sense of humor doubly pleasing in a
man who was so sensitive—one might almost say touchy.
In a letter to Fr. Austin Mills, of the Birmingham Oratory,
Newman relates how at Kilkenny, either as a joke or by
mistake, the Irish cabby "took him to the Protestant
Superintendent's palace, a certain O'Brien, who now for
fifteen years past has been writing against him, the author,
and calling him bad names." Unfortunately, perhaps, the
Superintendent was in London at the time.

At an Ursuline academy, Newman was compelled to
see all the girls dressed in their uniforms with ribbons
and medals, and was asked to make a speech. Newman,
the Oxford don, was never much of a hand at talking
formally to school-girls, but he did the best he could.
He tells his correspondent, "how he puzzled and fussed
himself what on earth he should say impromptu to a par-
cel of school-girls; and how, in his distress, he *did* make
what he considered his best speech; and how, when it was
ended, the Mother school-mistress did not know he had
made it, or even begun it, and still asked for his speech.
And how he would not, because he could not, make a
second speech; and how to make it up, he asked for a
holiday for the girls; and how the Mother school-mistress
flatly refused him by reason (as he verily believes) because she would not recognize and accept his speech, and

wanted another, and thought she had dressed up her girls for nothing; and how he nevertheless drank her raspberry vinegar, which much resembles a nun's anger, being a sweet acid, and how he thought to himself, it being his birthday, that he was full old to be forgiven if he could not at a moment act the spiritual jack pudding to a girl's school."

In Limerick, the Bishop, Dr. Ryan, did all he could to honor Newman, and entertained him at a large banquet with his clergy. It was in the pre-Volstead days, and apparently few of the guests had come under the influence of the great contemporary advocate of total abstinence, Father Matthew. Amid the convivial scenes of the evening, the Bishop announced that he appointed Dr. Newman vicar-general of the diocese. There was a thunder of applause, and the assembly broke out into songs of '98. The surprising thing is that Newman saw the humor of the situation, and in later years enjoyed recounting the incident.

With so much to discourage him, and so little of encouragement, Newman kept on doggedly. On June 3, 1854, he was formally installed as rector, and the opening of the School of Philosophy and Letters was set for the third of November following. The School began with 17 students, rising to 27 during the term. The second term began with 33 students, eight of whom lived with Newman in a rented house in Harcourt Street.

One of Newman's pet projects was a University Church. But there were ecclesiastical and financial complications. Existing parochial churches did not want to see within their territorial limits another church that might possibly draw people away from them; and Archbishop Cullen could not give any financial assistance. However, a small chapel was built facing St. Stephen's Green. Newman put into it what was left from the contributions for the expenses of the Achilli trial. This chapel is one of the few permanent things that came out of the whole University experiment, for it is now used by the National University of Ireland.

Contemporaneously with his installation in June, 1854, Newman started *The University Gazette*, editing it himself for a year. Besides information in regard to the University, Newman published in it a number of other addresses and papers, and his *Discourses on the Idea of a University*.

In the summer of 1856, a medical school was started. From the first, it was a success in attracting students and in giving standing to Catholic practitioners. In fact, the School of Medicine continued after the other departments of the University had been closed, and is still in existence.

Newman also established a school of science and a professorship of Celtic literature. He looked upon this latter as one of the few worth while accomplishments of the University. A stimulus was given to the study of Celtic and to research in Irish antiquities even outside the University, and the effects of this continued after the University had ceased to exist.

As regards the faculty, Newman tried to use local talent wherever possible, and he did have a majority of Irishmen on the staff. But in large measure he was forced to turn to his old Oxford friends, and to converts—and anyone who knows social and national and political feelings will realize how this still further complicated an already difficult situation. In fact, as early as September 30, 1854, Archbishop Cullen wrote a letter which Newman interpreted as an attempt to get rid of Mr. Ornsby and

Mr. Stewart, professors respectively of classics and ancient history.[1]

The foregoing outline of what was actually done in connection with the University, indicates how hard Newman must have labored during these few years. A great deal more was accomplished than an impartial observer would have expected possible in the face of the difficulties of the situation. Moreover, Newman did this in spite of the feeling that hung over him of actual and prospective misunderstandings with the leaders of the Irish episcopate,

[1] The following is the first published list of professors:

1. Dogmatic Theology, the Rev. Father Edmund O'Reilly, D.D., S.J.
2. Holy Scripture, the Very Rev. Patrick Leahy, D.D.
3. Archaeology and Irish History, Eugene O'Curry, Esq., M.R.I.A., etc., etc.
4. Political Economy, John O'Hagan, Esq., M.A.
5. Geography, J. H. Robertson, Esq.
6. Classical Literature, Robert Ornsby, Esq., M.A.
7. Ancient History, James Stewart, Esq., M.A.
8. Philosophy of History, Thomas W. Allies, Esq., M.A.
9. Political and Social Science, Aubrey de Vere, Esq.
10. Poetry, D. Florence Macarthy, Esq.
11. The Fine Arts, J. H. Pollen, Esq., M.A.
12. Logic, David Dunne, Esq.
13. Mathematics, Edward Butler, Esq., M.A.
14. Natural Philosophy, Henry Hennessy, Esq., M.A.
15. Civil Engineering, Terence Flanagan, Esq., M.I.C.E.
16. French Literature, M. Pierre le Page Renouf.
17. Italian Literature, Signor Marani.
18. Practice of Surgery, Andrew Ellis, Esq., F.R.C.S.
19. Anatomy (i), Thomas Hayden, Esq., L.R.C.S.I.
20. Anatomy (ii), Robert Cryan, Esq., L.R.C.S.I. and K. and Q.C.P.I.
21. Physiology and Pathology, Robert D. Lyons, Esq., M.B.T.C.D. and L.R.C.S.
22. Demonstrator in Anatomy, Henry Tyrrell, Esq., L.R.C.S.I.
23. Demonstrator in Anatomy, John O'Reilly, Esq., L.R.C.S.I.

and in spite of his never changed conviction, formed in 1854, that the University was doomed to failure. Mr. J. H. Pollen, the professor of fine arts, says that "Newman had a constant sense that he was in a hornet's nest. Some of the Bishops did not give him his proper place—having a conception of their position which was incompatible with their treating him as an equal. Newman on his side preserved towards them an attitude of painstaking politeness. He was also tried by the line taken by these prelates in respect of intellectual problems. 'They regard an intellectual man as on the road to perdition,' he said." [1]

As to Archbishop Cullen specifically, Newman wrote to Professor Ornsby: "Dr. Cullen wishes well to the University, but while he is ignorant as anybody *how* to do good he has not the heart to have perfect confidence in anyone... Here is the *origo mali;* an Archbishop who will not trust anyone." And Newman adds the delightful touch, "I wonder he does not cook his own dinners." [2]

Newman had agreed to give five years to the University, and his determination was not changed by the fact that two of these years had been frittered away without doing anything. So in April, 1856, he announced to Archbishop Cullen that he intended to resign the following June. And although Dr. Cullen urged Newman to remain, he was probably relieved on the whole, for he had gotten a bear by the tail and did not know how to let go. Bishop Patterson, in a letter to Wilfrid Ward, uses another figure. Archbishop Cullen had "hoped that he had

[1] Ward, *Life of Newman,* I, 355.

[2] *Ibid.,* 370. In reviewing the painful relations between Newman and Archbishop Cullen, one is reminded that the pen may be mightier than the crosier as well as than the sword. For Cardinal Cullen is almost forgotten, whereas Newman through his writings has won a place among the great religious leaders of all time.

found a splendid horse to do his work against the Queen's Colleges, but now he began to regard it as a Pegasus with wings and beyond his control. He saw fire coming from its nostrils, and while its feet nervously pawed the ground, Cullen stood by in dread of some new and unexpected flight into a medium beyond his reach and understanding." [1]

In 1857 Newman ceased to reside in Dublin. And although he continued as nominal head of the University for another year, practically he severed his connection with the experiment.

The whole attempt to found a Catholic University in Dublin would have been a farce, if it had not been pathetic. Here was one of the greatest men of the Victorian Era, or of any other age in England, wasting time and energy trying to establish a University on a shoestring, when the very men who had called him to the task did not support him. The financial side of the University must have seemed pitifully cheap to an Oxford man, even in those days. As rector, Newman received 400 pounds a year. The professors were to get 300 pounds with room and board. The University budget contemplated a total outlay of 5,000 pounds a year, with the School of Science and that of Medicine getting 1,000 pounds each, and Philosophy and Letters another 2,000 pounds.

It is true that education was not so costly at that time as it is now. Elaborate research laboratories were not customary, and the curriculum did not attempt to cover everything in the universe. But after making all due allowance for these limitations, and for the greater purchasing power of money in those days, $25,000 was too little for all the expenses of a first class University, including

[1] *Ibid.*, 370.

professors' salaries, laboratory material and equipment, the renting of buildings, the accumulation of a library, etc., etc. And $1500 a year was too small a salary for an outstanding professor, with an honored name, as Newman had, in the world of scholarship. No wonder the shoestring broke!

However, of all the paradoxical things connected with this educational abortion, the most surprising is the question of religious teaching. The University was supposed to safeguard Catholics against the dangers of Protestant Trinity and undenominational Queen's. But the safeguarding, apparently, was to be mostly negative, for Newman had to defend the idea of teaching religion to the undergraduates, and he wrote a long letter on the subject to the Dean of the Faculty of Philosophy and Letters.[1]

In the beginning, it seems, students could go through the University without even studying Catholic philosophy. For in Newman's *Campaign* is an official letter from the professor of logic in which he says: "According to the present system of studies and examinations, a student of the University may pass through his whole course without having attended a single lecture in Metaphysics, or having read a single line on the subject."

But in spite of all the lamentable failure, certain tangible results did come out of Newman's efforts. In addition to what has already been mentioned, some of the professors made worth while contributions to scholarship. For example, there is T. W. Allies' work on the philosophy of history, *The Formation of Christendom.* And certainly not least, were Newman's 1852 lectures on *The Idea of a University,* with his occasional addresses bearing on various phases of education. R. H. Hutton has said that *The*

[1] This letter is printed in *My Campaign in Ireland,* 156 *ff.*

Idea of a University had "a very great effect in stimulating the reforms which soon afterwards took place in the Universities of Oxford and Cambridge."[1] And in the United States, where the only thing on which those interested in higher education are agreed is in being dissatisfied with existing methods, Newman's lectures can still be read with profit.

The main thought of these nine discourses can be summed up as emphasizing the unity of education. Newman was always opposed to a purely secular education. As an Anglican, he had written anonymously a series of letters to *The Times*—republished under the curious title (Newman was seldom happy in titles) *The Tamworth Reading Room*—urging the importance of religious knowledge.[2]

It was only natural, therefore, that in establishing a Catholic University in Dublin, Newman should spend considerable time in vindicating the place of theology in a university. Three discourses out of the nine are given to this theme—"Theology as a Branch of Knowledge," "Bearing of Theology on Other Knowledge," and "Bearing of Other Knowledge on Theology." Newman shows that if a university is to dispense *universal* knowledge, it cannot afford to leave out theology, which is a branch of knowledge, and which gives a unity and coherence to all other knowledge in the light of ultimate ends.

But it would be a mistake to draw the hasty conclusion that Newman's idea of a university was a sort of glorified theological institution. Newman faced facts and kept his feet on the ground. He knew that most of his

---

[1] *Cardinal Newman*, 216.

[2] Incidentally, Newman showed such an incisive style and keen journalistic sense in these letters that *The Times* offered him a position on its staff at an attractive salary.

students expected to live in the world, and that he was bound to give them an effective training for such a life. "For why do we educate," asks Newman in his last discourse, "except to prepare for the world?" And then he goes on with as well balanced a statement of objectives and means of a liberal education as the educational world has ever had.

"If then a University is a direct preparation for this world, let it be what it professes. It is not a convent; it is not a seminary; it is a place to fit men of the world for the world. We cannot possibly keep them from plunging into the world, with all its ways and principles and maxims, when their time comes; but we can prepare them against the inevitable; and it is not the way to learn to swim in troubled waters never to have gone into them. . . Cut out from your class books all broad manifestations of the natural man; and these manifestations are waiting for your pupils' benefit at the very doors of your lecture room in living and breathing substance. They will meet him there in all the charm of novelty, and all the fascination of genius or of amiableness. To-day a pupil, to-morrow a member of the great world; to-day confined to the lives of the Saints, to-morrow thrown upon Babel. . . You have succeeded but in this—making the world his University."

Newman enforced with the utmost power the true purpose of a liberal education, that it is the pursuit of knowledge for the sake of knowledge, and not for the sake of any of the fruits of knowledge, however important. In fact, Newman repudiated the idea that the acquisition of knowledge is merely subsidiary even to religion. Some of his phrases have a curiously modern ring. They could have been written by Everett Dean Martin or Abraham Flexner.

It should be noted that these lectures say nothing about one function of a university—that of increasing and advancing human knowledge through research, scientific or otherwise. For in Newman's mind research was no part of a university's task. In the preface to the published discourses, he tells us that he would leave to academies and special societies the advancement of knowledge, while restricting a university to the teaching of existing knowledge. In this attitude, Newman was certainly going counter to what has been the modern development of universities through the world. And surely we could ill afford to do without the contributions that universities have made to the sum of human knowledge. Nor is there any prospect that universities will abandon the function of research.

Nevertheless, Newman was undoubtedly right in saying that "to discover and to teach are distinct functions; they are also distinct gifts, and are not commonly found united in the same person." Many a good research man has been hampered by having to teach; and many a good teacher has been spoiled by having to do research for the sake of academic advancement. Our universities might profitably recognize the distinction Newman insists upon, and by relieving their research men from teaching and their teachers from research, make all the more effective their double function of teaching and research.

It should be noted, too, that these discourses take the view that the object of a university "is intellectual, not moral." And this is all the more remarkable, as it seems in opposition to Newman's actual practice. At Oxford he had been the leader of a movement to recognize a responsibility on the part of the University for the moral life of the undergraduates. One of the first things he did on getting a position of authority was to undertake what was almost a crusade against drinking bouts. In Dublin he certainly expected to influence the moral life of the students through hostels, the sermons and religious exercises in the University chapel, and he even went so far as to consider leasing a theater so that the students would be protected from immoral plays. One would have expected Newman to take the view that good religious teaching must be dynamic, in the sense of moving the will as well as informing the intellect. Newman's own religious teaching was certainly of this nature. And, indeed, there would seem to be little reason for having a separate Catholic University, if it were to leave out the moral side of education.

Naturally, every educational problem cannot be treated in nine lectures. Lacunae are to be expected. But there are certain topics omitted that would seem to have fitted in naturally with the subjects of some of Newman's discourses. For instance, one looks in vain in the lectures on "The Bearing of Theology on Other Knowledge" or "The Bearing of Other Knowledge on Theology," for any treatment of the important question of academic freedom. However, in 1855, after the University was actually open, Newman insisted strongly on the freedom of scientific investigation in a lecture before the School of Science.[1]

"I say, then," declared Newman in this lecture, "that it is a matter of primary importance in the cultivation of those sciences, in which truth is discoverable by the human intellect, that the investigator should be free, independent, unshackled in his movement; that he should

[1] *Christianity and Scientific Investigation.*

be allowed and enabled to fix his mind intently, nay, exclusively, on his special object, without the risk of being distracted every other minute in the process and progress of his enquiry, by charges of temerariousness, or by warnings against extravagance or scandal."

Assuming that a scientific speculator or inquirer is not in conflict with dogma, nor interpreting the Scriptures, nor recklessly scandalizing the weak, Newman maintained "that he is not bound, in conducting his researches, to be every moment adjusting his course by the maxims of the schools or by popular traditions, or by those of any other science distinct from his own, or to be ever narrowly watching what those external sciences have to say to him, or to be determined to be edifying, or to be ever answering heretics and unbelievers; being confident, from the impulse of a generous faith, that, however his line of investigation may swerve now and then, and vary to and fro in its course, or threaten momentary collision or embarrassment with any other department of knowledge, theological or not, yet, if he lets it alone, it will be sure to come home, because truth can never be contrary to truth."

Was not Newman here following his old habit as Vicar of St. Mary's of talking to himself? Had Newman not already learned, by bitter personal experience, better than anyone in his audience, how strong was the opposition to any such freedom as he outlined? Perhaps Newman's ideas of academic freedom helped to make Dr. Cullen realize he had employed a Pegasus, as Bishop Patterson said, instead of a steady-going cart horse. And Newman knew that some of the prelates with whom he dealt looked upon "any intellectual man as on the road to perdition."

Newman's was a forlorn hope, but he had nailed his flag to the masthead and he would not haul it down. Which nautical figure is carried out by Newman himself in another paragraph of the same lecture. "If we reason," says Newman, "we must submit to the conditions of reason. We cannot use it by halves; we must use it as proceeding from Him who has also given us Revelation; and to be ever interrupting its processes, and diverting its attention by objections brought from a higher knowledge, is parallel to a landsman's dismay at the change in the course of a vessel on which he has deliberately embarked, and argues surely some distrust either in the powers of Reason on the one hand, or the certainty of Revealed Truth on the other. The passenger should not have embarked at all, if he did not reckon on the chance of a rough sea, of currents, of wind and tide, of rocks and shoals; and we should act more wisely in discountenancing altogether the exercise of Reason than in being alarmed and impatient under the suspense, delay, and anxiety which, from the nature of the case, may be found to attach to it. Let us eschew altogether secular history, and science, and philosophy for good and all, if we are not to be allowed to be sure that Revelation is so true that the altercations and perplexities of human opinion cannot really or eventually injure its authority."

There was a vein of pathetic prophecy running through this discourse. Newman was a sort of reversed Balaam. He began as the prophet of a reasonable academic freedom, and then in spite of himself he wrote what could well have been the summary of his own bitter disappointments for the next twenty years.

"Great minds," pleaded Newman, "need elbow room, not indeed in the domain of faith, but of thought. And so, indeed, do lesser minds, and all minds. . . Yet if you insist that in their speculations, researches, or conclusions in their particular science, it is not enough that they submit to the Church generally, and acknowledge its dogmas, but that they must get up all that divines have taught or the multitudes believed on religious matters, you simply crush and stamp out the flame within them, and they can do nothing at all."

We must be big enough, and sure enough of truth, to make allowances for mistakes. For, as Newman says with a touching humility because of its unmistakable personal reference, "every human system, every human writer, is open to just criticism."

"But what then?" continues Newman. "Make him shut up his portfolio; good! And then perhaps you lose what, on the whole, and in spite of incidental mistakes, would have been one of the ablest defences of Revealed Truth (directly or indirectly, according to the subject) ever given to the world."

Naturally, with his usual care and prudence, Newman safeguarded himself against an exaggerated and dangerous academic license. In the concluding paragraph of this lecture, he wrote: "On the other hand, it must of course be remembered, Gentlemen, that I am supposing all along good faith, honest intentions, a loyal Catholic spirit, and a deep sense of responsibility. I am supposing, in the scientific enquirer, a due fear of giving scandal, of seeming to countenance views which he does not really countenance, and of siding with parties from whom he heartily differs. I am supposing that he is fully alive to the existence and the power of the infidelity of the age; that he keeps in mind the moral weakness and the intellectual confusion of the majority of men; and that he has no wish at all that any one soul should get harm from certain speculations to-day, though he may have the satisfaction of being sure that those speculations will, as far as they are erroneous or misunderstood, be corrected in the course of the next half-century."

No doubt Newman was "fully alive to the existence and the power" of the reactionaries of his time; no doubt he kept "in mind the moral weakness and the intellectual confusion" of his opponents. But if he were going to head a university, he had to head it as he conceived it should be. He could not compromise the cause of truth.

Newman's lecture, *Christianity and Scientific Investigation,* was written before the theory of evolution set the theological world agog. But it is significant that neither here nor elsewhere did Newman take up a reconciliation of religion with specific scientific theories. He contented himself with laying down principles, partly because he did not feel himself competent to speak as a scientist, and partly because he knew scientific attitudes changed rapidly. It seemed to him somewhat undignified for eternal religious truth to be tied up with the scientific outlook of any one generation.

The whole experience of the University fiasco was very trying to Newman. There was not only failure—there was disillusionment. Although Newman was intensely interested in education, he would never have entered upon so unpromising an experiment except that the supreme authority in the Church had approved it. In a touching passage in the first of his discourses on the idea of a university, Newman had said that all history showed the Pope was always on the winning side, and he was merely following the guidance of the Holy See. To find that this time the Pope was not to win, was hard. And to have the

Pope lose, not merely because of the formidable array of worldly obstacles against him, but also, and perhaps primarily, because the Catholic body was split by jealousies of one sort or another, was doubly hard.

Wilfrid Ward says that the events of these years— from 1853 to 1858—"did much to break his spirit." [1] But this seems to be a misunderstanding of Newman. A man of Newman's sensitiveness, one who lived superbly the ideal of a gentleman described in that famous passage of his *Idea of a University,* naturally suffered from the rough handling of men who were not gentlemen. But no man whose spirit had been broken could have written the *Apologia,* or could have entered the lists so successfully against the premier debater of England, Gladstone, in defending Catholic teaching on the relations between Church and State. Some men going through the same experiences as Newman would have become morbid, hypersensitive, over-critical, a trial to everyone around them. But in spite of the very cutting passages we find in the original edition of the *Apologia,* we may say that Newman came through this suffering chastened in spirit, mellowed, sweeter-tempered. Newman was metal tried in the fire and found to be all gold.

Newman had expected, and some of his friends had hoped, that the University in Dublin would have been for the Catholics of the whole of Great Britain. However, the English bishops were not associated directly with the University, and they gave Newman practically no support. And so when it was evident that the University in Dublin would fail, some of Newman's friends suggested that he transfer his energies to a similar institution in England,

[1] *Life of Newman,* I, 386.

where he would be more likely to have the support of the English bishops. It is not surprising that Newman had no relish for such an undertaking. He had gone to Ireland only because the Synod of Thurles and the Pope had approved the plan; without a similar high ecclesiastical sanction, he would never embark on any other scheme that from every worldly standpoint had so many obstacles in the way.

Nevertheless, Newman realized the need of doing something for the higher education of Catholics. As religious tests for attendance at Oxford and Cambridge had been withdrawn in 1854, Catholic gentlemen were sending their sons to these universities in increasing numbers. Newman preferred a separate Catholic university. But failing in that, he considered the next best thing was to make the attendance of Catholics at the English universities as innocuous as possible.

Cardinal Wiseman, with his deep trust in men and his confidence that Catholicism could hold its own in the modern world, had at first rather welcomed this movement of Catholics towards the English universities. Wiseman was too much in touch with the laity not to feel the deepest sympathy with their desire to enjoy the same intellectual advantages possessed by their fellow countrymen. That Catholics should once more be trained in the universities raised by their forefathers, in this day when so many of the noblest sons of Oxford were returning to the Church, seemed to Cardinal Wiseman like the fulfillment of one of the dearest dreams of his heart.

It is not surprising, therefore, that under such circumstances Newman's thoughts should turn to some plan whereby the Catholic youth, without extreme danger to their faith, could enjoy the training under which he had so marvellously developed. To found a Catholic house at Oxford where his voice might again be heard and his influence felt in university circles, not only in training Catholic undergraduates, but in explaining the Catholic Faith to Anglicans and others, or in defending before the graduates of the University the first principles of revealed religion, seemed to Newman to be the greatest service he could render to the Church, now that he could get no support in founding a separate Catholic university.

"How are you to prepare young Catholics," wrote Newman, "for taking part in life, for filling stations in a Protestant country such as England, without going to the English Universities? Impossible. Either then refuse to let Catholics avail themselves of these privileges, of going into Parliament, of taking their seat in the House of Lords, of becoming Lawyers, Commissioners, etc., etc., *or* let them go *there, where alone* they will be able to put themselves on a par with Protestants. Argument first.

"2. They will get more harm in London life than at Oxford or Cambridge. A boy of 19 goes to some London office, with no restraint—he goes at that age to Oxford or Cambridge, and is at least under *some* restraint.

"3. Why are you not consistent, and forbid him to go into the Army? Why don't you forbid him to go to such an 'Academy' at Woolwich? He may get at Woolwich as much harm in his faith and morals as at the Universities." [1]

Oxford was in the Birmingham diocese, and so came under Bishop Ullathorne. In April, 1866, Ullathorne offered the Oxford mission to Newman. Newman had bought five acres in Oxford in 1864, and now started collecting funds for the establishment of a branch Oratory.

[1] Ward, *Life of Newman*, II, 70.

But in order that there might be no last moment hitch, authorization was sought from Propaganda for the undertaking. However, Manning, who had become Archbishop of Westminster in 1865, was vehemently opposed to the attendance of Catholics at Oxford. Manning was sincerely convinced that instead of de-Protestantizing Oxford, Oxford would de-Catholicize the Catholics. And undoubtedly he could make out a plausible case *a priori*. Oxford and Cambridge were still Protestant, the chief training schools for Anglican ministers, and still closing all positions of emolument to Catholics. What Manning did not see, but Newman did, and experience has proved, was that attendance of Catholics at Oxford and Cambridge was the lesser of the evils with which Catholics were confronted.

Through Mgr. Talbot and what Bishop Ullathorne called "backstairs politics," "a mischievous camarilla," Manning represented to Rome the fatal consequences of allowing Newman with his influence and prestige to settle in Oxford, because it would seem to indicate that Catholics were fully protected in their attendance at the University. Propaganda was alarmed, and Cardinal Reisach made a visit to England to investigate the whole situation. Then happened one of those things that made Newman wonder at the fairness and justice and common sense of men in high office. Cardinal Reisach consulted only those who had been carefully handpicked by Manning. Although supposedly investigating the establishment of an Oratory at Oxford, Reisach *never saw Newman, the superior of the Birmingham Oratory*, the man who had applied to Propaganda for permission to establish a branch house. No wonder that Newman was hurt, and felt that Manning, who during this time was writing to him in terms of affection, had double-crossed him.

The outcome was that Propaganda issued permission to establish a branch Oratory at Oxford—provided Dr. Newman was not allowed to go there! The communication was sent to Ullathorne as the Ordinary of the diocese. With all the good intentions in the world, but with very poor judgment, Ullathorne kept from Newman the condition on which the permission was granted. Ullathorne's excuse was that he hoped to get this condition rescinded before Newman knew anything about it, and so save him the deep wound which such an attitude on the part of Propaganda would cause. But Ullathorne had not counted sufficiently on the indiscretion of some of those in the secret. News of the condition became public, and Ullathorne was compelled to tell Newman. It was one more blow on an old man whose head was already battered.

One Saturday morning, Newman took a walk with Fr. Neville, the priest who was to go to Oxford next day. Newman was full of the Oxford project, and Fr. Neville has thus described the conversation: "Newman, sunshine on his face, talked of the prospect. 'Earlier failures do not matter now,' said he; 'I see that I have been reserved by God for this. There are signs of a religious reaction in Oxford against the liberalism and indifferentism of ten years ago. It is evidently a moment when a strong and persuasive assertion of Christian and Catholic principles will be invaluable. Such men as Mark Pattison may conceivably be won over. Although I am not young, I feel as full of life and thought as ever I did. It may prove to be the inauguration of a second Oxford Movement.' " [1]

When Newman and Fr. Neville returned to the Oratory, the servant who opened the door gave Newman a

[1] Ward, *Life of Newman*, II, 138.

long blue envelope from Ullathorne. Newman read the letter and said to Fr. Neville: "All is over. I am not allowed to go."

Newman immediately abandoned the idea of a branch Oratory at Oxford. And as this was a foregone conclusion from the condition laid down by Propaganda, it would have been much more tactful to have made the refusal of permission absolute, without mentioning Newman by name. To single Newman out as the one undesirable element in the proposition, showed unnecessary cruelty. When Mr. Martin, an ecclesiastical student in Rome, and the Roman correspondent of *The Weekly Register*, hinted in a letter to this paper that the Pope had "inhibited" Newman's Oxford mission because of suspicions in Rome regarding Newman's orthodoxy, he was certainly going beyond the intentions of Propaganda. But Mr. Martin was putting an interpretation upon Propaganda's action that was only too acceptable to Manning and many others in England, and Propaganda might have foreseen such an interpretation.

Manning was not prepared for the indignation expressed by Newman's friends at this insult to the man who had so recently done such yeoman service for English Catholics by his *Apologia* and by his reply to Pusey's *Eirenicon*. Considering the discipline of the Catholic Church, Newman's friends could not attack the "instruction" of Propaganda. But they could avow their disgust at the insinuation of *The Weekly Register*, and they could express their loyalty to Newman. This they did in an address signed by upwards of two hundred, including all the most prominent members of the English laity—William George Ward being a striking exception—and headed by Lord Howard, the deputy Earl Marshal and guardian to the young Duke of Norfolk.

"TO THE VERY REVEREND JOHN HENRY NEWMAN.

"We, the undersigned, have been deeply pained at some anonymous attacks which have been made upon you. They may be of little importance in themselves, but we feel that every blow that touches you inflicts a wound upon the Catholic Church in this country. We hope, therefore, that you will not think it presumptuous in us to express our gratitude for all we owe you, and to assure you how heartily we appreciate the services which, under God, you have been the means of rendering to our holy religion."

Newman knew that Manning was back of the opposition to his going to Oxford, and he knew that Rome accepted Manning as the mouthpiece of the Church in England. Moreover, Newman was fully aware that this address identifying him with the Church in the phrase, "every blow that touches you inflicts a wound upon the Catholic Church in this country," would make Manning intensely angry. But in Newman's answer to the address, there was no conciliating the powers that were for the sake of policy, no truckling to powerful enemies. On April 12, 1867, Newman answered with dignity and spirit:

"I acknowledge without delay the high honor done me in the Memorial addressed to me by so many Catholic noblemen and gentlemen... The attacks of opponents are never hard to bear when the person who is the object of them is conscious to himself that they are undeserved, but in the present instance I have small cause indeed for pain or regret at their occurrence, since they have at once elicited in my behalf the warm feelings of so many dear friends who know me well, and of so many others whose good opinion is the more impartial for the very reason that I am personally not known to them. Of such men, whether friends or strangers to me, I would a hundred times rather receive the generous sympathy than have escaped the misrepresentations which are the occasion of their showing it."

The very next day, April 13, 1867, Manning wrote to his confidant at the court of Pius IX, Mgr. Talbot, urging him not to let Propaganda be alarmed at the address to Newman signed by so many influential laymen. "If it will only be *firm* and *clear*, we shall get through this and more." A week later, in answer to a letter of Talbot, Manning wrote again: "This Address of the laity is as you say a revelation of the absence of Catholic instinct, and the presence of a spirit dangerous in many... As it stands it implies that in Dr. Newman's writings there is nothing open to censure, and that to touch him is to wound the Catholic Church. But if Rome should touch him?"

That Rome should touch Newman, in the sense of condemning certain of his writings, is just what Manning wanted. And when, during the next pontificate, the English laity again moved, at that time under the leadership of the Duke of Norfolk, and Leo XIII made Newman a cardinal, it was one of the hardest things Manning ever had to bear. Rome touched Newman, but in a way Manning never intended. And Rome's scarlet touch was a positive proof that Manning was wrong in supposing there was anything rightly censurable in Newman's writings.

"The final relinquishment of the Oxford scheme,"

writes Ward, "left the extreme party triumphant; but it left the practical problem of higher education for English Catholics unsolved... Catholics were authoritatively warned against Oxford and Cambridge; but where else were they to go for University training? It was part of what Newman afterwards called the policy of 'Nihilism' pursued by the authorities. Actual difficulties were not faced; practicable remedies were not found." [1]

Manning, indeed, made a gesture in founding a Catholic college in Kensington. It ran for a few years, and involved Manning in serious financial difficulties. Mgr. Capel, the rector, had to break with Manning, and spent the remainder of his days very successfully in the United States. Wilfrid Ward, who was one of the few students the college ever had, deplored the fact that he had been sent there by his father. Ward's well-considered opinion, as expressed in his life of Newman, was that the college was "a ludicrous failure."

Abbot Cuthbert Butler, of Downside Abbey, who was also a student in Manning's college, writes of the ill-fated attempt in his *Life of Bishop Ullathorne:* "It was opened in October, 1874; the first year there were but sixteen students; the second year there were twenty-eight (among whom was the present writer, who must gratefully acknowledge the debt he has ever since owed to the high quality of the instruction and formation received there); the third year the number mounted up, I believe, to fifty. But at the end of the fourth year, the summer of 1878, the college had to be wound up in hopeless bankruptcy, and worse—'a heavy cross, a grave scandal,' Manning calls it. Manning was the only one who really had his heart in it; the bishops did not believe

[1] II, 187.

in it—we have seen that in 1864 they had declared the idea to be impracticable; the laity did not want it—it did not meet their desires or needs, though they contributed generously to it. Manning kept it wholly in his own control and management, allowing neither laity nor religious orders, nor even the bishops, any real share in its government. Seldom has a masterful man succeeded so well in getting his own way so completely, to meet with failure so speedy and so entire." [1]

The complete failure of his pet college was doubtless a cross for Manning, and one that was not made any lighter by the fact that the judgment of Newman, the speculative thinker, was thereby justified as against his own, the practical man of affairs. But for the cause of Catholic education—or the education of Catholics—the perfectly evident failure was a blessing.

Thus was Newman justified, even during his own and Manning's lifetime. And Manning was hardly dead before Herbert Vaughan, his protégé, and successor as Archbishop of Westminster, took steps to reverse Manning's policy regarding the attendance of Catholics at Oxford. Manning was buried on January 21, 1892, and on January 4, 1895, at the meeting of the bishops, Vaughan urged that the Holy See should be petitioned to withdraw the admonition against the attendance of Catholics at the universities.

"It only remains to be added," says Snead-Cox in his *Life of Cardinal Vaughan*, "that the experiment of Catholics attending the universities seems to have been successful from every point of view, and that Cardinal Vaughan lived long enough to be able to acknowledge that the fears of those who had resisted the change had

[1] II, 36.

been so far happily disappointed. In a memorandum for Propaganda, written some five years before his death, after alluding to the leave given to Catholic laymen and then to ecclesiastics to go to the Universities, he said: 'I must report most favorably of these two permissions. Catholics have done themselves credit in both Universities.' " [1]

Purcell wrote in his *Life of Cardinal Manning:* "What Dr. Manning did not anticipate but experience has shown, the frequentation of the Universities by Catholics well trained in their own secondary schools has not turned to their detriment, morally or spiritually, or lessened their fidelity to the Church; but, on the contrary, has to no small extent quickened their zeal in defence of religion, whilst the advantages of University training have placed them on an intellectual level with their non-Catholic countrymen." [2]

After a much longer experience, the settled judgment of English Catholics, from Cardinal Bourne down, seems to be that this was the best solution of a difficult problem. It took the English a long time to get over what Newman called the policy of "Nihilism," and grateful as one may be for their having gotten over it finally, yet one may also regret that they did not act sooner. "The regret of Ullathorne's biographer," writes Cuthbert Butler, "must be that, it seeming certain his sympathies were with Newman and those in favour of the movement [for Catholics to go to Oxford], he did not act with greater courage at the fateful meetings in 1864 and '65, and join his voice to those of Clifford and William Vaughan of Plymouth." [3] Ullathorne succumbed to that temptation, unfortunately common to ecclesiastics as well as to civil officials, to do

[1] II, 85.   [2] II, 290.   [3] II, 38.

what the higher authorities are thought to wish, rather than what they themselves think will be for the best interest of the Church or of their country. The fact that Newman rose above this time-serving, to act with purity of intention, according to his lights, without respect for persons, makes him stand out as such an interesting figure.

Several years ago I was in correspondence with the heads of the Catholic houses for clerics at Oxford. All of them were enthusiastic over the results of Catholics attending the University. One head of a house wrote that "it has made *men* of every one who has come to Oxford. There has been, on the other hand, no loss, little or great." Father O'Dowd, of St. Charles House, the residence for clerics from the Birmingham diocese, replied: "It is obvious that to get in touch with the educated people of a country it is necessary to be educated according to their fashion and standing. That is why both at Oxford and Cambridge the Bishops have established houses in connection with the Universities... I think I could say without exaggeration that the men who have been through the University training are not only more efficient but more safe than the others as a class... It is hoped that they will begin to lift up the education of future priests from the very beginning. It is really the only way of breaking through the narrow ring in which the system is that A educates B, and B educates C without reference to any of the educational currents flowing through the country at large... The dangers of fresh air seem to me smaller, taking them in the main, than those of a stuffy and hothouse training."

Father Charles Plater, the famous Jesuit, wrote in the same strain, using the very same figure of speech. "Personally I think," he said, "that the opening up of Oxford to Catholic priests and clerics has been one of the greatest blessings the Catholic body has received since the Reformation. It has enabled us to get into touch with the thought of the day and to influence it. It has brought us out in the open... I think the hothouse policy a bad one. We cannot hope to shield our young men from the microbes of infidelity and immorality, which exist outside universities as well as within them. What we have to do is to develop healthy Catholic constitutions that will resist their attacks."

Butler sums up the results of all this controversy over education: "And Newman: his position, consistently maintained in many letters and in the Dublin lectures on *The Idea of a University,* was that the normal and the desirable thing everywhere would be a Catholic University under the guidance of the Church as at Louvain... But this he held to be impracticable in England. He was altogether against the idea of a Catholic college or hall at Oxford or Cambridge. And so he advocated that Catholics should enter the existing non-Catholic colleges, but on the condition that strong Catholic influences should be provided in each place to give the young Catholics the religious support and guidance they needed. This is exactly what has been done, and in a measure and manner probably far beyond anything Newman ever dreamed of."

The Jesuits, Benedictines, Dominicans, Capuchins, and the diocese of Birmingham have houses at Oxford; and among women the Religious of the Holy Child and the Religious of the Sacred Heart have residences. In addition, numbers of other clerics and members of various sisterhoods attend the University. There are few stronger Catholic centers to-day in England than this Oxford from which Newman was excluded. This tremendous change in attitude on the part of Catholics "is Newman's signal victory in English Catholic party politics, whereby the idea he stood for, and fought for, and suffered for, did after his death come triumphantly into its own." [1]

[1] *Life of Ullathorne,* II, 38.

CHAPTER IV

FURTHER BUFFETINGS

"Don't you see this, if nothing else, puts a great
obex to my writing? ... *Now,* if I, as a private
priest, put anything into print, Propaganda answers me at once. How can I fight with such a
chain on my arm? It is like the Persians driven
to fight under the lash. There was true private
judgment in the primitive and medieval schools,
—there are no schools now, no private judgment (in the religious sense of the phrase), no
freedom, that is, of opinion. That is, no exercise
of intellect. Now, the system goes on by the
tradition of the intellect of former times."

(LETTER TO MISS BOWLES)

NEWMAN'S idea of a university at Dublin, was that
of a center where Catholics would be trained to meet the
difficulties of the day in the intellectual world. The failure
of his attempt to found a university did not make the
need for such training of Catholics any less acute. And
so he turned to other ways of meeting the problems of the
hour.

It seemed providential to Newman, therefore, that in
August, 1857, there should come from Cardinal Wiseman
a letter making the definite proposal for Newman to edit
the new English version of the Scriptures which the Synod
of Oscott in 1855 had recommended.

The official English translation of the Bible for

Catholics had been made by men connected with the English college at Douay. The New Testament had been published at Rheims in 1852, and the Old Testament at Douay in 1609-1610. As a consequence, the work is sometimes called the Rheims version, although more frequently the Douay. It is generally conceded that the English of the Douay Bible lacks the beauty of the Protestant (King James) Version. But the actual Bible in use among English Catholics in the 1850's—and still in use, for that matter—was the Douay as revised by Dr. Challoner, Vicar Apostolic of the London District, in the 1740's.

"Looking at Dr. Challoner's labors on the Old Testament as a whole," wrote Newman, "we may pronounce that they issue in little short of a new translation. They can as little be said to be made on the basis of the Douay, as on the basis of the Protestant Version. Of course, there must be a certain resemblance between any two Catholic translations whatever, because they are both translations of the same Vulgate; but this connection between the Douay and Challoner being allowed for, Challoner's Version is even nearer to the Protestant than it is to the Douay; nearer, that is, not in grammatical structure, but in phraseology and diction." [1]

If the plan of the new translation had been carried into effect, Newman would undoubtedly have produced a work of supreme excellence from the standpoint of English, and that would have been highly desirable. Moreover, Newman's introductions and notes would certainly have met the needs of modern English readers much more effectively than the at times rather naïve explanations of Dr. Challoner.

[1] *Tracts Theological and Ecclesiastical,* 414.

But in spite of admiration for Newman as an English stylist, and of respect for his intellectual powers, it must be admitted that he was not a Biblical scholar. And it is very doubtful if, at that time, Newman could have gathered around him in England the Catholic scholars sufficiently versed in the original languages of the Bible, and in all the questions of textual and higher criticism, to produce a new translation of any great value in the scholarly world.

William George Ward, for instance, was asked by Newman to translate the Psalms. And this in itself is an indication of the lack of real scholars to do the work. For in replying to Newman's invitation, Ward admitted quite frankly that he had "not the very slightest knowledge of Hebrew." Undoubtedly, the whole work would have been merely a translation of the Latin Vulgate—that is, a translation of a translation. Nor would there have been any critical examination of the Vulgate text itself, such as is now going on in Rome.

However, the translation itself would have been the least important part of the work. Newman knew the more fundamental Scriptural difficulties, and he would have seen to it that they were met frankly in notes and introductions. His own part in the work, besides a detailed supervision, was to have been an exhaustive general introduction including a defense of theism and of revealed religion. Newman mentioned this idea in the same letter to Ward in which he asked Ward to translate the Psalms. And Ward, answering with the experience of a man who, although a layman, had taught dogmatic theology in a Catholic seminary, replied:

"I must fully agree with you that nothing is more clamorously required than an argument for Theism. You would be really surprised how much harm, even among ecclesiastical students, is done by the existing books. They grow up, half unconsciously, with the conviction that there is something argumentatively rotten at the foundation; and that the only safe way of keeping the faith is the resolute blinding of the reason. Dr. Errington amused me very much two years ago. For first he said it was shocking to say that every detail of Theism was not adequately proved by the existing arguments; and then when I raised particular difficulties, he replied at once: 'Do you venture not to see force in an argument which satisfied the great mind of St. Thomas, *etc., etc.*,' thus shifting in fact the whole thing *from* reason to grounds of faith. As if I *could* believe, even on the authority of the Church, that such or such an argument convinces *me*. Certainly a greater calamity could not befall one sceptically tempted than to come across the Catholic treatises 'in quibus *invictissime probatur*' everything held by Catholics: and all others are held up to hatred and derision as an incredible compound of knavery and folly." [1]

Besides his own labors on the introduction, Newman had immediately set other men to work, and he had expended what he says was for him a large sum, expecting to be reimbursed by the bishops. More than a year went by in this way without hearing anything farther from Wiseman or the other members of the hierarchy. And then out of a clear sky, Wiseman forwarded to Newman through Bishop Ullathorne (without even the courtesy of a covering note of his own) a letter from the American bishops saying that Archbishop Kenrick of Baltimore was engaged on a translation of the Bible and suggesting that

[1] Ward, *Life of Newman,* I, 421.

Newman coöperate with him. Apart from the question of distance, such coöperation would undoubtedly have been difficult for a man of Newman's temperament. But as between coöperation (even though implying some degree of subordination on Newman's part) and complete abandonment of his work, coöperation would seem to have been the wiser course.[1]

But Newman dropped the work of translation—together with the money so far expended—and tore up what he had written on his introduction. It was a pity that Newman did not continue the defense of theism and a consideration of Biblical problems independently of a translation, for no English Catholic of his time was so well qualified to discuss the difficulties of the modern mind in accepting the Bible as divinely revealed. Newman realized, for instance, that much of the supposed conflict between the Bible and science was due to a misuse of the Scriptures by believers who wanted to make the Bible a textbook of science. He was merely expressing what had all along been his consistent attitude, when in 1884 he wrote: "It seems unworthy of divine greatness, that the Almighty should in His revelation of Himself to us undertake mere secular duties, and assume the office of a narrator, as such, or an historian or geographer, except so far as the secular matters bear directly on revealed truth." [2]

With the abandonment of the new translation of the

[1] Two years later Newman heard from Archbishop Kenrick that as no word had come from the English bishops, he (Kenrick) was going on with his translation. So Newman could at least have the consolation of knowing that it was not only the laity or simple priests like himself with whom Wiseman and the other bishops were lax in their correspondence.

[2] *The Nineteenth Century,* February, 1884, p. 189.

Bible, Newman turned to other activities, and among them was the establishment of a secondary school. In the ranks of the recent converts to Catholicism there was considerable dissatisfaction with existing Catholic schools. Ushaw, Stonyhurst, Downside, Oscott, and other Catholic schools were in rural districts, were connected with theological seminaries, and in discipline and studies were better calculated to prepare for a seminary than for the world or for an English university. As a consequence, Newman had often been urged to lend his name to a Catholic institution resembling more closely the English public schools. In May, 1859, with many misgivings, he finally acceded and opened the Oratory School in Edgbaston, Birmingham.

From the first the Oratory School was a success, in the sense that it secured attendance and had the patronage of influential families. But every departure from the traditional Catholic methods was the object of almost violent criticism. And conducting a preparatory school, Newman was immediately involved in the question of Catholics' attending Oxford and Cambridge. Naturally, he had to prepare young men for these universities if their parents insisted upon it. And there were those who interpreted this preparation as a very effective encouragement of attendance where attendance should be discouraged by every loyal Catholic.

This Oratory School was to furnish a striking illustration of Newman's loyalty to his friends in spite of consequences. Mrs. Wootten, a devoted friend of Newman who had been converted through his influence, became the matron. At Christmas, 1861, the masters protested against the very special position accorded by Newman to Mrs. Wootten, and demanded that she be removed. Newman resolutely declined, and they represented that if he persisted they would all have to resign.

Here was a strike involving the whole teaching force. Most men would have calculated the probable injury to the school, and would have sacrificed Mrs. Wootten. They would have argued that she should have been willing to resign, rather than run the risk of destroying the whole institution. And probably Mrs. Wootten took this view. But Newman would never allow threats to make him desert a friend. He accepted the resignations of the staff, and kept Mrs. Wootten.[1] Moreover, he pulled the School through the crisis without serious harm.

---

[1] During his sojourn in Dublin Newman gave a similar example of loyalty to his friends. As soon as Dr. Cullen found that Newman was on speaking terms with Frederick Lucas, a Catholic journalist who was very outspoken—too violently outspoken, in fact—on the ecclesiastical authorities, he grew cold to Newman. Abp. Cullen, writes Newman, "warned me against him, and I, of course, would not be warned. . . I never, of course, would give up Lucas as a friend. I differed with him, but I thought him honest and good."

A man's character, after all, is the most interesting thing about him, and Newman's loyalty is one of his outstanding characteristics. Some men in Newman's position would have argued: "Dr. Cullen is my ecclesiastical superior. His friendship is absolutely necessary for the success of the University. That undertaking is bigger than any individual, either myself or Lucas. And surely Lucas must see this. He should understand that I am simply asking him to make for the good of the cause a sacrifice he ought to be perfectly willing to make."

But Newman was not such a friend. He was staunch and true to Lucas. Feeling that Cullen was prejudiced, he was determined to stick to Lucas to the end. If it injured the University, the injury came not from him, but from Cullen. On Cullen's conscience must rest the blame. Some years later, Manning wrote of Newman: "He has a sort of sensitiveness about standing by friends even when in the wrong, which is very honorable to his generosity." And if friendship deserves all that poets and philosophers have said of it, surely a man who can be as true as was Newman to a friend, deserves our praise and admiration.

That the education of the Catholic mind was essential for the effective defense of the Church, Newman had urged as rector of the abortive Catholic University in Dublin, and he knew that a preparatory school could not go very far in that direction. Newman had projected for the University a scholarly organ known as *The Atlantis,* and a few issues appeared. In one of the numbers was Newman's essay called *The Benedictine Centuries,* a study of theological conservatism. Newman was now to turn his energies more completely to the field of journalism. And as Capes, Simpson, Acton, and others of his friends were contributors to *The Rambler,* a Catholic magazine taking a more liberal stand than the conservative *Dublin Review,* it was only natural that Newman should use its pages.

Undoubtedly, the temper of a nation at war is different from the temper of the same nation at peace. Anyone who remembers the trying days in America during 1917 and 1918, and who recalls the absurd things leading to a suspicion of pro-Germanism, will understand to some extent what has been the attitude of many Catholics since the Protestant Revolt. What would have been tolerated or applauded during the Renaissance, would have been scrutinized after the Protestant Revolt by hundreds of heresy hunters for the slightest indication of anything off-color.

Moreover, politics became involved with theology. In France, to be a democrat was to make the royalists accuse one of theological heresy. Lamennais was condemned, and refused to submit. Gregory XVI, who had censured Lamennais, was a friend of autocratic Austria and the inveterate foe of the revolutionary and democratic movement. Rome was constantly harassed by the machinations of the Carbonari, and Pope Gregory lived in an atmosphere of suspicion. Although his successor, Pius IX, for some time held out a hope of something different, the murder of his minister De Rossi, and his own enforced flight to Gaeta, turned him into another Gregory.

Nevertheless, this intransigent attitude did not meet the needs of the times. At best, it was calculated to preserve what the Church already held. It could not go out and convert the modern world. Gradually, Catholics were losing intellectual leadership, because the world around them was going ahead independently and they would pay no attention to it. Newman has said that he was not a theologian, but a controversialist. He might better have said that he was a missionary. Newman longed to bring others into the light of religious truths that he himself professed. But to do this, he had to speak their language, and that language was modern. He had to distinguish carefully between what was of faith and what was not of faith.

Also, Newman's outlook was historical. He realized that many of the difficulties of the Church in the past had come from over-zealous advocates or defendants identifying her with the local and the transitory. Newman had no intention whatever of taking over modern science. On the contrary, he deliberately said that we should avoid the tying up of religious truth with scientific theories which are changing so rapidly. But Newman did want to be able to say that this or that historical fact could be admitted without repudiating any dogma of faith; that this or that scientific fact or theory did not contradict anything in the Catholic creed. Working in Germany and France and other countries were Catholic scholars trying to do this for their respective audiences. France had *Le*

Correspondant, founded by Montalembert; and in Germany, there was the *Katholik,* of Munich. Newman wanted *The Rambler* to accomplish for England what these magazines were doing for the Continent.

All around him in England, Newman realized that there was a seething world of thought with no sufficient Catholic counterpoise. It was the hey-day of John Stuart Mill and Utilitarianism; Darwin's *Origin of Species* was published in 1859; Huxley was in his prime and preaching an old infidelity under the new name of "Agnosticism"; higher and lower criticisms were fast blasting away the foundations of Protestant bibliolatry. The sort of training that W. G. Ward and others have described as being given at this time in the English seminaries, was not calculated to meet the evident dangers in the situation, to produce a clergy capable of leading a laity exposed to such an environment. Failing a university, the only hope of helping Catholics living in this atmosphere was a strong periodical literature.

There were two Catholic magazines in the field. One was *The Dublin Review,* founded in 1836 by Daniel O'Connell and Wiseman. After 1845, Wiseman's contributions became fewer and fewer, although he still owned and controlled *The Dublin.* In 1858, *The Dublin Review* was edited by W. G. Ward, and it had become ponderous, dull, and dreary. It was recognized as almost dead.

The other Catholic magazine, *The Rambler,* was a monthly. It had been founded by a group of brilliant converts, and was edited by laymen who claimed considerable independence. In 1858, *The Rambler* became the property of Lord Acton, a pupil of Döllinger. He was then only twenty-four, but was already recognized as remarkably learned.   Richard Simpson became the editor. Acton stood "for the position that all questions of philosophy, politics, history, science, short of defined dogma, were legitimate objects of free investigation, and should be pursued to their issues irrespective of the results for Catholic apologetics and controversy." A Catholic periodical conducted along such lines would require almost superhuman tact to avoid trouble with the ecclesiastical authorities, and unfortunately *The Rambler* group was not conspicuous for tact. Some of the writers, as notably Simpson, the editor, seemed to take delight in putting statements in such a way as to shock everyday Catholic sentiment, and unnecessarily to antagonize the bishops.

Towards the end of 1859, things reached a crisis because *The Rambler* had criticized the attitude of the bishops in regard to the royal commission on schools. The bishops were offended, and drastic action was suggested to assert their authority. But before taking this step, Ullathorne was deputed to approach Newman, who was on friendly terms with *The Rambler* people, to see if it were possible to bring about a change in the tone of the magazine.

The owners, Acton and Simpson, pressed Newman to undertake the editorship himself. Apparently Ullathorne also urged this course on Newman. After a month of hesitation, with forebodings and yet with hopefulness, Newman yielded to the necessities of the situation and accepted the editorship. Cardinal Wiseman was satisfied, and curiously enough W. G. Ward, editing the rival *Dublin,* was delighted.

Success in editing a magazine that already had a bad name in conservative circles depended upon the co-operation of a number of people, and especially of the bishops.

After all his experience, Newman might well have had forebodings as to the necessary coöperation. And looking back upon the events, it seems clear that he might better have devoted himself to something that he could have done alone, instead of making success depend upon others working with him. For instance, Newman might have worked out his defense of theism, or he could have been a mere contributor to existing Catholic magazines. In fact, it would have been wiser for the whole *Rambler* group to have written for secular journals, rather than to have attempted to conduct a distinctively Catholic periodical. For, from the nature of the case, bishops can pass over what a Catholic writes in a secular journal, when they would feel obliged to notice what appears in a professedly Catholic organ.

Moreover, it is probable that some non-Catholic magazines are read by more Catholics than any Catholic periodical of similar scholarship. Consequently, by writing for such magazines, a man like Acton would be influencing Catholics to a greater extent than if he wrote for an exclusively Catholic monthly or quarterly. In addition, he would be influencing non-Catholics a great deal more than would be the case if his articles appeared in a Catholic paper. For Catholic magazines have difficulty in securing Catholic readers, and are almost wholly neglected by non-Catholics.

Undertaking this difficult and disagreeable task of editing *The Rambler*, partly at least as a favor to Ullathorne, Newman might reasonably have expected his firm support during a fair trial. But the May number, the first under Newman's editing, had hardly appeared when Ullathorne went to see Newman, and advised him to give up the editorship. In his interview, Ullathorne said "Catholics never had a doubt; it pained them to know that things could be considered doubtful which they had ever implicitly believed. *The Rambler* was irritating."

Newman stated his own position strongly, and urged the need of meeting the difficulties confronting thinking laymen to-day. The Bishop did not allow any weight at all to Newman's representations and said "something like, 'Who are the laity?' I answered (not in these *words*) that the Church would look foolish without them."[1]

The outcome of the meeting between Ullathorne and Newman, was that Newman agreed to resign as editor after the next issue, the July number. The Bishop's action was in reality a great blow to Newman. This was the third important task in three years—the other two were the Catholic University and the translation of the Scriptures—that Newman had undertaken in hope, only to see them fail because he could not get coöperation from those set over Israel.

However, Newman had the consolation of knowing that his resignation was deplored by the more keen-sighted among the converts. Some of them thought it a sign that the ecclesiastical authorities failed to realize the needs of the times. "It seems to me," wrote Mr. Thompson, "that we must wait for a convert Bishop for such a periodical as the times demand." In a few years, ironically enough, they were to have a convert bishop in Manning, who certainly was less liberal than Wiseman or Ullathorne. "I cannot but admire and acquiesce in your spirit," wrote Henry Wilberforce to Newman, "but I feel deeply that our Bishops do not understand England and the English. Either the Catholic laity will kick, or, what I rather fear, they will more and more fall below Protes-

[1] Butler, *Life of Ullathorne*, I, 314.

tants in intellectual training and have no influence on the public mind." [1]

In the July number of *The Rambler*, Newman had an article called *Consulting the Faithful in Matters of Doctrine*. It was a vindication of the place of the *Sensus fidelium*, the belief of the faithful, among the recognized sources of theology and doctrine, and a plea for giving it its due weight, as had been done very fully in the case of the definition of the Immaculate Conception, in 1854. For the main line of his argument, Newman went back to the history of the Arian controversy with which he was so familiar. During the confused fifty years that followed Nicaea, so Newman contended, it was the body of the faithful—the inferior clergy, the monks, the laity—who were the supporters of Athanasius and the defenders of the Nicene Faith, while bishops wavered and compromised by the hundred at council after council. At this crisis, it was the *Ecclesia discens*, the Church learning, rather than the *Ecclesia docens*, the Church teaching, that preserved the Catholic Faith.

This was Newman's answer to Ullathorne's question, "Who are the laity?" Under the circumstances, Newman can hardly be excused from imprudence in making such an answer, and it is not surprising that the essay caused much fluttering in theological dovecots. No one dared to question Newman's array of facts, but the line of his argument was held to be tantamount to saying that the teaching authority of the Church had failed in so great an emergency. Bishop Brown, of Newport, delated the article to Rome. Propaganda took up the case, and when at the end of the year Ullathorne was called to Rome over the affairs of the Church in Australia, Cardinal Barnabó

[1] Ward, *Life of Newman*, I, 499, 501.

took the opportunity of consulting him on the incriminating article.

On Ullathorne's return Newman in consultation with him prepared a letter to Cardinal Wiseman who was then in Rome. In this letter Newman said:

"I will request, then, of Your Eminence's kindness three things:

"1. The passages of the article on which the Cardinal Prefect of Propaganda desires an explanation.

"2. A copy of the translations in which His Eminence has read them.

"3. The dogmatic propositions which they have been represented as infringing or otherwise impairing.

"If Your Eminence does this for me, I will engage, with the blessing of God, in the course of a month from the receipt of the information:

"1. To accept *ex animo* in their fullness and integrity the dogmatic propositions implicated.

"2. To explain the animus and argument of the writer of the article in strict accordance with those propositions.

"3. To show that the English text and context of the article is [sic] absolutely in accordance with them."

This was a dignified, humble, and sincere statement. If it had been presented to Cardinal Barnabó by Wiseman, it would have saved Newman a great deal of trouble. But Wiseman, with the knowledge of Manning who was with him in Rome, did not present the letter. Wiseman simply allowed things to drift. And Newman, who had had no direct communication from Propaganda, naturally thought that the matter had been settled. But inasmuch as Cardinal Barnabó had communicated directly with

Bishop Ullathorne, it is difficult to see why Newman's letter was not addressed to Ullathorne, and sent by him directly to Barnabó. The whole affair is an illustration of the roundabout way used by some ecclesiastics, of which Newman so often complained. If Barnabó had written to Newman himself, as one man to another, immediately specifying what was thought wrong with the article, Newman would have replied directly and frankly, and everybody would have been satisfied.

In regard to *The Rambler* article, Abbot Butler remarks: "The thing was a piece of unfortunate bungling, for which Wiseman must take the principal blame, but neither Manning nor Talbot can be acquitted of a share in the responsibility." [1] In an anonymous pamphlet in 1869, the statement was made that Manning had deliberately intercepted and suppressed Newman's letter in order to put him in bad odor at Rome. This assertion was unfounded. But it seems true that Manning considered Newman dangerous theologically, and looked upon him as the leader of a disaffected group, who ought to be suppressed as far as policy would allow.

In a letter to Mgr. Talbot, February 25, 1866, Manning had written: "Whether he [Newman] knows it or not, he has become the centre of those who hold low views about the Holy See, are anti-Roman, cold and silent, to say no more, about the Temporal Power, national, English, critical of Catholic devotions, and always on the lower side... It is the old Anglican, patristic, literary, Oxford tone transplanted into the Church. It takes the line of deprecating exaggerations, foreign devotions, Ultramontanism, anti-national sympathies. In one word, it is

---

[1] Butler, *Life of Ullathorne*, I, 321.

worldly Catholicism, and it will have the world on its side, and will deceive many." [1]

This letter of Manning was in answer to one of Talbot dated February 20, 1866: "I am afraid that *The Rambler* and the old school of Catholics will rally round Newman in opposition to you and Rome. Stand firm, do not yield a bit in the line you have taken. . . I repeat myself, continue to stand forward as the advocate of Roman views in England. . . You will have battles to fight, because every Englishman is naturally anti-Roman. To be Roman is to an Englishman an effort. Dr. Newman is more English than the English. *His spirit must be crushed.*" [2]

On the other hand, Manning was jealous of appearances. He did not wish to come out publicly as opposed to Newman, nor as having had an open break with him. He did not regard publicity with equanimity. And so in July, 1867, Manning tried through Canon Oakeley to straighten out matters with Newman. Those who wish to go into an extended narrative of the matter should read the chapter entitled "Archbishop Manning and J. H. Newman" in Purcell's *Life of Manning.*

Of course, Newman did not know of these letters of Manning and Talbot which have just been quoted. But when Manning approached him through Oakeley, Newman replied as if he had had a sort of clairvoyant view of Manning's correspondence with Talbot. Newman wrote: "The question is whether his [Manning's] house has not been a centre from which a powerful antagonism has been carried on against me; whether persons about the Archbishop have not said strong things against me

[1] Purcell, *Life of Manning*, II, 323.
[2] *Ibid.*, II, 322. Italics added.

both here and at Rome; and whether, instead of showing dissatisfaction publicly of acts which were public, he has not allowed the world to identify the acts of his *entourage* with himself. No one dreams of accusing me of thwarting him—indeed the idea would be absurd, for I have not the power. The world accuses him without provocation of thwarting me.[1] And the *prima facie* proof of this is, (1) that his *entourage* acts with violence against me. (2) That instead of taking any step to prevent them, he contents himself with denying his having done anything against me himself, and with deeply lamenting that there should be a distance between us.

"The world thinks, and I think, that he has virtually intervened in the Oxford Oratory matter—and the world and I have to be convinced to the contrary, or we shall continue to think so."

The end of a lengthy correspondence was this gem from Newman to Manning:

"The Oratory, 3rd November, 1869.

"MY DEAR ARCHBISHOP:

"Thank you for your kind letter.

"I can only repeat what I said when you last heard from me, I do not know whether I am standing on my head or my heels when I have active relations with you. In spite of my friendly feelings, this is the judgment of my intellect.

"Yours affectionately in Christ,

"JOHN H. NEWMAN."

In an autobiographical note, Manning commented on this: "His last was in terms which made a reply hardly

---

[1] Evidently, Newman means: "The world accuses him of thwarting me without provocation"—a good example of Newman's carelessness in regard to the proper position of qualifying phrases.

fitting on my part. For years we never wrote and never met." [1]

Purcell adds: "After the year 1869, owing to poor Mgr. Talbot's removal from the Vatican to an asylum at Passy, there is no further direct nor contemporary evidence recorded of Manning's opinion in regard to John Henry Newman. Mgr. Talbot had no successor capable of interpreting at the Vatican Manning's judgment on men and things in Catholic England." I have found no evidence as to how long this mental disease was coming on Talbot. Newman might have dated it back a number of years! Talbot was a good example of the fact that the most dangerous people are not those in asylums, but those outside, not yet insane enough to be recognized as crazy.

The Rambler had finally come to an end in 1862. The bad odor into which it had fallen, and the delation of his own article, reflected upon Newman as its one-time editor. And this suspicion was accentuated by Newman's attitude on the Temporal Power of the Pope. "He came to be, to use his own phrase, 'under a cloud,' a man suspected in many quarters as not thoroughly orthodox. At the end of September 1861, Simpson, who was still communicating with Newman as to the future of *The Rambler,* enclosed a letter from Mr. Burns, the publisher, objecting to Newman's connection with any Review as injurious to its prospects of success. 'The great objection to Newman,' Mr. Burns wrote, 'is his, ... for one reason or another, unpopularity.' " [2]

Critical times were preparing in Rome, and it was almost impossible for a man of Newman's prominence to avoid expressing himself on the question of the Temporal

[1] Purcell, II, 346.
[2] Ward, I, 526.

Power. Since the restoration of Pius IX in 1849, the Papal States had been kept in order by French and Austrian troops. Piedmont was a growing power in Italy, and under Cavour it bought France's acquiescence in a United Italy by promise of the cession of Savoy and Nice. In 1859, the situation was further complicated for the Pope by war between Austria, on the one hand, and Italy and France, on the other. By the summer of 1860 Pius held, besides Rome, only the provinces of Frosinore and Velletri. But the secular world looked on with indifference.

This indifference of the secular world goaded Catholics into expressions of indignant loyalty. And like all emotional crises, it produced its exaggerations. Ten years after the Italians had established their government in Rome, Manning was angrily impatient with the Temporal Power, and came to think that the Italian occupation of the Eternal City was a divine chastisement.[1] But in 1861, Manning thought Newman semi-heretical for holding much milder views, and Manning and Wiseman were among the leaders in the Catholic demonstration in England favoring the Temporal Power. Manning's views took what Newman held to be a very extreme color. Even in Rome itself they met with a not unmixed approval. And the first draft of his lectures on the subject had to be remodelled to escape theological censure.

In the midst of this excitement, Newman wrote to a Mr. Monteith, that, as the Temporal Power "had been created by a series of secular events, so we could not be surprised if, as it rose, so it was destined to fall." And Newman quoted to "a young layman Lord Palmerston's words, that, as Dr. Sumner made an excellent Archbishop,

[1] Cf. Shane Leslie, *Henry Edward Manning*, 263.

yet it did not follow that he would succeed as Prime Minister, so the Holy Father had far too much on his hands as Pastor of the Catholic Flock to acquit himself well as the Temporal Ruler of a territory over and above his special *ecclesiastical* training."

Writing of these events in 1882, Newman said: "What I was especially anxious about was that there should be no attempt to make the Temporal Power a doctrine *de fide;* and that for two reasons. (*a*) Perhaps it was in God's Providence to cease to be. (*b*) It was not right to frighten, worry, irritate Catholics, by forcing on them as *de fide* what was not." [1]

However, Newman did not intend that the Pope should be a subject of some secular power. Apparently, he had in mind something like the settlement that was actually made by Pius XI in 1929. But Newman was sixty years ahead of his time. What can be said now with perfect loyalty, was then taboo by men like Manning and William George Ward. Their language would be a condemnation of Pius XI, whereas Newman's would be in complete accord with the present situation at Rome. At the time, however, Newman's careful weighing of historical facts and eternal principles merely earned him the suspicion, and even the hatred, of certain powerful factions of the Catholic Church in England.

Closely connected with the question of the Temporal Power of the Pope over the Papal States, is the question of what should be the relations of the Pope as spiritual head of the Church to secular temporal sovereigns; and as a sort of subdivision of this larger question, what should be the relations between the Church locally and any State? Should there be a union between Church and

[1] Ward, I, 521.

State? Is a union between Church and State such an ideal situation that Catholics should normally try to secure it?

T. W. Allies, a professor of history in Newman's ill-fated university attempt, and later the author of *The Formation of Christendom,* was representative of a goodly number of Catholics in thinking of the Middle Ages as the Ages of Faith, as a period when the Church had the opportunity of working out her purposes more perfectly than at any other time in history, and consequently, that, as there was union of Church and State in the Middle Ages, such a union is really the ideal condition.

In some correspondence with Allies, Newman shows that he probed much deeper into this problem than do many Catholics. Under date of November 22, 1860, Newman wrote: "I do not see my way to hold that 'Catholic civilization,' as you describe it, is *in fact* (I do not say in the abstract), but in fact, has been, or will be, a good, or *per se* desirable. . . . During the Middle Ages Rome is spoken of, not only as the world [in the sense of the phrase, the world, the flesh, and the devil], but even as Babylon. How strong is St. Thomas of Canterbury upon it! How the saints are used to look upon the Pontifical Court as in fact almost a road to perdition! . . . Surely Christian society was the world, and nothing short of it.

"Again, the noblest aspect of man is not the social, but the intellectual. In the Middle Ages Christianity has impressed its image on the social framework. It never has been able to do so on literature and science. As to the *Middle Ages,* the *prima facie* judgment passed on a philosopher was that he was in league with the evil powers. . . If, then, Christianity has not compelled the *intellect* of the world, viewed in the mass, to confess

Christ, why insist as a great gain on its having compelled the *social* framework of the world to confess Him?" [1]

Newman then gets back to the fundamental end of the Church—which is sometimes lost sight of—the salvation of souls. And Newman states the problem of the relation of Church and State in terms of saving souls. "Have we any reason to suppose," Newman asks, "that more souls were saved (relatively to the number of Christians) under the Christian Theocracy than under the Roman Emperors, or under the English Georges? There are no means, of course, of proving the point either way; but are we prepared in *matter of fact* to hold the affirmative? If not, *cui bono* the medieval system?"

A few weeks later (December 4, 1860), in another letter to Allies, Newman returns to this question of saving souls. "My position is, that there is no *probability in facts* (*i.e.*, no *evidence*) that one organization of society saves more souls than another.

"And further, that there *is* an *antecedent probability* the other way (*viz.*, that one organization of society is *not* in fact better suited for this great object than another, except accidentally)...

"To illustrate or recommend what I maintain, take the Episcopate as Constantine found it as Nicaea in 325; and take it again as Theodosius inherited it in 381 at Constantinople... *Quaere* as to the fact which of the two Episcopates was in the better state, as to personal sanctity, and as to the power of saving souls?...

"Take, again, the *de facto* state of the French clergy, as in the last century and in ours: is it clear that, in proportion to their numbers, the clergy of the eighteenth

[1] Mary H. Allies, *Thomas William Allies*, 121-122.

century saved more souls than the clergy of the nine-teenth?

"Again, take Rome, in which the medieval system has continued up to this day, and which is honeycombed with secret societies. Have we any reason to think that more souls are saved (in proportion to the Catholic popu-lation) in the diocese of Rome [with its union of Church and State and the Pope as a temporal sovereign] than in the diocese of Dublin [where we have separation of Church and State and a Protestant sovereign]?

"On the other hand," continues Newman, "where are the clear instances in your favour, granting the fore-going *ex parte?* When has the medieval system acted with undeniably greater effect (in appearance) in saving souls than another system? That can hardly be included in the divine Purpose, which cannot be clearly shown to have special *fructus animarum*."

These expressions of Newman's opinion on the im-portant question of Church and State are taken from private letters. Newman never published such views. And for the most part, during the years immediately following *The Rambler* fiasco, Newman withdrew himself more and more into private life, until his supreme moment came in an opportunity afforded most unwittingly by Kingsley. Old age was upon him, his years (as he thought) must be few, and his whole life as a Catholic had been one buffeting after another. The Achilli trial, the University in Dublin, the translation of the Scriptures, his editing of *The Rambler* had all failed. Newman had found the Catholic Faith consoling, but many of the Catholic faith-ful intolerable.

Newman's friends wondered at his silence, and James

Laird Patterson wrote to ask the reason. There is a somewhat bitter irony underlying Newman's answer:

"Seven reasons for not writing more books.
"I do not write
"(1) because in matters of controversy I am *miles
emeritus, rude donatus.*
"(2) because no one serves on parliamentary com-
mittees after he is sixty.
"(3) because Rigaud's steam engine which was hard
to start was hard to stop.
"(4) because Hannibal's elephants never could learn
the goose-step.
"(5) because Garibaldi's chaplains in ordinary never
do write.
"(6) because books that do not sell do not pay.
"(7) because just now I am teaching little boys
nonsense verses."

The Catholic Church has often been credited with
great astuteness in utilizing diverse minds and tempera-
ments in forwarding its one end. But certainly the concrete organization in England showed little of this
traditional astuteness, when it forced a genius like Newman to occupy his incomparable talents in teaching
nonsense verses to little boys.

Newman's discouragement naturally became known,
and people put their own construction upon it. Certain
gossips, whose tribe unfortunately is not practicing birth
control, any more than it is practicing tongue control,
circulated silly and mischievous statements about Newman. Among other things, it was said that he had preached
in favor of Garibaldi, had subscribed to the Garibaldi

fund, etc. People who prided themselves on their faith, as contrasted with Newman's, were—as they thought— showing their faith by failing in justice and charity. Perhaps if Faber and his admirers had put as much emphasis on respect for the reputation of others, as they did on unessential devotions, Newman might have been spared all this suffering and idleness.

Reports gradually magnified in the telling, and became invested with convincing detail. It is human nature that those who make charges against others should desire the satisfaction of saying, "I told you so!" And consequently, those who had been accusing Newman of disloyalty and heresy, really wanted to see him justify by actual defection the charges they had made. Then the wish proving father to the thought, they began to whisper that Newman had left the Church.

At any rate, in July, 1862, it was openly stated in the *Stamford Morning Advertiser*, and repeated in *The Globe*, that Newman had left the "Brompton Oratory" (*sic*) and was going to return to the Church of England. Newman, goaded to the utmost, promptly sent a letter to *The Globe* that shows in some of its phrases the rawness of his feelings:

"The paragraph is utterly unfounded in every portion of it. . .

"I have not had one moment's wavering of trust in the Catholic Church ever since I was received into her fold. I hold, and ever have held, that her Sovereign Pontiff is the centre of unity and the Vicar of Christ; and I have ever had, and have still, an unclouded faith in her creed in all its articles; and a supreme satisfaction in her worship, discipline, and teaching; and an eager longing, and a hope against hope, that the many dear friends whom I have left in Protestantism may be partakers of my happiness.

"This being my state of mind, to add, as I hereby go on to do, that I have no intention, and never had any intention, of leaving the Catholic Church and becoming a Protestant again, would be superfluous, except that Protestants are always on the look-out for some loophole or evasion in a Catholic's statement of fact. Therefore, in order to give full satisfaction, if I can, I do hereby profess 'ex animo,' with an absolute internal assent and consent, that Protestantism is the dreariest of possible religions; that the thought of the Anglican service makes me shiver, and the thought of the Thirty-nine Articles makes me shudder. Return to the Church of England! No! 'The net is broken and we are delivered.' I should be a consummate fool (to use a mild term) if in my old age I left 'the land flowing with milk and honey' for the city of confusion and the house of bondage."

One can understand how irritated Newman was at such unfounded rumors. And yet, it is to be regretted that he used phrases which were calculated to offend some of his old friends among the Anglicans. But there is an indication of character here that must not be overlooked in estimating Newman.

Such an emphatic denial of any intention of leaving the Catholic Church effectively stopped this particular rumor. But Newman remained "under a cloud." Catholics were whispering and wondering. And *The Saturday Review,* commenting on Newman's letter to *The Globe,* said that he had disappointed friends and enemies by doing nothing since becoming a Catholic.

Then Newman, under date of January 21, 1863, in his journal proceeds to give in detail why he has done nothing. "The Church," he wrote, "must be prepared for converts, as well as converts prepared for the Church. . . To me conversions were not the first thing, but the edification [building up] of Catholics. . . To aim then at improving the condition, the status, of the Catholic body, by a careful survey of their argumentative basis, of their position relatively to the philosophy and the character of the day, by giving them juster views, by enlarging and refining their minds, in one word, by education, is (in their view) more than a superfluity or a hobby, it is an insult. It implies that they are deficient in material points. Now from first to last, education, in this large sense of the word, has been my line, and, over and above the disappointment it has caused as putting conversions comparatively in the background, and the offence it has given by insisting that there was room for improvement among Catholics, it has seriously annoyed the governing body here and at Rome:—at Rome on the side of the philosophy of polemic. I should wish to attempt to meet the great infidel, *etc.*, questions of the day, but both Propaganda and the Episcopate, doing nothing themselves, look with extreme jealousy on any one who attempts it." [1]

A few months later, Newman wrote to Miss Bowles, sister of his companion at Littlemore: "Don't you see this, if nothing else, puts a great obex to my writing? This age of the Church is peculiar,—in former times, primitive or medieval, there was not the extreme centralization which is now in use. If a private theologian said anything free, another answered him. If the controversy grew, then it went to a Bishop, a theological faculty, or to some foreign University. The Holy See was but the Court of ultimate appeal. *Now,* if I, as a private priest,

[1] Ward, I, 583.

put anything into print, Propaganda answers me at once. How can I fight with such a chain on my arm? It is like the Persians driven to fight under the lash. There was true private judgment in the primitive and medieval schools,—there are no schools now, no private judgment (in the religious sense of the phrase), no freedom, that is, of opinion. That is, no exercise of the intellect. Now, the system goes on by the tradition of the intellect of former times." [1]

Newman added: "Nor need we fret under a state of things, much as we may feel it, which is incomparably less painful than the state of the Church before Hildebrand, and again in the fifteenth century." But nevertheless, Newman did fret. He loved the Catholic Church so much that it pained him to see opportunities go by default, to know that chances were wasted, that many minds were set back by the attitude of ultra-conservative, over-fearful friends. He knew that his concept of Catholicism was orthodox and correct, but he felt powerless to present it to the world in the face of the manœuvres of what he was later to call an "insolent and aggressive faction." All that Newman could do was to busy himself with the routine duties of a priest, and cultivate the cherished friendships of earlier days. So at this time he renewed his association with W. J. Copeland, his former curate at St. Mary's, Oxford. Newman's letters about turkey at Christmas, and various light details, show a man of affectionate longing for his friends, of dependence upon human comfort, of humorous outlook on the commonplaces of life.

To his beloved Ambrose St. John, Newman could always show his delicate sense of humor, his deep affec-

[1] *Ibid.,* I, 588.

tion, his underlying joy in living. "When I got here [Rednal, a country home of the Oratorians] last night, poor Mrs. Catton was in a dreadful state. She had quite forgotten I was coming, thinking only of your cow, which was all but given over. She was crying and sobbing, had been up four nights, and was to be up that night. And her great distress was that poor Father Ambrose was so very unfortunate; he had lost so much, and really it was not her fault if the cow died." And again from Rednal: "I hope you will come to-morrow—the clematis smells sweetly and the fuchsias are gorgeous. As to the poor dog, I think she is starved."

Newman had reconciled himself to an existence of such quiet domesticities, when suddenly his whole life was changed by an almost chance remark in a review of Froude's *History of England*.

CHAPTER V
APOLOGIA PRO VITA SUA

"I begin to see: he thought me a gentleman at the very time that he said I taught lying on system. After all, it is not I, but Mr. Kingsley who did not mean what he said." (APOLOGIA)

THE History of England from the Fall of Wolsey to the Defeat of the Spanish Armada by James A. Froude, the brother of Newman's early friend Hurrell Froude, began to appear in 1856 and was completed in 1870. It was, as every historian knows, a grandiose diatribe against Catholicism and a panegyric of Protestantism. A review of some of its volumes appeared in *Macmillan's Magazine* in January, 1863; and the reviewer (whose name was not signed) utilized the opportunity to make a special attack of his own on the Catholic Church. This would doubtless have passed without any particular notice, except that he lugged in Newman for a perfectly gratuitous insult.

"Truth for its own sake," wrote the reviewer, "had never been a virtue of the Roman clergy. Father Newman informs us that it need not, and on the whole ought not to be; that cunning is the weapon which Heaven has given to the saints wherewith to withstand the brute male force of the wicked world which marries and is given in marriage. Whether his notion be doctrinally correct or not, it is at least historically so."

When this insulting reference to himself was called to his attention, Newman's first move was to write the house of Macmillan, publishers of the magazine in which the review had appeared.

"The Oratory, Dec. 30, 1863.

"GENTLEMEN:

"I do not write to you with any controversial purpose, which would be preposterous; but I address you simply because of your special interest in a Magazine which bears your name.

"That highly respected name you have associated with a Magazine of which the January number has been sent to me by this morning's post, with a pencil mark calling my attention to page 217.

"There, apropos of Queen Elizabeth, I read as follows:—

" 'Truth for its own sake, had never been a virtue with the Roman clergy. Father Newman informs us that it need not, and on the whole ought not to be; that cunning is the weapon which Heaven has given to the saints wherewith to withstand the brute male force of the wicked world which marries and is given in marriage. Whether his notion be doctrinally correct or not, it is at least historically so.'

"There is no reference at the foot of the page to any words of mine, much less any quotation from my writings, in justification of this statement.

"I should not dream of expostulating with the writer of such a passage, nor with the editor who could insert it without appending evidence in proof of its allegations. Nor do I want any reparation from either of them. I neither complain of them for their act, nor should I thank them if they reversed it. Nor do I even write to you with any desire of troubling you to send me an answer. I do but wish to draw the attention of yourselves, as gentlemen, to a grave and gratuitous slander, which I feel confident you will be sorry to find associated with a name so eminent as yours.

"I am, Gentlemen,
"Your obedient Servant,
"JOHN H. NEWMAN."

Apparently, the publishers immediately communicated with the reviewer, who was no less a person than Charles Kingsley, the Anglican clergyman, "Christian Socialist," and popular novelist. Under date of January 6, 1864, Kingsley wrote to Newman: "that my words were just, I believed from many passages of your writings; but the document to which I expressly referred was one of your Sermons on 'Subjects of the Day,' No. XX, in the volume published in 1844, and entitled 'Wisdom and Innocence.' .. I am most happy to hear from you that I mistook (as I understand from your letter) your meaning; and I shall be most happy, on your showing that I have wronged you, to retract my accusation as publicly as I have made it."

Kingsley enclosed to Newman the draft of a letter of explanation and apology to appear in *Macmillan's Magazine*. The letter included the reference to Newman's sermon—preached and published while an Anglican, be it noted—and continued: "Dr. Newman has, by letter, expressed in the strongest terms his denial of the meaning which I have put upon his words. No man knows the use of words better than Dr. Newman; no man, therefore, has a better right to define what he does, or does not, mean by them. It only remains, therefore, for me to express my hearty regret at having so seriously mistaken him; and my hearty pleasure at finding him on the side of Truth, in this, or any other matter."

Besides the obvious defect of appealing to Newman's Protestant writings, there was an implication in this letter that an ordinary man would have interpreted Newman's words as Kingsley did, and that it was because of a special meaning attached to them by Newman that Newman slips out of the accusation. Also, the general tone

of the letter seems rather condescending. Newman pointed
out these considerations, and the apology as it actually
appeared ran:

"To the Editor of Macmillan's Magazine.
"Sir,
       "In your last number I made certain allegations against
the teaching of Dr. John Henry Newman, which I thought
were justified by a Sermon of his, entitled 'Wisdom and Innocence' (Sermon 20 of 'Sermons bearing on Subjects of the
Day'). Dr. Newman has by letter expressed, in the strongest
terms, his denial of the meaning which I have put upon his
words. It only remains, therefore, for me to express my hearty
regret at having so seriously mistaken him."

This letter was not perfect. But it does appear that
Kingsley was trying to do the handsome thing, although
in a blundering sort of way. Newman might have accepted
the apology, and the world would never have had his incomparable *Apologia*. It has been ordinarily supposed
that Newman's irritation got the better of his charity, and
that he scored Kingsley so unmercifully in the first edition
of his *Apologia* because he could not restrain himself.

But J. S. Fletcher and Wilfrid Meynell remarked
that Newman's passion in the *Apologia* was simulated and
nicely calculated for effect. And Wilfrid Ward writing
much later, in an introduction to the Oxford University
Press edition of the *Apologia*—incidentally an edition giving by a typographical device the various readings of
the different editions—maintains that "Newman's use of
strong language was then due to that close knowledge of
the effect produced by words on the public mind which
was so marked a feature in his conduct of the whole controversy. The overmastering passion which carried his
readers away was not real but simulated. Doubtless there

will be some who will resent this method as histrionic. They will say that Newman was acting a part, that the charm of sincerity is absent from words so carefully calculated. But this appears to me a false estimate. It was no case of using language which he did not consider to be, in itself, justified, with the sole object of producing a certain controversial effect. On the contrary, he evidently thought an indignant denial and angry language the appropriate retort richly deserved by Kingsley's accusation, and representing truly his own view though not any lively personal feeling. He was using the words appropriate to the situation, as an old man, past all lively feeling, may express in answer to some exceptional public testimonial overpowering emotions of gratitude, of which he is physically incapable, and which are yet the feelings appropriate to the situation."

In justification of this view of Newman's apparent emotion in the *Apologia,* Ward quotes Newman's own words from a letter to Sir William Cope, in which he says that he had no personal feeling against Kingsley. But even if Ward's interpretation of this letter were warranted by the actual words, it must be remembered that this letter was written in 1875, after the death of Kingsley and ten years after the *Apologia*. It is possible, therefore, that Newman failed to recall accurately the state of his feelings at the time of the *Apologia*.

Moreover, as Newman wrote his reply to Kingsley at top speed, working sometimes over twenty hours a day, it does not seem probable that he had time to play a part and calculate effects, as Ward maintains. At any rate, there are those, as Ward anticipated, who resent Newman's feigning of emotions which he did not feel. They would prefer to have Newman fail in charity, because he was carried off his feet by the excitement of the moment, rather than that he should deliberately and cruelly crush Kingsley, cold-bloodedly to gain an advantage for his own reputation.

A more plausible suggestion than Ward's, and one which harmonizes with Newman's letter to Cope, is that Newman had no personal antagonism towards Kingsley, but a very real hatred of that Protestant bigotry which he looked upon Kingsley as personifying. For Kingsley was bitterly anti-Catholic. His popular novels, *Westward Ho* and *Hereward the Wake,* are filled with bigoted passages. Newman was really not attacking Kingsley, an individual person, so much as the Protestant prejudice which Kingsley so well represented. And the feeling Newman shows in the *Apologia* was no exaggeration of the feeling he actually entertained against Protestant bigotry.

But be that as it may, Newman was not satisfied with the letter of Kingsley as it finally appeared in *Macmillan's.* And to show his disapproval, Newman reprinted the original review with its offensive statement, the correspondence between himself and Kingsley and Macmillan in regard to it, with Kingsley's apology, and added some comments on the whole episode.

"Mr. Kingsley begins then," wrote Newman, "by exclaiming,—'Oh the chicanery, the wholesale fraud, the vile hypocrisy, the conscience-killing tyranny of Rome! We have not far to seek for an evidence of it. There's Father Newman to wit: one living specimen is worth a hundred dead ones. He, a Priest writing of Priests, tells us that lying is never any harm.'

"I interpose: 'You are taking a most extraordinary liberty with my name. If I have said this, tell me when and where.'

"Mr. Kingsley replies: 'You said it, Reverend Sir, in a sermon which you preached when a Protestant, as Vicar of St. Mary's, and published in 1844; and I could read you a very salutary lecture on the effects which that Sermon had at the time on my opinion of you.'

"I make answer: 'Oh ... *Not,* it seems, as a Priest speaking of Priests;—but let us have the passage.'

"Mr. Kingsley relaxes: 'Do you know, I like your *tone.* From your *tone* I rejoice, greatly rejoice, to be able to believe that you did not mean what you said.'

"I rejoin: 'Mean it!—I maintain I never *said* it, whether as a Protestant or as a Catholic.'

"Mr. Kingsley replies: 'I waive that point.'

"I object: 'Is it possible! What? Waive the main question! I either said it or I didn't. You have made a monstrous charge against me; direct, distinct, public. You are bound to prove it as directly, as distinctly, as publicly;—or to own you can't.'

" 'Well,' says Mr. Kingsley, 'if you are quite sure you did not say it, I'll take your word for it; I really will.'

"My *word!* I am dumb. Somehow I thought that it was my *word* that happened to be on trial. The *word* of a Professor of lying that he does not lie!

"But Mr. Kingsley reassures me: 'We are both gentlemen,' he says; 'I have done as much as one English gentleman can expect of another.'

"I begin to see: he thought me a gentleman at the very time that he said I taught lying on system. After all, it is not I, but Mr. Kingsley who did not mean what he said."

All this was no doubt very irritating to Kingsley. Yet if he had been able to reflect calmly, he might have seen that the man who could punch as many holes as this in his armor was more than his match in a dialectical duel. Kingsley would have been well advised to have accepted as closing the incident the final statement of Newman in this first pamphlet:

"While I feel that Mr. Kingsley's February explanation is miserably insufficient in itself for his January enormity, still I also feel that the Correspondence, which lies between these two acts of his constitutes a real satisfaction to those principles of historical and literary justice to which he has given so rude a shock. Accordingly, I have put it into print, and make no further criticism on Mr. Kingsley."

But Kingsley, with the same obtuseness he had shown previously, would not let the matter rest. He resented having been put upon the defensive by the brilliant intellectual fence of Newman, and he came back for more punishment. It was the dull, stolid, bull goaded to fury by the toreador. Newman had stuck his darts in Kingsley's hide in a dozen places, and Kingsley simply put his head down and rushed blindly for the spot he thought Newman was occupying.

Kingsley replied to Newman with a pamphlet of thirty-five pages, called *What, then, Does Dr. Newman Mean?* It was dull, heavy, ill-tempered, and yet shrewdly calculated to arouse Protestant prejudices against Newman. The old rallying cries of Mariolatry, the Church above the Bible, the condition of Catholic countries, immured nuns, equivocation were raised, and Kingsley no doubt felt that he had completely silenced Newman. But considering the final outcome, Kingsley's first words in this pamphlet are singularly inept: "Dr. Newman has made a great mistake. He has published a correspondence between himself and me, with certain 'Reflexions' and a title page, which cannot be allowed to pass without a re-joinder." In the event, it was Kingsley, not Newman, who had made a great mistake. As Professor Erskine has pithily said, Kingsley, who had written the lines,

> "Be good, sweet child,
> And let who can be clever,"

as if goodness and cleverness were somehow in contra-diction, learned to his cost that Newman was both *good* and *clever*.

In his original review and in his subsequent pamphlet, Kingsley had not only attacked Newman personally, but he had also maligned the whole Catholic clergy, and to some extent the whole Church. If Newman could vindi-cate his own honor, and at the same time the honor of the Catholic priesthood, he would be doing a great deal to ingratiate himself with the Catholic people. The sus-picions then attaching to Newman in Catholic circles would be dissipated. His name would be wiped clean of all aspersions as to his orthodoxy. And of the two sus-picions—that of Protestants concerning his truthfulness and that of Catholics concerning his orthodoxy—the latter was probably the harder to bear. Consequently, Newman had ample reasons for replying to Kingsley. It was a dangerous game, as Newman realized, and only phenomenal success could bring victory. But the stake was worth the danger. Newman risked his all, and his victory was as romantic as that of any medieval knight in searching for the Holy Grail.

Newman decided to answer Kingsley with a history of his religious opinions. He hit upon the happy expedient of issuing his reply in weekly instalments. The first part came out on April 21, 1864. This first number, and the second, were devoted to a consideration of Kingsley's method of disputation, and the true mode of meeting Mr. Kingsley. These parts abounded in the same brilliant controversial thrusts that Newman's previous *Reflections* had exhibited. They caught the public attention, and prepared the way for the entirely different sections dealing with a history of Newman's religious opinions. A detailed answer to Kingsley's charges concluded the issues as a sort of appendix. In this answer, Newman humorously summed up Kingsley's mistakes as thirty-nine articles.

Newman's victory over Kingsley was so complete and the vindication of his own character so triumphant, that there is danger of looking upon them as easily won. To recover some appreciation of his gigantic task, one must remember that he was looked upon by many Protestants as a renegade from the true faith, a traitor to the Church of his birth, who had joined the arch-enemy of all good Christians and become a hanger-on at the court of Anti-Christ. When Kingsley insinuated that for years before his open break with the Anglican Church, Newman had been really a Catholic occupying a Protestant pulpit, he was arousing a degree of personal prejudice that might naturally have daunted the boldest.

And when Kingsley taxed Newman with the teaching of certain Catholic moralists about equivocation, Newman might well call it an attempt to poison the wells. For it was not only an appeal to Protestant prejudice, it was also a driving of the witness out of court. "He is down on me," wrote Newman, "with the odious name of 'St. Alfonso da Liguori,' and 'Scavini,' and 'Neyraguet,' and 'the Romish moralists,' and their 'compeers and pupils,' and I am at once merged and whirled away in the gulph of notorious quibblers, and hypocrites, and rogues."

To show how this lugging in of St. Alfonso was intended to forestall any explanation or defence on his part, Newman quotes Kingsley: "I am *henceforth* in doubt and *fear,* as much as any honest man can be, concerning every word Dr. Newman may write. *How can I tell that I shall not be the dupe of some cunning equivocation,* of one of the three kinds laid down as permissible by the blessed Alfonso da Liguori and his pupils, even when confirmed by an oath, because 'then we do not deceive our neighbor, but allow him to deceive himself?' . . . It is admissible, therefore, to use words and sentences which have a double signification, and leave the hapless hearer to take which of them he may choose. *What proof have I, then, that by 'mean* it? I never said it!' Dr. Newman does not signify, I did not say it, but I did mean it?"

Newman promises to answer these insinuations and questions in their proper place, and goes on with a flaming eloquence and transparent sincerity: "Here I will but say that I scorn and detest lying, and quibbling, and double-tongued practice, and slyness, and cunning, and smoothness, and cant and pretence, quite as much as any Protestants hate them; and I pray to be kept from the snare of them; but all this is just now by the bye; my present subject is Mr. Kingsley; what I insist upon here, now that I am bringing this portion of my discussion to a close, is this unmanly attempt of his, in his concluding pages, to cut the ground from under my feet;—to poison by anticipation the public mind against me, John Henry Newman, and to infuse into the imagination of my readers, suspicion and mistrust of everything I may say in reply. This I call *poisoning the wells.*"

If Kingsley's profession of not being able to know

when Newman was taking advantage of an equivocation, justified by his own Catholic moralists, was to take effect with his Protestant readers, then Newman's answer was foredoomed to failure. The more plausible was the answer, the more cunning and insincere it would seem. And a detached observer, considering the amount of Protestant prejudice in England, would have said that the odds were strongly against Newman. But Newman was an Englishman and knew his fellow countrymen. He knew that in spite of bigotry and prejudice, Englishmen are at bottom fair, and that they have an instinctive sympathy for the underdog. Newman expresses his confidence that his readers will *believe* him, no matter what they may think of him otherwise. And he ends this first part of his *Apologia* with the striking paragraph:

"And now I am in a train of thought higher and more serene than any which slanders can disturb. Away with you, Mr. Kingsley, and fly into space. Your name shall occur again as little as I can help, in the course of these pages. I shall henceforth occupy myself not with you, but with your charges."

The next part of the *Apologia*, published April 28, 1864, was devoted to showing that the true and best way of meeting Mr. Kingsley was to give a history of Newman's religious opinions, and to let his readers judge of the sincerity of his convictions at any one time. He shrinks from the labor involved, and from the publicity of the thing, but he determines to take all England into his confidence.

And then in the third part, which now constitutes the opening chapter of the *Apologia*, Newman begins with his childhood religious influences, and carries us up to the year

1833. In boyhood, he had been Evangelical, with the typical conversion about sixteen years of age, and the conviction that God wanted him to lead a life of celibacy.[1] So far from being a Papist in disguise, Newman during this period was anti-Roman. And yet he traces with unerring finger how he had received from various Protestant sources remnants of the old Faith.

Of the present *Apologia*, this first section up to the year 1833 is by far the most interesting. Newman's history of his religious opinions from then on until his final submission to Rome in 1845, becomes so involved in forgotten controversies and technical theological questions, that it loses much of its interest for the general reader. But to those who can go through Newman's account, his progress towards the final dénouement is as convincing and inexorable—given Newman—as a Greek tragedy. Modern liberals and indifferentists, constituting such an overwhelming percentage of the public, cannot follow Newman to Rome, but they can admire his single-hearted obedience to his conscience. All suspicion of insincerity, equivocation, double-dealing vanishes. Newman comes through the ordeal of self-revelation with an honesty of purpose which no one would ever again dare question. Kingsley's charges are so effectively disposed of, as Newman had hoped, that the appendix answering those charges in detail is hardly necessary, and probably not one in twenty of the readers of the *Apologia* ever dips into the appendix.

[1] The name of St. Paula is irrevocably associated with that of St. Jerome, the Lady Clare with Francis of Assisi, St. Jane Frances de Chantal with St. Francis de Sales, with interacting influence for good in their seeking of God. But no woman ever came into Newman's life in such a way.

There were some who thought that Newman had been too severe with Kingsley in the opening sections and in the appendix. And when the *Apologia* was reprinted, Newman omitted the parts which friends had questioned. Also, he revised the language throughout in the direction of mildness. What was appropriate in the heat of the discussion, and when his reputation hung in the balance, was out of place after his complete victory and vindication. The changes can be followed in the Oxford University Press edition.

The writing of the *Apologia* was a serious emotional and physical strain on Newman. While working on the third part, Newman's diary records that he wrote for sixteen hours at a stretch. The limit was reached on part five, and given in this entry: "At my 'Apologia' for twenty-two hours running." Newman wrote everything himself in longhand, for he had no secretary to whom he could dictate, and it was before the days of typewriters. In sending back some proofs he wrote: "Excuse my penmanship. My fingers have been walking nearly twenty miles a day." Father H. I. D. Ryder, who was with him at the time in the Oratory, tells us that sometimes Newman wrote throughout the night, "and he has been found with his head in his hands crying like a child over the, to him, well nigh impossibly painful task of public confession." [1]

And the labor was made all the greater by the need of checking his memory of events in the Oxford Movement against his own letters in so far as he had copies of them, against published records, and against the memory of others such as Rogers and Church. For although the

[1] Ward, *Life of Newman*, II, 23.

Apologia was mostly autobiographical, the history of Newman's religious opinions involved others, too, and it is a striking illustration of Newman's powers that writing under such tension his narrative should never have been seriously accused of any notable error.

In taking the line he did, of letting the history of his opinions vouch for his sincerity, Newman gambled magnificently. As far as the British public was concerned, Kingsley had the popular side, and his pamphlet showed a natural confidence in the strength of his position, and a contempt for his opponent. But Newman won the final verdict. Almost from the first, Newman had the papers with him. *The Saturday Review, The Times,* and *The Spectator* set the tone for the rest. Richard Holt Hutton, a known admirer of Kingsley and a sympathizer with the theology of Frederick Denison Maurice, wrote in *The Spectator:* "Mr. Kingsley is a choice though perhaps too helpless victim for the full exercise of Father Newman's powers. But he has high feelings and generous courage enough to make us feel that the sacrifice is no ordinary one; yet the title of one of his books,—*Loose Thoughts for Loose Thinkers*—represents too closely the character of his rough but manly intellect, so that a more opportune Protestant ram for Father Newman's sacrificial knife could scarcely have been found."

There were a few articles and books written in reply to Newman. But for the most part, the English public recognized that Kingsley's charge had been swallowed up as completely as his Mary who called the cattle home across the sands of Dee. Never again, during the quarter of a century remaining to him, would Newman's sincerity be challenged. No matter how Protestant prejudice might still attribute equivocation and careless handling of the truth to Catholics generally, Newman would be an exception.[1]

Newman and Kingsley, unfortunately, never met. But on February 13, 1875, just after Kingsley's death, Newman wrote to Sir William Cope: "As to Mr. Kingsley, much less could I feel any resentment against him when he had been thus accidentally the instrument, in the good Providence of God, by whom I had the opportunity given me, which otherwise I should not have had, of vindicating my character and conduct in my 'Apologia.' I had heard, too, a few years back from a friend that she had chanced to go to Chester Cathedral and found Mr. Kingsley preaching about me, kindly, though of course, with criticisms on me... I have always hoped to meet him, feeling sure that there would be no embarrassment on my

[1] Professor G. G. Coulton, of Cambridge, in his "Romanism and Truth," (I, 11) has quoted from the *Apologia* Newman's contention that the Catholic system "tends not only to the liberty, but to the courage, of the individual theologian or controversialist." Then he puts beside this passages from Newman's private letters of the time in which he says: "There are no schools now, no private judgment (in the religious sense of the phrase), no freedom, that is, of opinion. That is, no exercise of the intellect." He thinks that Newman "deliberately gives the reader to understand the exact opposite, on a question of capital importance, of what in private letters he was confessing to be the truth." But Newman was not lying in the *Apologia* passage. The reconciliation of the two statements is this: in his reply to Kingsley he was describing the Catholic system as he conceived it essentially to be, and as he thought it had been historically; in his letters, he was describing what he thought was an accidental and temporary situation under Pius IX. In fact, in the very letters quoted by Coulton, Newman writes: "All this will be overruled; it may lead to much temporary mischief, but it will be overruled." "This age of the Church is peculiar...this is a way of things which, in God's own time, will work its own cure, of necessity."

part, and I said Mass for his soul as soon as I heard of his death." [1]

It is pleasant to look back upon these two actors in the most romantic literary drama of the nineteenth century—the victor without arrogance in his signal triumph, and the defeated taking his painful whipping without a whimper.

The *Apologia* was a national event; it marked a crisis in Newman's life. Henceforth Newman was taken to the heart of the British public, and his writings received an attention they had never before obtained. Newman had become a first page character, there to rub elbows familiarly with prime ministers, and victorious generals, and primates of all England. Although he held no official position in his Church, it was to Newman rather than to anyone else that the reading public turned for an explanation of any seemingly offensive point of Catholic teaching.

In Catholic circles, moreover, Newman stood forth as the great champion of the priesthood, a valiant defender against one of the most vigorous and respected writers of the day. Bishop Ullathorne wrote a letter expressing the wide appreciation among Catholics of Newman's work of recent years, and the diocesan Synod, June 2, 1864, was used as an occasion to present an address to Newman. The German Catholics, assembled in the Congress of Wurzburg in September, 1864, also sent an address of congratulation. And particularly gratifying to Newman was an address signed by one hundred and ten of the clergy of Manning's diocese, because he felt that Westminster had been a center of opposition to him for years. The Academia of the Catholic Religion, founded by Manning, also joined in the general chorus of praise.

[1] Ward, *Life of Newman,* II, 46.

The surprising thing is, that, in the midst of all this hearty satisfaction over Newman's achievement, there were some dissatisfied critics in the ranks of the Catholics. Not only were the criticisms of captious theologians a sore trial to Newman, but they made him feel the difficulty of writing further, as his friends wished, and taking advantage of having won the ear of the British public. "As to my writing more," he complains to Mr. Hope-Scott in a letter of July 6, "speaking in confidence, I do not know how to do it. One cannot speak ten words without ten objections being made to each. . . It would matter little, if I might be quiet under criticism—but I never can be sure that great lies may not be told about me at Rome, and so I may be put on my defence. A writer in a Review of this month says (he knows personally) that persons in Rome within this three years spoke publicly of the probability of my leaving the Church. And Mgr. Talbot put about that I had subscribed to Garibaldi, and took credit for having concealed my delinquencies from the Pope." [1]

The verdict of more than half a century is that Newman's *Apologia* deserves to rank with *The Confessions* of St. Augustine, and with all the other great autobiographical religious writings of Christendom. It is a wonderfully moving picture that we have of this old man, writing in an obscure house in Birmingham, actually changing in a few short weeks the tone of British public opinion towards himself and towards his Church, and achieving for himself an immortal place in English letters and in English religious history.

Writing with the perspective of 1890, Richard Holt Hutton says that the *Apologia* "has done more to break

[1] Ward, *Life of Newman*, II, 43.

down the English distrust of Roman Catholics, and to bring about a hearty good fellowship between them and the members of other Churches, than all the rest of the religious literature of our time put together." [1]

Sixty years after its publication, Bertram Newman— who is not related to the Cardinal—summed up its present position in the world of letters: "The *Apologia* holds its place as one of the great autobiographies in literature, and as a classic which most educated people may be expected to have read in, if not read through. It retains in a full measure the quality of charm, a quality which defies analysis in letters as in life. It is distinguished by its utter absence of any sort of pose, which is not very common in religious or other biographies. The simple and dignified manner in which a sensitive and reserved nature undertook the very uncongenial task of intimate self-revelation lends it a rare attractiveness." "The *Apologia* wrought a literal revolution in the general estimation of its author; Newman's fame had a 'second spring' to which there cannot be many parallels. Kingsley frankly and generously acknowledged that he had 'crossed swords with one who was too strong for him.' " [2]

Dr. S. Parkes Cadman, although belonging to that liberal school so much deplored by Newman, pays his measure of tribute to the success of Newman's history of his religious opinions. "The book," says Cadman, "revealed Newman in all his grandeur and his weakness. Those who had long been indifferent or angry, turned to him again, and a generation that had arisen since the days of relentless war judged him more justly. He now lived under kindlier skies, and once more felt that responsive

---

[1] *Cardinal Newman*, 230.
[2] *Cardinal Newman*, 157, 160.

warmth of sympathy which was so necessary to his temperament and gifts." "The *Apologia* is an acknowledged masterpiece of literary portraiture. Certain passages in it are of the highest quality; the characterizations are as fine and close as need be, bold and pitilessly outright." [1]

Professor Gates, of Harvard, has written: "Probably no book so uncompromisingly autobiographical as the *Apologia* seems from first to last so free from egotism and leaves so charming an impression of frankness and simplicity... There is never any real doubt in your mind of his courage and manly English temper, or of his readiness to meet you fairly on the grounds of debate." [2]

Seldom has a book met such a unanimity of praise for so long a time from men of such different religious and literary outlooks. Professor J. J. Reilly, of Hunter College, as a Catholic might be expected to succumb to its charm, and write: "No work ever written had a more immediate effect in revolutionizing public opinion; no vindication from damaging suspicion ever proved so striking and so complete." [3] But Professor Charles Sarolea, of Edinburgh University, was a man who had drifted away from the Church which Newman entered, and yet he is equally enthusiastic: "The innuendo of Kingsley was as clumsy as it was unfair. The reply of Newman was a merciless execution." [4]

The comparison of Newman with Augustine and Pascal has so often been made that it is almost trite. But there is nothing trite in Algernon Cecil's remarkable paragraph on the *Apologia*. "That beautiful book sets him

[1] *Three Religious Leaders of Oxford*, 570, 446.
[2] *Selections from the prose Writings of John Henry Cardinal Newman*, introd.
[3] *Newman as a Man of Letters*, 253.
[4] *Cardinal Newman and His Influence*, 55.

beside the four or five famous people who have dared plainly and without reserve to write their own spiritual biography. It is a task that requires either great conceit or great humility. Augustine did it to catch souls for the Kingdom of God; Rousseau did it to prove himself a good citizen of the world; Amiel (if Amiel was a great man) did it to be quit of the groanings which could not be uttered. But of the four that have been named, Newman's book, like his character, is by far the noblest. Neither the sensuality of Augustine, nor the egotism of Rousseau, nor the weakness of Amiel soils its pages. From first to last his candle burnt with a clear, steady flame, and Kingsley had taken away the bushel that covered it." [1]

But the *Apologia* did more for Newman than to gain for him a place in English letters. The clearing of his reputation with his old friends, and with Protestants generally, and the position which his success secured for him with the body of Catholics, gave him a peace of soul in sharp contrast with his depression just before the tilt with Kingsley. On October 30, 1867, Newman wrote in his journal:

"I never was in such happy circumstances as now, and I do not know how I can fancy I shall continue without some or other real cross. I am my own master,—I have my time my own—I am surrounded with comforts and conveniences—I am in easy circumstances, I have no cares, I have good health—I have no pain of mind or body. I enjoy life only too well. The weight of years falls on me as snow, gently though surely, but I do not feel it yet. I am surrounded with dear friends—my reputation has been cleared by the *Apologia*. What can I want but greater gratitude and love towards the Giver of all these

[1] *Six Oxford Thinkers*, 104.

good things? There is no state of life I prefer to my own
—I would not change my position for that of anyone I
know—I am simply content—there is nothing I desire—
I should be puzzled to know what to ask, if I were free to
ask... For myself I am as covered with blessings and as
full of God's gifts, as is conceivable. And I have nothing
to ask for but pardon and grace, and a happy death."

And yet in that same entry in his journal, Newman
had indicated that there was something he could, and
really did, ask for, one thing that still troubled him: "And
now, alas," he wrote, "I fear that in one sense the iron has
entered into my soul. I mean that confidence in any superiors whatever can never blossom again within me. I never
shall feel easy with them. I shall, I feel, always think
they will be taking some advantage of me,—that at length
their way will lie across mine, and that my efforts will be
displeasing to them. I shall ever be suspicious that they or
theirs have secret unkind thoughts of me, and that they
deal with me with some *arrière pensée*. And, as it is my
happiness so to be placed as not to have much intercourse
with them, therefore, while I hope ever loyally to fulfill
their orders, it is my highest gain and most earnest request of them, that they would let me alone—and, since
I do not want to initiate any new plan of any kind, that,
if they can, they would keep their hands off me. Whether
or not they will consent to this is more than I can say, for
they seem to wish to ostracise me. But in saying this,
I repeat what I said when I began to write, I am now
in a state of quiescence, and fear as little as I hope. And
I do not expect this state of mind to be reversed. God
forbid I should liken them to the 'Scribes and Pharisees'
—but still I obey them, as Scribes and Pharisees were to

be obeyed, as God's representatives, not from any devotion to *them*."

The iron had entered Newman's soul, and the injustice done him by certain maximizers in Catholic circles, and more particularly at the center of the Catholic world, Rome, still rankled. Under the same date of October 30, 1867, Newman recorded:

"I have said to Cardinal Barnabó: 'Viderit Deus.' I have lodged my cause with Him—and, while I hope ever by His grace to be obedient, I have now as little desire as I have hope to gain the praise of such as him in anything I shall do henceforth. A.B. and others have been too much for me. They have too deeply impressed the minds of the authorities at Rome against me to let the truth about me have fair play while I live; and when one ceases to hope, one ceases to fear. They have done their worst—and, as Almighty God in 1864 cleared up my conduct in the sight of Protestants at the end of twenty years, so as regards my Catholic course, at length, after I am gone hence, 'Deus viderit.' "

But Newman's Roman Catholic course was to be cleared before his death by the red hat of a cardinal, and cleared in almost as spectacular a manner as the *Apologia* had cleared his Anglican defection. Newman was to win the heart of Catholic Rome as he had won the heart of Catholic England—by the sheer force of doing God's will as he saw it.

CHAPTER VI

PAPAL INFALLIBILITY

> "Certainly if I am obliged to bring religion into
> after dinner toasts (which does not seem quite
> the thing), I shall drink—to the Pope, if you
> please—still, to conscience first, and to the Pope
> afterwards."
>
> (LETTER TO THE DUKE OF NORFOLK)

THE Protestant Revolt of the sixteenth century has
had profound results for the Catholic Church. The defection of the northern nations left the Catholic Church
restricted in membership, and dominantly Latin in complexion. Effective intellectual leadership for Europe as
a whole was lost to the Church, and to a large extent
moral leadership, also.

An almost inevitable reaction to Protestantism was
an emphasis within the Church upon authority. And so,
although the Church was weakened by the Revolt, the
Papacy was strengthened. The post-Tridentine Pope has
been in some ways much more influential in Catholic
circles than his predecessors. An Innocent III, of course,
or a Hildebrand, had been powerful figures in earlier
centuries. But the hierarchy was relatively independent
of them. The effect of Protestantism has been to empha-

size Rome as the center of unity for those who have remained faithful.

It is true that for some time after the sixteenth century, the French were still somewhat centrifugal. The nation that had given a number of Popes to the Church, and had transported the Government of the Church to French soil, was disinclined to yield too much to Rome, when Rome was held by an Italian. Moreover, the political supremacy of France under Louis XIV did not make matters any easier for the sovereign of the Vatican.

A union of Church and State, where the bishops are appointed by the State, is likely, when the State is as strong and autocratic as was France under Louis XIV, to lead to the dominance of the Church by the State. Naturally, the State will appoint as bishops those priests who are loyal to it, rather than loyal to the interests of a weak temporal sovereign on the other side of the Alps. And a temporal sovereign with enough territory to make spoliation tempting, and yet without enough military power to defend himself, will think twice before offending this neighboring State, which more than once has sent its troops into the Italian Peninsula. It is said that during the Kulturkampf in Germany, when the Catholic hierarchy was successfully opposing the oppressive laws of an almost deified Prussian State, Bismarck regretted that the Pope no longer had a seaport to which he might send a few threatening battleships.

But one of the by-products of the French Revolution at the end of the eighteenth century was the weakening of Gallicanism. As far as the Catholic world was concerned, the papacy came out of the Napoleonic débâcle stronger than ever. Spain and Austria, the greatest of the Catholic countries left in Europe, were mere puny infants compared with the Gallican France of the Grand Monarch. The fear of the Pope was directed not against autocratic governments, which professed a certain loyalty to the Church, and which supported the Church temporally, but against the dangerous excesses associated in his mind with democracy. And it is no wonder that an institution which had suffered as the Catholic Church had suffered at the hands of irresponsible revolutionists should look with suspicion on anything derived from the hated Liberté, Egalité, Fraternité.

All new movements have their extremists, and the democratic movement certainly had some remarkable specimens in Danton, Murat, and Robespierre. On the other hand, all old institutions have their bitter-enders, men who confuse the accidental with the essential, and who fight as fiercely for the one as for the other. Among these extremists on either side there is no willingness to consider things calmly, to work patiently for slow changes, to weigh the good and the bad in institutions and proposals. One stands committed to things as they are; the other wants the complete destruction of the established order.

Change in the political order, therefore, almost invariably originates outside the Church. And being outside, it is looked upon with suspicion. Where Church and State are united, revolt against the State becomes in the eyes of the extremists religious heresy or schism. The Inquisition is a tool of the civil government, as well as an arm of the Church. Consequently, it is easy for ecclesiastics to label their political opponents with the badge of religious disloyalty. The task of distinguishing between what is religious and what is political becomes extremely difficult.

Moreover, it is hard for the bitter-enders to recognize a real and permanent change. They hark back to previous conditions. They are constantly hoping that the old régime will be restored by some political *coup*. They do not judge things by eternal principles, but by comparison with what once was. At the same time, the bitter-enders will make no compromise with the forces in the saddle. They deliberately widen the breach between themselves and the world outside. Figuratively speaking, they descend once more into the catacombs, hoping for some Constantine who will bring them forth into victory and power.

In France, the extreme bitter-enders among the Catholics were particularly active and intransigent. The Party represented by *L'Univers,* under Louis Veuillot, "tended to withdraw Catholics from contact with a wicked world, to take little interest in and have little belief in the progress of thought outside the 'visible fold,' and to extend to the non-Catholic world in general the feeling of suspicion which had been engendered by persecution. Veuillot looked in short to a state of war as most hopeful, and to a Catholic party as a compact phalanx resisting the encroachments of modern society and of the fatal secularist spirit." [1]

Just as some men take delight in shocking the simple faith of the traditional believer, so Veuillot and his friends took delight in shocking the common sense and critical judgment of the modern man. "The collection together of all the most startling suppositions which individual theologians have tolerated, and the advocacy in some cases of forms of expression which appeared to most readers to go even beyond what could be tolerated, were

[1] *W. G. Ward and the Catholic Revival,* 113.

extremely trying to those who considered that an age which did not understand the depth and beauty of Catholicism had to be won and not further repelled.... Frederic Ozanam speaks on the subject with painful feeling. 'This·school ... goes about looking for the boldest paradoxes, the most disputable propositions, provided that they irritate the modern spirit. It represents truth to men not by the side which attracts them but by that which repels them. It does not propose to bring back unbelievers, but to stir up the passions of believers.' "[1]

If Veuillot had lived in the days of St. Paul, he would probably have looked upon the Apostle of the Gentiles as a dangerous innovator. Veuillot would have taken his stand firmly on the ground of tradition, and absolutely fixed procedure, with everything dogmatically final. For Veuillot, to introduce the policy of allowing Gentiles to eat the spiritual food of the Children of Abraham would have been unadulterated treachery. To suggest that circumcision was not essential for converts would have roused the deepest ire of this essentially bitter-ender. Wilfrid Ward describes this spirit when he goes on to say:

"They [Veuillot and his school] tended to view current Catholic teaching, apart from matters of faith, as more or less final in its form. They were little ready to see the necessity, for the sake of accuracy, of viewing it in the light of modern discoveries, and thereby correcting its expression. They were little alive to the possibility of such modifications being called for as the discovery of Copernicanism introduced in the current interpretation of *Josué*. If traditional expressions of belief conflicted with modern scientific theories, no doubt could arise but that the science of an evil day was wrong. If individual

[1] *Ibid.*, 121.

Catholics had difficulties as to such collisions, it showed a want of faith in them... Hence the tendency of the school to uncompromising views... The careful separation of good and bad elements in the character of an enemy of the Church, or the delicate weighing of the certain, the probable, the possible, the impossible, in dogmatic belief, seemed to them to savour of that plausible and corroding rationalism which attenuates and ends by destroying the deepest and most vital differences of opinion."

Opposed to Veuillot in France was *Le Correspondant,* founded by Montalembert, and representing a desire to bring about as great a rapprochement as Catholic dogma would allow between the Church and the modern world. This school held that, on questions apart from what had been doctrinally defined, the Church had traditionally and historically allowed a certain amount of freedom. As contrasted with the offhand method of a papal definition every time some journalist raised a problem, they preferred the slow method of thorough discussion.

In England, the fact that prior to 1850 there was no established hierarchy, that the country was governed by Vicars Apostolic much more completely dependent upon the Holy See than a bishop in ordinary, tended to exalt the influence of Rome. On the other hand, the fewness of Catholics and their comparative isolation preserved them from the intellectual currents agitating their fellow religionists in continental Europe. But once Catholics came out of their shell, and began to look around them, they took sides. And it is rather interesting to note that generally the "old" Catholics were "liberal" and the converts "ultramontane." Manning and W. G. Ward and Talbot were the leaders in England of a group corresponding largely to Veuillot and his followers in France, and *The Dublin Review,* edited by Ward, took the place of *L'Univers.*

Newman's appreciation of the dangers of liberalism, of the great temptation it was to many minds, of the impossibility of meeting these dangers by a mere policy of "nihilism," or of prohibitions and restraints, led him to sympathize with the less reactionary group among the Catholics of England. It was because of this sympathy that he had attempted to establish the university in Dublin; failing in this, to have a house at Oxford; and later to become associated with *The Rambler.*

At bottom, however, it was Newman's historical sense that made it impossible for him to accept the intransigent attitude of Veuillot. Newman knew that Veuillot's theories did not correspond with the historical development of the Church. Rome had rarely initiated anything. She had been the court of last appeal to decide between rival theologians or schools of theology. The initiative had come from outside. And Newman felt that there should still be this historical freedom of discussion on theological questions, with an appeal to Rome only when necessary.

Veuillot and his school, however, wanted Rome to be always deciding questions. W. G. Ward said that he would have liked a daily infallible document with his morning *Times* to read at breakfast.

At any rate, there was a decided increase in the number of papal documents issued under Pius IX. As each came out, there was a tendency for the maximizers to call it infallible, whether careful theological opinion would do so or not. A papal document supposedly in line with their own attitude on any question was a convenient club with which to bang their opponents, and to make that club infallible rendered it all the bigger and more devastating.

In August, 1863, a Catholic Congress was held at Malines under the presidency of the Archbishop. On Thursday, the 20th, Count de Montalembert, the leader of the French liberal Catholics, delivered his address on "A Free Church in a Free State." Incidentally, it has been claimed that this slogan was coined by the liberal Catholics, as asserting the rights of the Church against a despotic State. Montalembert even charged Cavour with stealing his conception and using it from a different point of view.[1] The following day, August 21, Montalembert spoke on "Freedom of Conscience."

A month later, a meeting of nearly one hundred German Catholic scholars took place at the Benedictine Monastery in Munich upon the invitation of Abbot Haneburg, Döllinger, and Alzog, the Church historian. At this meeting, Döllinger outlined what he considered the necessary policy of Catholic scholars in meeting the problems of the day. The drift of the address was away from the traditional scholastic treatment of theological questions.

The addresses of both Montalembert and Döllinger were probably capable of a moderate interpretation that would have been acceptable at Rome. But they were also capable of an extreme interpretation. The maximizers proceeded to the extreme interpretation. And they were unwittingly aided in this by some liberal Catholics adopting the same extreme views. *The Home and Foreign Review,* under Acton—the successor of *The Rambler*—welcomed the addresses and interpreted them in a way that was offensive to a middle-of-the-roader like Newman. This *Home and Foreign* interpretation immediately determined

[1] Luigi Luzzatti, *God in Freedom,* 171.

the policy of W. G. Ward in *The Dublin Review,* and he proceeded to denounce with great heat what he called "liberal Catholicism."

Underlying the whole question was the infallible authority of papal documents, and so Ward wrote a number of articles dealing with this problem. In the light of what the Vatican Council finally defined in 1870, it is interesting to note that Ward's "main contention was that all the doctrinal instructions in the Pope's official public letters, which claim to guide Catholic belief, are strictly infallible; although neither the incidental statements (*obiter dicta*), nor the doctrinal statements of letters whose primary purport was disciplinary, are infallible. Papal condemnations were, he held, infallible not only when they declared an opinion or work heretical, but when they branded it with some lesser censure. Papal letters might be *ex cathedra* and infallible, although in form only addressed to a single individual provided that the Pope designed them for general guidance. Further, he maintained that the Pope did in fact intend very frequently to give infallible instruction in such letters. Once more, although the matter of papal teaching *ex cathedra* is 'faith and morals,' he maintained that such decisions might be immediately ('in their proximate relations') concerned with philosophy, politics, history, or physics, provided that the ultimate object of the decisions was the safe-guarding of revealed truth." [1]

Newman condemned emphatically the liberalism of the Munich school, as interpreted by the extremists, but he thought that Ward went too far in the opposite direction. One of Newman's Oratorians, Henry I. D. Ryder, wrote a book on the interpretation of papal documents in

[1] *Ward and the Catholic Revival,* 165.

answer to Ward. And it is very significant that so Ultramontane a man as Manning, "although almost entirely in harmony with Ward's general views, refused to maintain, as Ward did, that the principles of '89 were condemned. Newman had hopes of the philosophical and historical movement represented by the Munich school, Manning of the movement of Lacordaire and Montalembert, that they might be factors in the Catholic Revival; and they shrunk from pressing logical conclusions which might kill the prospect." And on Manning's advice, Ward's essay on "Liberty of Conscience," answering Montalembert's Malines address, was withdrawn from publication, lest its strictures on Montalembert might give offence.

Newman's attitude was so subtle and complex that it is extremely difficult to do it justice. He was misunderstood by Acton and his friends, who could not reconcile Newman's intellectual sympathy for freedom with his complete submission to authority; and Newman was misunderstood by Ward and Manning, who could not believe that his submission to authority was really genuine, when he also professed a belief in the necessity of freedom. Here was another reason justifying the title of Abbé Brémond's book, *The Mystery of Newman.* As Manning put it, Newman was a difficult man to understand. The best treatment of Newman's attitude towards the liberal and ultramontane movements is the chapter called, "Ward, Newman and Liberal Catholicism," in Wilfrid Ward's *William George Ward and the Catholic Revival.*

"As to the ... province of authority in the progress of theology," writes Ward, "Newman held with Lacordaire that authority and liberty are equally necessary. While Ward proposed to build theological science mainly on the decisions of authority as a positive foundation, Newman regarded the action of Rome as primarily negative. With the writers of the *Home and Foreign* he eloquently vindicated the importance of originality and of scientific methods; but adhering still to a *via media* he considered that each party neglected a necessary element."

"Newman's belief in the necessity of submission to authority had always been strong; but so had his belief in the necessity of a boldness and freedom of thought... His agreement with Ward in principles, which from time to time he emphasised, was matched by his strong dislike of Ward's uncompromising and emphatic assertions of principle at moments which he considered inopportune, and of his relentless application of one set of principles without consideration of another set equally essential to a just conclusion... The consequence was that, from those who did not understand him, he incurred, as in the days of Tract 90, the charge of over-subtlety, and of a reserve incompatible with the plain speaking which the situation demanded."

Moreover, Newman felt that the traditions of the Church were a safeguard for freedom of thought. These traditions were a guarantee that new definitions, making a demand for something entirely novel, should not be promulgated. In his *Apologia*, Newman writes: "I submit ... to the universally received traditions of the Church in which lies the matter of those new dogmatic definitions which are from time to time made, and which in all times are the clothing and illustration of the Catholic dogma as already defined... Nothing can be imposed on me (in time to come) different in kind from what I hold already, much less contrary to it."

"In Newman's eyes the province of authority not

only as a discipline for individuals, but as an actual security for prudent action, and general well-being, and sound thinking in the long run, was of the highest importance; while the leaders of the Munich school, as subsequent events showed still more clearly, did not recognize this subtler aspect of it, although they allowed in some measure the individual's duty of submission. Authority as defining dogmas of faith, or as maintaining discipline, was understood by them. But its complex action in giving breathing time, checking precipitation, protecting weak minds, occasionally enforcing the superior importance of other interests over the intellectual, acting at times justly as a ruling power by condemnations which were not philosophically exact, and might be ultimately cancelled—such manifestations of authority were not understood or valued by so exclusively and intellectual a school. 'The Pope is a ruler, not a philosopher,' Newman said; and he held that this truth was one which both the Munich school and *The Dublin Review* were apt, for opposite reasons, to forget. The former grudged intellectual submission to what made no pretence of exhaustive scientific treatment, the latter tended to build Catholic thought on preventive decrees." [1]

In a well-known passage of his *Apologia* Newman goes into this question of the relation between the individual and authority in considerable detail. It is best to give Newman's own words in this regard, as any paraphrase on so important and subtle a matter might easily create a false impression. In fact, any condensation may do this, and so the reader should preferably go to the *Apologia* itself, rather than be content with a mere extract.

[1] Ward, *op. cit.*, 208.

"Every exercise of Infallibility," writes Newman, "is brought out into act by an intense and varied operation of the reason, both as its ally and as its opponent, and provokes again, when it has done its work, a reaction of reason against it; and, as in a civil polity, the State exists and endures by means of the rivalry and collision, the encroachments and defeats of its constituent parts, so in like manner Catholic Christendom is no simple exhibition of religious absolutism, but presents a continuous picture of authority and private judgment alternately advancing and retreating as the ebb and flow of the tide; it is a vast assemblage of human beings, with wilful intellects and wild passions, brought together into one by the beauty and the majesty of a superhuman power, into what may be called a large reformatory or training-school, not as if into a hospital or into a prison, not in order to be put to bed, not to be buried alive, but (if I may change my metaphor) brought together as if into some moral factory, for the melting, refining, and moulding by an incessant, noisy process, of the raw material of human nature, so excellent, so dangerous, so incapable of divine purposes.

"St. Paul says in one place that his Apostolical power is given him to edification and not to destruction. There can be no better account of the Infallibility of the Church. It is a supply for a need, and it does not go beyond that need. Its object is, and its effect also, not to enfeeble the freedom and vigor of human thought in religious speculation, but to resist and control its extravagance. . .

"It is individuals, and not the Holy See, that have taken the initiative, and given the lead to the Catholic mind in theological inquiry. Indeed, it is one of the reproaches urged against the Roman Church that it has originated nothing, and has only served as a sort of *remora* or break in the development of doctrine. And it is an objection which I really embrace as a truth; for such I conceive to be the main purpose of this extraordinary gift. It is said, and truly, that the Church of Rome possessed no great mind in the whole period of persecution. Afterwards, for a long while, it has not a single doctor to show; St. Leo, its first, is the teacher of one point of doctrine; St. Gregory, who stands at the very extremity of the first great age of the Church, has no place in dogma or philosophy. The great luminary of the western world is, as we know, St. Augustine; he, no infallible teacher, has formed the intellect of Christian Europe; indeed, to the African Church generally we must look for the best early exposition of Latin ideas. Moreover, of the African divines, the first in order of time, and not the least influential, is the strong-minded Tertullian. Nor is the Eastern intellect, as such, without its share in the formation of the Latin Teaching. The free thought of Origen is visible in the writings of the Western Doctors, Hilary and Ambrose; and the independent mind of Jerome has enriched his own vigorous comments on Scripture from the stores of the scarcely orthodox Eusebius. Heretical questionings have been transmuted by the same living power of the Church into salutary truths. The case is the same as regards the Ecumenical Councils. Authority in its most imposing exhibition, grave bishops, laden with the traditions and rivalries of particular nations or places, have been guided in their decisions by the commanding genius of individuals, sometimes young and of inferior rank. Not that uninspired intellect overruled the superhuman gift which was committed to the Council, which would be a self-contradictory assertion, but that in that process of inquiry and deliberation which ended in an infallible enunciation, individual reason was paramount. Thus Malchion, a mere presbyter, was the instrument of the great Council of Antioch in the third century meeting and refuting, for the assembled Fathers, the heretical Patriarch of that see. Parallel to this instance is the influence, so well known, of a young deacon, St. Athanasius, with the 318 Fathers at Nicaea. In medieval times we read of St. Anselm at Bari, as the champion of the Council there held against the Greeks. At Trent, the writings of St. Bonaventura, and what is more to the point, the address of a priest and theologian, Salmeron, had a critical effect on some of the definitions of dogma. In some of these cases the influence might be partly moral, but in others it was that of a discursive knowledge of Ecclesiastical writers, a scientific acquaintance with theology, and a force of thought in the treatment of doctrine." [1]

What Newman feared from the attitude of men like Ward and Manning was the gross injustice of impugning the orthodoxy of their opponents, when that orthodoxy would be judged by an appeal to inflamed prejudices, rather than by calm reason. And Newman felt that this was a much greater injustice in the field of Catholicism than in any other line of human activity. For a man's relations to the Catholic Church are different from his relations to any other society.

For instance, if an army officer advocates a policy that is repudiated by his government, he can resign. There are plenty of other things he can do besides soldiering. No man has to be an army officer. If a politician stands for something that his party denounces, he can either go over to another party, or he can give up politics. In the extremest case imaginable, a man can leave

[1] *Apologia*, 252, 265.

one country and go to another. No one is bound irrevocably to any particular nation. Many Americans are living in London and Paris.

But with a Catholic, there is no way of dropping
out of the Church with a good conscience, as long as one
believes in the Church. As a priest, Newman had to remain a priest. Newman could not resign, as an army
officer can, and go back into lay life; Newman could
not change Churches; he could not go to any part of
the globe where he would not still be a Catholic. For
anyone, therefore, recklessly to throw suspicion on his
loyalty to the Church, or anyone else's loyalty, seemed
to Newman the height of injustice and uncharitableness.
It was to inflict a lasting and irremediable injury.

Newman's tendency, therefore, was to proceed very
cautiously in determining what one had to hold as a loyal
Catholic. He did not wish to put any undue strain on
individuals. He has said in one of his sermons that of the
two sins, minimizing Catholic doctrine and maximizing
Catholic doctrine—that is, subtracting from or adding to
Catholic dogma—the greater sin was that of maximizing.
For by maximizing one might be driving out of the
Church, and so depriving of the help of the sacramental
life of membership, a great many persons who might
otherwise have remained faithful. Whereas in minimizing,
one might be making it possible for many minds to remain
at peace and in touch with the sacraments, ultimately
to come to a deeper and broader faith.

It has been necessary to go thus into detail in regard
to Newman's attitude towards Liberalism and Ultramontanism, towards minimizing and maximizing, because the
next few years were to try him severely by raising innumerable questions on these lines. In former pontificates,

encyclical letters had been rather rare. But Piux IX introduced the custom of issuing frequent allocutions and encyclicals on questions of the day. And in 1864 the hearts of Ward and of those who shared his views were warmed by the appearance of the now famous *Syllabus Errorum* and the encyclical *Quanta Cura*. The encyclical renewed the papal protests of fifteen years, and the *Syllabus* was a list of the propositions condemned as erroneous in earlier documents of Pius IX. Newman was to show, later on, that these two documents were capable of an interpretation recommending them to the good sense of such liberal-minded statesmen as Gladstone. But for the time being, this calm and reasoned interpretation was lost in the clamor of the extreme maximizers. And it is not surprising that the interpretation of these extremists was taken by the non-Catholic world as correct and official.

For a generation or more, these maximizers had been crying that there was an essential conflict between the Church and everything modern. The terms "liberal" and "liberalism" became epithets equivalent to heretical and anathema. The maximizers welcomed the *Syllabus* as confirming everything they had been saying, and immediately raised it to the dignity of an infallible document.

On the other hand, moderate Catholics, like Dupanloup, Bishop of Orleans, regretted the appearance of the *Syllabus Errorum* for the very reason that they feared it would be misinterpreted by the world at large—a fear that has been amply justified by the event. When Ward, six months after the publication of the *Syllabus*, wrote in *The Weekly Register* that undoubtedly it was infallible, Newman was disturbed. Newman was afraid that many unthinking Catholics would be driven towards Liberalism by such false statements. He did not look upon the *Syl-*

labus as infallible, and he knew that theologians of note were of the same opinion. Father O'Reilly, a well known Jesuit theologian of Ireland, had expressed such a view to him privately. But when Newman proposed that they should jointly prepare a letter to offset Ward's confident assertion, Father O'Reilly "was not disposed to move in the matter or to repeat in writing at a critical juncture the opinion he had given earlier." [1]

"Newman felt himself powerless to act. But he did not rest until he had pressed his question home in Rome itself; and eighteen months later he had the satisfaction of learning from Ambrose St. John that the Roman theologians with whom he conversed agreed with himself in withholding from the Encyclical the character of an infallible utterance." [2]

Cardinal Wiseman died in February, 1865. But Newman's hopes that now Manning's dominance in Rome would cease were short-lived. For Manning became Archbishop of Westminster, and so was more strongly entrenched than ever. Newman had to wait not only for the death of Wiseman, but of Pius IX, for a change of atmosphere. Fortunately, Newman was long-lived.

In his period of watchful waiting, Newman was renewing more of his old Anglican friendships. In September, 1865, he went to Hursley to visit Keble, and as Pusey was visiting at the same time, it was a reunion of the three old leaders of the Tractarian Movement. There was a pathos about the meeting that Newman has described in letters of the time. "When I got to Keble's door," Newman wrote to Mrs. Froude, "he happened to be at it, but we did not know each other, and I was obliged to

[1] Ward, *Life of Newman*, II, 84.
[2] *Ibid.*, II, 85.

show him my card. . . . There was something awful in three
men meeting in old age who had worked together in their
best days. Vanity of vanities, all is vanity, was the sad
burden of the whole—once so united, now so broken up,
so counter to each other. . . . Keble is deaf—, but, what is
worse, his speech is much impaired—and I think he *thinks*
more slowly. Pusey was full of plans, full of meetings.
He has since made an important speech at Norwich on
the interpretation of Scripture, which will do good, and
of this he was full. Then, he was just on publishing his
book which he calls an *Eirenicon,* and he was full of it,
though he was cautious of letting out all that was in it....
It is anything but an Eirenicon—it is likely to make
Catholics very angry—and justly angry."

The force of Pusey's *Eirenicon* depended mainly
upon his acceptance of the extreme views of Ward, Veuillot, and others as being authoritative. Newman answered,
in a very friendly way, and disclaimed any such authori-
tativeness for the views which Pusey had attributed to
the whole Church. Thus Newman could kill two birds
with one controversial stone—as a champion of the Catholic Church he could answer Pusey, and at the same time
he could to a large extent pull the claws of Ward and Co.
For a man of Newman's subtle mind and keen appreciation of irony, there must have been a gentle humor in a
situation that kept Ward from attacking him for fear of
seeming to side with Pusey against the Catholic protagonist.

Newman's letter to Pusey received seven columns in
The Times review. And it is significant that the reviewer
picked out for praise a characteristic of Newman's controversial style to which some Catholics strongly objected.
For he notes "the English habit of not letting off the

blunders and follies of his own side, and of daring to think that a cause is better served by outspoken independence of judgment than by fulsome, unmitigated puffing."

At the same time that Newman was giving an example in his own writing of the best type of controversy, he wrote a private letter to Fr. Coleridge, S.J., editor of the Jesuit organ, *The Month,* pointing out how an article called *Archbishop Manning on the Reunion of Christendom* (April, 1866) was full of maladresse:

"1. 'The great name of Bossuet has been *foolishly* invoked by Dr. Pusey,' p. 384.

"2. 'There can be no more mistake about the fact than about *the impression which Dr. Pusey has meant to produce* on his readers,' p. 387, note.

"3. 'How does this . . . differ *from the artifice of an unscrupulous* advocate?' p. 388.

"4. 'Great confusion of thought,' p. 388.

"5. 'In happy unconsciousness of the absurdity of his language,' p. 389.

"6. 'This language shows as much *confusion or ignorance,* etc.,' p. 389.

"7. 'He does not *understand* that . . . ,' p. 389.

"8. 'He *talks* of a continual flow, etc.,' p. 389.

"9. 'This is very *childish,*' p. 389.

"10. 'Dr. Pusey must have deliberately ignored the distinction,' p. 389.

"It must be recollected that your object is to convince those who respect and love Dr. Pusey that he has written hastily and rashly and gone beyond his measure. Now if even I feel pained to read such things said of him, what do you suppose is the feeling of those who look up to him as their guide? They are as indignant at finding him thus treated as you are for his treatment of Catholic doctrine. They close their ears and hearts. Yet these are the very people you write for. You don't write to convince the good Fathers at No. 9 [the residence of the Jesuits in London], but to say a word in season to *his* followers and to *his* friends—to dispose them to look kindly on Catholics and Catholic doctrine,—to entertain the possibility that they have misjudged us, and that they are needlessly, as well as dangerously, keeping away from us, —but to mix up your irrefutable matter with a personal attack on Pusey, is as if you were to load your gun carefully, and then as deliberately administer some drops of water at the touch-hole." All of which is very sound advice for apologists in general.

However, there were Catholic critics of Newman's answer to Pusey. Manning and Talbot had some correspondence in which they "deplored" and "viewed with alarm" certain passages. *The Tablet* of March 10, 1866, published a letter by a Mr. E. R. Martin which was quite offensive to Newman. But such strictures were not allowed to pass unanswered, and there were many who took Newman's side in letters to *The Tablet*. Among them was Bishop Clifford and Newman's own Bishop, Ullathorne. On April 7, 1866, Ullathorne wrote: "Is petty cavilling from Catholics without authority to be the present reward for a masterly exposition of the subject most difficult for Protestants to comprehend, and which has made that subject classical in the English tongue?" [1]

One question which would naturally have come into Newman's answer to Pusey was that of papal infallibility. Newman deliberately avoided infallibility, because he felt that the state of Catholic sentiment at the time, with all

[1] Butler, *Life of Ullathorne*, I, 366.

the external troubles of the Pope, did not allow a calm discussion. But events moved swiftly in such a direction that Newman could not long avoid discussing in some detail the problem of papal infallibility. The extreme Ultramontanes were pushing for a condition of affairs that Newman felt would do tremendous harm to the Church. Newman could have made his own the words of Archbishop Sibour, of Paris, in 1853:

"We defended the independence of the spiritual power against the pretensions of the temporal power, but we respected the constitution of the State and the constitution of the Church. We did not do away with all intermediate power, all hierarchy, all reasonable discussion, all legitimate resistance, all individuality, all spontaneity. The Pope and the Emperor were not, the one the whole Church, the other the whole State. Doubtless there are times when the Pope may set himself above all the rules which are only for ordinary times, and when his power is as extensive as the necessities of the Church. The old Ultramontanes kept this in mind, but they did not make the exception a rule. The new Ultramontanes have pushed everything to extremes, and have abounded in hostile arguments against all liberties—those of the State as well as those of the Church. If such systems were not calculated to compromise the most serious religious interests at the present time, and especially at a future day, one might be content with despising them; but when one has a presentiment of the evils they are preparing for us, it is difficult to be silent and resigned."

The Ultramontanes were doing everything possible to make the infallibility of the Pope a dogma of faith. And those Catholics who wonder at Newman's opposition to the definition, and who ridicule the fantastic ideas non-

Catholics have of papal infallibility, should go back to the writings of the extreme Ultramontanes of that day to find just how they were speaking of this prerogative of the Pope.

For instance, Veuillot wrote: "We all know certainly only one thing, that no man knows anything except the Man with whom God is forever, the Man who carries the thought of God. We must . . . unswervingly follow his *inspired* directions." And again: "We must affirm squarely the authority and the *omnipotence* of the Pope, as the source of all authority, spiritual and *temporal*. The proclamation of the dogma of the infallibility of the Pope has no other object."

One of Newman's contentions, in union with *Le Correspondant,* was that definitions came about after a prolonged study and discussion, and Veuillot ridiculed this idea. "The *Correspondant* wants them to discuss, and wishes the Holy Ghost to take time in forming an opinion. It has a hundred arguments to prove how much time is indispensable to the Holy Ghost."

In October, 1869, Veuillot's organ, *L'Univers,* printed a hymn addressed to Pius IX, paraphrasing the words used by the Church to the Holy Ghost in the *Veni Creator* on Whitsunday:

> "Pater pauperum,
> Dator munerum,
> Lumen cordium,
> Emitte cœlitus
> Lucis tuæ radium."

And next month came a version of one of the hymns in the Roman Breviary, in which the word "Pius" was substituted for "Deus" in the opening line:

> "Rerum Pius tenax vigor."

William George Ward never went to such almost blasphemous lengths as did Veuillot. But Ward claimed that his was the only Catholic view, and that anyone who disagreed with him was a "minimiser," "anti-papal," "unsound," "disloyal." The cheerful ease with which he consigned to hell those who differed with him earned for him the nickname, "Damnation Ward."

When the Vatican Council assembled in 1869, it was certain that the definition of papal infallibility would be urged by a strong party. Newman feared that the definition might be couched in language which would seem to countenance the extravagant views of Veuillot and his followers. But Newman felt powerless to influence matters, and when Bishop Ullathorne asked him to be his theologian at the Council, he refused. However, Newman did write a private letter to Ullathorne, dated January 28, 1870.

"MY DEAR LORD:

I thank your Lordship very heartily for your most interesting and seasonable letter. Such letters (if they could be circulated) could do much to reassure the many minds which are at present disturbed when they look towards Rome. Rome ought to be a name to lighten the heart at all times,.. But now we have the greatest meeting which has ever been, and that in Rome, infusing into us by the accredited organs of Rome (such as the *Civiltá,* the *Armonia,* the *Univers,* and the *Tablet*) little else than fear and dismay. Where we are all at rest and have no doubts, and, at least practically, not to say doctrinally, hold the Holy Father to be infallible, there is thunder in the clear sky, and we are told to prepare for something, we know not what, to try our faith, we know not how. ... As to myself personally, please God, I do not expect any trial at all, but I cannot help suffering with the various souls that are suffering. I look with anxiety at the prospect of having to defend decisions which may not be difficult to my private judgment, but may be most difficult to defend logically in the face of historical facts. What have we done to be treated as the Faithful never were treated before? When has definition of doctrine *de fide* been a luxury of devotion and not a stern and painful necessity? Why should an aggressive and insolent faction be allowed to make the hearts of the just to mourn whom the Lord hath not made sorrowful? . . I assure you, my dear Lord, that some of the truest minds are driven one way and another, . . ; one day determining to give up theology as a bad job and recklessly to believe henceforth almost that the Pope is impeccable; at another tempted to believe all the worst that a book like Janus [1] says; . . and then again angry with the Holy See for listening to the flattery of a clique of Jesuits, Redemptorists and Converts."

Ullathorne showed this letter to Bishop Clifford, and Clifford took a copy. Apparently through Clifford's indiscretion, the letter got into the papers and caused no small tempest. On the other hand, Newman's letter found an echo in many English hearts. Several bishops wrote to Newman expressing their agreement, and thanking him for having written as he did. It is noteworthy that Bishop Brown of Newport, the man who had delated Newman's article in *The Rambler*, was among those who sided with Newman. "I cannot resist my desire of thanking you," wrote Bishop Brown, "for the admirable letter you wrote Dr. Ullathorne, and I am rejoiced at finding it in print. With every word of it my feelings and judgment fully coincide—though it would not be prudent in me to give publicity. Yet in regard to the *Tablet,* I have not hesitated

[1] *Janus* was the popular title of a controversial book which was published on the eve of the Vatican Council and which attempted to show that the proposed doctrine of papal infallibility was contrary to historical facts. It was partisan and bitter. Though published anonymously, it was soon known to be the work of Döllinger, the prominent church historian and the leader of the "Munich school."

to express loudly my disapproval, also my apprehension of the serious evil likely to ensue from the course pursued by Herbert Vaughan and his party in England."

Bishop Goss, of Liverpool, was even more emphatic than Bishop Brown. "I wish to signify my adhesion," he wrote, "to your condemnation of an aggressive and insolent faction. The *Dublin Review*, the *Tablet*, and Archbishop Manning have taken upon themselves not merely to advocate the infallibility, but to denounce everybody else as little less than heretics and infidels, and as committing the unpardonable sin against the Holy Ghost, whose decision and ruling they forestalled."

The dramatic circumstances of the final passing of the definition of papal infallibility in the midst of a violent electrical storm, have often been related. Equally dramatic were the political events marching swiftly to the climax of the Italian troops entering Rome, and Pius immuring himself in the Vatican. Newman comments on both incidents in a letter to Mrs. Froude:

"As little as possible," writes Newman, "was passed at the Council—nothing about the Pope which I have not myself always held. But it is impossible to deny that it was done with an imperiousness and overbearing wilfulness which has been a great scandal—and I cannot think thunder and lightning a mark of approbation, as some persons wish to make out, and the sudden destruction of the Pope's temporal power does not seem a sign of approval either. It suggests too the thought, that to be at once infallible in religion and a despot in temporals, is perhaps too much for mortal man. Very likely there will be some reaction for a time in his favour, but not permanently—and then, unless the Council, when reassembled, qualifies the dogma by some considerable safeguards, which is not unlikely, perhaps the secularly defenceless state of the Pope will oblige him to court the Catholic body in its separate nations with a considerateness and kindness, which of late years the Holy See has not shown, and which may effectively prevent a tyrannous use of his spiritual power. But all these things are in God's hands, and we are blind."

The definition of infallibility as finally passed by the Vatican Council was really a defeat for Veuillot, Ward and their extreme party. For it was quite moderate in its terms, and fell far short of what they had been claiming. Before the Council they would have denounced as heretical anyone who limited the papal infallibility as it was actually limited by the Council. But, unfortunately, the extremists made so much noise before the event that their idea of papal infallibility is the one remaining in the mind of the public. Catholics are still suffering from the misunderstanding engendered by irresponsible and heated protagonists. If those who are not Catholics think that papal infallibility means the supremacy of the Pope over all temporal sovereigns, including the power of deposing the King of England or the President of the United States, their erroneous conception is largely due to the fact that Veuillot and those like him said just this.

Papal infallibility as defined by the Vatican Council merely means that under certain conditions the decrees of the Pope, apart from a general council, are irreformable, and enjoy the same infallibility as that which Christ wished His Church to have. These conditions are: (1) that the Pope should speak to the whole world, and not only to a portion of the Church; (2) that he should speak as the supreme head of the Church and not simply as a private theologian; (3) that he should speak on a question of faith or morals that has been revealed in Scripture or Tradition; (4) that he should indicate clearly his intention of using his infallible prerogative.

Hence papal infallibility does not mean that the Pope is inspired, that he cannot commit sin, or even that he cannot err. Infallibility really allows for all the historical difficulties which can be brought forward, and which troubled Newman in regard to the attitude of the extremists. Moreover, papal infallibility does not mean that the Pope is a temporal sovereign set over the whole world of temporalities, in such a way that no Catholic can any longer be a loyal subject of any civil State.

William Ewart Gladstone, several times Prime Minister of England, accepted the extreme interpretation of papal infallibility that Veuillot and his associates had so assiduously preached, and in November, 1874, published his attack under the title, *The Vatican Decrees and Their Bearing on Civil Allegiance.* Gladstone made much of Cardinal Manning's lecture on *Caesarism and Ultramontanism.* In that lecture, Manning had put extreme emphasis on an undying contest between the Pope and the civil power.

Once again, as with Kingsley and Pusey, Gladstone's pamphlet afforded Newman a chance to give a backhanded slap at Manning. Commenting on Gladstone's attitude, Newman wrote to Lord Blatchford: "Gladstone's excuse is, I suppose, the extravagance of Archbishop Manning in his *Caesarism,* and he will do us a service if he gives us an opportunity of speaking. We can speak against Gladstone, while it would not be decent to speak against Manning."

Newman's answer to Gladstone took the form of a letter to the Duke of Norfolk, and under that title it appears in his collected works, in the second volume of the *Difficulties of Anglicans*. This letter—it is really a book of over two hundred pages—remains to this day the best answer in English to the charges of civil disloyalty brought against Catholics. On the emphatic resurgence of these charges during Mr. Alfred Smith's campaign for the presidency in the United States in 1928, nothing was written that can at all compare in thoroughness and persuasiveness with Newman's treatment of the question. In the half century that has elapsed since the appearance of Newman's book, it has held the field without competition. And it does not seem that anything better will be produced in the future.

Besides being the best answer so far given to the charges of civil disloyalty, this letter to the Duke of Norfolk is an excellent example of Newman's controversial methods. Others have suggested that Gladstone's attack was due to his chagrin at the defeat of his Irish University Bill through the opposition of the Catholic bishops in Ireland. But not so Newman. To ridicule Gladstone, and impugn his motives, might be good politics, as discounting his influence with Catholics. But it was not good controversy in the sense of convincing Gladstone of the error of his ways, or of getting the British public to look calmly on the papal claims. See how much more wisely and Christianly Newman went about the task. For in the dedicatory note to the Duke of Norfolk, he wrote:

"I deeply grieve that Mr. Gladstone has felt it his duty to speak with such extraordinary severity of our Religion and of ourselves... Yet not a little may be said in explanation of a step which so many of his admirers and well-wishers deplore. I own to a deep feeling that Catholics may in good measure thank themselves, and no one else, for having alienated from them so religious a mind. There are those among us, as it must be confessed, who for years past have conducted themselves as if no responsibility attached to wild words and overbearing deeds; who have stated truths in the most paradoxical form, and stretched principles till they were close on snapping; and who at length, having done their best to set the house on fire, leave to others the task of putting out the flame. The English people are sufficiently sensitive to the claims of the Pope, without having them, as if in defiance, flourished in their faces... I have one difficulty to overcome in the present excitement of the public mind against our Religion, caused partly by the chronic extravagance of knots of Catholics here and there."

In Gladstone's attack, the Catholics of England were confronted with much the same charges as those which from time to time have been brought against the Catholics of the United States. Newman thus states the question in the opening paragraph of his *Letter:* "The main question which Mr. Gladstone has started I consider to be this: Can Catholics be trustworthy subjects of the State? has not a foreign Power a hold over their consciences such that it may at any time be used to the serious perplexity and injury of the civil government under which they live?"

Consequently, in his answer, Newman goes at length into the whole question of the liberty of conscience enjoyed by Catholics. He contends that conscience, in a true sense of that word, is supreme, and is to be followed at all costs even against ecclesiastical authority, including the Pope himself. In support of this contention, Newman first quotes the Fourth Lateran Council, that a man acting against his conscience loses his soul. Then Newman goes on: "The celebrated school known as the Salmanticanses, or Carmelites of Salamanca, lay down the broad proposition that conscience is ever to be obeyed whether it tells truly or erroneously, and that whether the error is the fault of the person thus erring or not. They say that this opinion is certain, and refer, as agreeing with them, to St. Thomas, St. Bonaventure, Cajetan," and twenty others.

In addition, Newman quotes several other theologians of note, including the famous Jesuit, Busenbaum. And to show that this opinion is held among all schools in the Church, Antonio Corduba, a Spanish Franciscan, is cited as saying: "In no manner is it lawful to act against conscience, even though a Law, or a Superior commands it."

The French Dominican, Natalis Alexander, is quoted: "If, in the judgment of conscience, though a mistaken conscience, a man is persuaded that what his superior commands is displeasing to God, he is bound not to obey." And Newman adds: "The word 'Superior' certainly includes the Pope; Cardinal Jacobatius brings out this point clearly in his authoritative work on Councils, which is contained in Labbe's Collection, introducing the Pope by name."

But Newman is not satisfied with this abstract treatment of the problem of conscience. He gives two concrete cases of when a priest would be obliged to disobey the Pope. "If the Pope told the English bishops," writes Newman, "to order their priests to stir themselves energetically in favor of teetotalism, and a particular priest was fully persuaded that abstinence from wine, *etc.*, was practically a Gnostic error, and therefore felt that he could not so exert himself without sin; or suppose that there was a Papal order to hold lotteries in each mission for some religious object, and a priest could say in God's sight that he believed lotteries to be morally wrong, that priest in either of these cases would commit a sin *hic et nunc* if he obeyed the Pope, whether he was right or wrong in his opinion, and, if wrong, although he had not taken proper pains to get at the truth of the matter."

Newman ends this section on conscience with the words we have put at the beginning of the chapter: "Certainly, if I am obliged to bring religion into after-dinner toasts (which does not seem quite the thing), I shall drink —to the Pope, if you please—still, to Conscience first, and to the Pope afterwards."

In the section of his *Letter* called "Divided Allegiance," Newman admits that historically there have been conflicts between the Pope and various civil States. He grants that theoretically there might be a conflict between the Holy See and England. "Certainly in the event of such a collision of jurisdictions," he writes, "there are cases in which we should obey the Pope and disobey the State. Suppose, for instance, an act was passed in Parliament binding Catholics to attend Protestant services every week, and the Pope distinctly told us not to do so, for it was to violate our duty to our faith; I should obey the Pope and not the law."

During the Great War there were sociologists—of a sort—who suggested the possibility of the State sanctioning polygamy to repair more quickly the loss of man power suffered by the military operations. Suppose that Mr. Gladstone, or any other Protestant, were confronted with a State reviving the old levirate marriage, and commanding him, although already married, to take the wife of his deceased brother and raise up children by her in his brother's name? What would Mr. Gladstone do?

Would he obey the State, or obey his own Church, and his own conscience?

It has been urged that the difference between Gladstone or any other Protestant in such a situation, and a Catholic, is that the Catholic is obeying not his own conscience, not the behest of a democratic organization governed by citizens of his own country, but the dictate of a foreign authority to which he attributes infallibility. Consequently, the Catholic must obey that foreign authority. He has no choice; it is a mere quibble to say that he follows his conscience, because his conscience has previously told him that whatever this foreign authority commands is right.

Newman has answered this objection sufficiently by the second case he gives in which a Catholic should disobey the Pope. "But now, on the other hand," he proceeds, "could the case ever occur in which I should act with the Civil Power, and not with the Pope? Now, here again, when I begin to imagine instances, Catholics will cry out . . . that instances never can occur. I know they cannot; I know the Pope never can do what I am going to suppose; but, then, since it cannot possibly happen in fact, there is no harm in just saying what I should (hypothetically) do, if it did happen." How ingeniously does Newman thus take care of the sensibilities of Catholics and forestall criticism!

"I say then in certain (impossible) cases I should side, not with the Pope, but with the Civil Power. For instance, let us suppose members of Parliament, or of the Privy Council, took an oath that they would not acknowledge the right of succession of a Prince of Wales, if he became a Catholic: in that case I should not consider the Pope could release me from that oath, had I bound

myself by it. Of course, I might exert myself to the utmost
to get the act repealed which bound me; again, if I could
not, I might retire from Parliament or office, and so rid
myself of the engagement I had made; but I should be
clear that, though the Pope bade all Catholics to stand
firm in one phalanx for the Catholic Succession, still,
while I remained in office, or in my place in Parliament,
I could not do as he bade me.

"Again, were I actually a soldier or sailor in her
Majesty's service, and sent to take part in a war which I
could not in my conscience see to be unjust, and should
the Pope suddenly bid all Catholic soldiers and sailors to
retire from the service, here again, taking advice of others
as best I could, I should not obey him."

This attitude of Newman is buttressed by quotations
from Cardinal Bellarmine, the famous Jesuit defender of
the Papacy, and from Cardinal Turrecremata. The latter
says: "Were the Pope to command anything against Holy
Scripture, or the articles of faith, or the truth of the sacraments, or the commands of the natural or divine law, he
ought not to be obeyed." There is implied here that some
conscience besides the Pope's decides that the Pope is
commanding what is against the natural or the divine law,
and consequently it is not correct to say that a Catholic
must always submit his judgment to the judgment of the
Pope.

Bellarmine is even more to the point as regards civil
allegiance, for he says: "As it is lawful to resist the Pope,
if he assaulted a man's person, so it is lawful to resist
him, if he assaulted souls, or *troubled the state* (turbanti
republicam), and much more if he strove to destroy the
Church. It is lawful, I say, to resist him, by not doing
what he commands, and hindering the execution of his

will." Certainly the individual citizen in many situations would be able to judge whether or not the Pope was troubling the State of which he was a subject.

The Vatican decree on papal infallibility had been the occasion of Gladstone's attack on Catholic loyalty. But the real ammunition used by Gladstone was taken from the Encyclical of 1864 and the *Syllabus Errorum.* Consequently, Newman devotes a section to each of these documents, and he shows quite conclusively that Gladstone was misrepresenting them. The Pope "has condemned free speech, free writing, a free press, toleration of nonconformity, liberty of conscience," Gladstone had written. And Newman asks: "Now is not this accusation of a very wholesale character? Who would not understand it to mean that the Pope has pronounced a universal anathema against *all* these liberties *in toto,* and that English law, on the contrary, allowed those liberties *in toto,* which the Pope had condemned?"

It is easy for Newman to bring out that English law does not allow all these liberties without any restriction whatever. And after showing that, he goes on: "But let us see, on the other hand, what the proposition really is, the condemnation of which leads him to say, that the Pope has unrestrictedly 'condemned those who maintain *the* liberty of the Press, *the* liberty of conscience and worship, and *the* liberty of speech,' has condemned 'free speech, free writing, and a free press.' The condemned proposition speaks as follows:

" 'Liberty of conscience and worship is the *inherent right* of all men. 2. It ought to be proclaimed in *every* rightly constituted society. 3. It is a right to *all sorts of liberty* (omnimodam libertatem) such that it ought not to be restrained by any authority, ecclesiastical *or civil,* as

far as public speaking, printing, or any other manifesta-
tion of opinion is concerned.'

"Now is there any government on earth," asks Newman, "that could stand the strain of such a doctrine as
this? . . What is the right of conscience thus inherent in
our nature, thus necessary for all states? The proposition
tells us. It is the liberty of *every* one to give *public* utterance, in *every* possible shape, by *every* possible channel,
without *any* let or hindrance from God or man, to *all* his
notions *whatsoever*.

"Which of the two in this matter is peremptory and
sweeping in his utterance, the author of this thesis himself, or the Pope who has condemned what the other has
uttered? . . What if a man's conscience embraces the
duty of regicide? or infanticide? or free love? . . Has Mr.
Gladstone really no better complaint to make against the
Pope's condemnations than this? Perhaps he will say,
Why should the Pope take the trouble to condemn what
is so wild? But he does: and to say that he condemns
something which he does not condemn, and then to in-
veigh against him on the ground of that something else,
is neither just nor logical."

To many persons Gladstone's interpretation will
seem to be the common sense meaning of the Pope's
words, and Newman's explanation will appear strained.
But this is because they forget that papal utterances are
technical documents, and experts are needed to interpret
them just as much as experts are needed to interpret our
civil law. There is an old saying that he who is his own
lawyer has a fool for a client. This applies to ecclesiastical
or canon law, as well as to civil law. The untrained man
who undertakes to interpret the technical language of
papal documents is likely to give vent to something very

foolish—as foolish, indeed, as what the supposititious Russian Count said in Newman's lecture on *The Present Position of Catholics in England.*

The happy hunting ground, however, of those attacking the Catholic Church is not so much any particular Encyclical as it is the *Syllabus Errorum.* This compilation of eighty propositions is so easily accessible and so compact that everybody digs something out of it. But the remarkable thing is that even careful writers, scholarly men, seem not to understand the nature of the *Syllabus.* The *Syllabus Errorum* is a resumé, or a sort of table of contents or index, of propositions contained in various documents issued by Pius IX. Any man who wishes to quote the *Syllabus* should go back to the original documents— the references are given after each proposition—to find out the exact meaning of any particular proposition. Merely to quote the *Syllabus* is like quoting the summary in a table of contents, and attributing some condensed statement to an author, without looking in the body of the book.

Newman gives a number of instances illustrating how Gladstone had misinterpreted the Pope's meaning because he had not gone back to the original documents. I shall quote only one such illustration. "For instance," writes Newman, take Gladstone's "own 16th (the 77th of the 'erroneous Propositions'), that, 'It is no longer expedient that the Catholic Religion should be established to the exclusion of all others.' When we turn to the Allocution, which is the ground of its being put into the Syllabus, what do we find there? First, that the Pope was speaking, not of States universally, but of one particular State, Spain, definitely Spain; secondly, that he was not noting the erroneous proposition directly, or categorically, but was protesting against the breach in many ways of the Concordat on the part of the Spanish government; further, that he was not referring to any work containing the said proposition, nor contemplating any proposition at all; nor, on the other hand, using any word of condemnation whatever, nor using any harsher term of the Government in question than an expression of 'his wonder and distress.' "

No lawyer would go into court quoting the table of contents of some statute book, without ever looking at the statute itself. Why do lawyers, as well as others, persist in doing just this in regard to the *Syllabus*, in spite of the lesson that Newman administered to Gladstone? Every controversialist with whom I am familiar who has quoted the *Syllabus* against the Church has fallen into the same error. If one were to go over the literature of the American presidential campaign of 1928, one could compile a much longer *Syllabus Errorum* than that of Pius IX, but it would be a collection of erroneous quotations and inferences.

Newman fulfilled his task admirably in answering Gladstone, and his success was generously recognized in Catholic and Protestant circles. There were some rumblings of discontent among the extreme Ultramontanes, but for the most part they were compelled to keep quiet. Cardinal Franchi, the then Prefect of Propaganda, wrote a confidential letter to Manning and to Ullathorne, saying that Propaganda had been notified that Newman's answer to Gladstone contained censurable propositions.

In his reply to Franchi's letter, Manning urged that no *public* action should be taken against Newman, and generally defended Newman's line of reasoning. Manning was a statesman, and once confronted with the actual situation of a powerful political leader like Gladstone attacking Catholic loyalty, he recognized the imperative need of careful, accurate limitation of the journalistic excesses of the maximizers.[1]

Eight months later, October 22, 1875, Franchi returned to the charge with a more specific letter to Ullathorne. Newman's statement "the Rock of Peter on its summit enjoys a pure and serene atmosphere, but there is a great deal of Roman *malaria* at the foot of it," was called "troppo irreverente to the Curia Romana"; and certain statements were said to be "false and contrary to genuine history." Abbot Butler makes the comment: "The reader who may refer to these passages, will probably be surprised at the kind of strictures on Popes deemed objectionable at Rome in 1875; he will rejoice in the change wrought in this Roman sensitiveness as to the political acts of Popes by the enlightened policy of Leo XIII. One wonders how Pastor's *History*—e.g., the volume on Paul IV, one of the cases in point—would have fared in the days of Pio Nono."

Ullathorne again replied to Franchi that it would be inadvisable to do anything about the matter, and added: "Father Newman has often complained that the authorities at Rome do not deal with him directly and openly, but by intermediaries and secretly. I strongly urge that if anything is to be done, he be written to directly and openly."

That Newman's dignified, courteous, conciliatory method of controversy was effective is shown very strikingly by Gladstone's later conduct. For as early as 1877, Gladstone referred to Newman "in a public speech in terms which were so laudatory as to seem to him extrava-

[1] Butler, *Life of Ullathorne*, II, 103.

gant. 'Although,' he writes to Church, 'I am truly grateful for Gladstone's kindness, I am frightened at it. It was to most men's apprehensions out of place, and I dread the reaction.' " [1]

But there was no such adverse reaction as Newman feared. Following hard upon the heels of his success in replying to Gladstone, came particularly gratifying honors from Newman's beloved Oxford. His old college, Trinity, made him an honorary Fellow at the end of 1877, and Newman, who had been occupying himself in editing his writings, dedicated the new edition of his *Development of Christian Doctrine* to the Reverend Samuel Wayte, president of Trinity. Oriel also honored him, and James Bryce was eager to have his picture painted by Ouless.

However, Newman's satisfaction in his controversial success, and in these honors, was tempered by the loss of his beloved Ambrose St. John. The affection between Newman and St. John is worthy to be placed beside that of Francis of Assisi and the Lady Clare, of Francis de Sales and Jane Frances de Chantal, or, more appropriately, perhaps, as "surpassing the love of man for woman," of David and Jonathan. Writing to Lord Blatchford a few days after St. John's death, Newman said:

"The Oratory, May 31, 1875.

"From the first he loved me with an intensity of love, which was unaccountable. At Rome 28 years ago he was always so working for and relieving me of all trouble, that being young and Saxon-looking, the Romans called him my Angel Guardian. As far as this world was concerned I was his first and last. He has not intermitted this love for an hour up to his last breath."

[1] Ward, *Life of Newman*, II, 425.

Ambrose St. John had overworked on his translation of Fessler's history of the Vatican Council, which was to help Newman in his reply to Gladstone. There was fear for a time that St. John would lose his mind. And it is to this Newman refers in a letter to Mother Imelda Poole: "I thank God for having given him to me for so long.

"I thank Him for taking him away when there was a chance for him of a living death.

"I thank Him for having given me this warning to make haste myself and prepare for His coming."

CHAPTER VII

THE CRIMSON SUNSET

"May He support us all the day long, till the shades lengthen, and the evening comes, and the busy world is hushed, and the fever of life is over, and our work is done: then in His mercy, may He give us a safe lodging, and a holy rest, and peace at the end." (COLLECT BY JOHN HENRY NEWMAN IN THE REVISED EDITION OF THE BOOK OF COMMON PRAYER OF THE PROTESTANT EPISCOPAL CHURCH.)

THE fundamental religious question in which Newman had a special interest was the way in which we reach certitude. For a time, as we have seen, Newman had uncritically and unquestioningly accepted the Evangelical attitude on personal experience. Then, largely under the influence of the Oxford Noëtics, he had realized the insufficiency of this theory from a philosophical standpoint, and under Hurrell Froude's leadership had begun that religious Odyssey which ultimately carried him to Rome.

In his Oxford University Sermons, Newman had considered one aspect after another of this problem of religious certitude, but naturally without exhausting the subject. The essay on *The Development of Christian Doctrine* touched on another phase of the same general problem. One of his lectures in Dublin returned to the question, and Newman had intended to go into the matter fully in his prolegomena to the ill-fated translation of the Bible.

With a sure sense of values, Newman realized that the current Catholic apologetic was powerless against the skepticism of the age. We have noticed the strong language which W. G. Ward used about the teaching in the seminaries. Both Catholics and Protestants were inclined to look upon the traditional arguments for Christianity as so conclusive that no fair-minded man could sincerely fail to accept them. As a consequence, all agnostics and unbelievers were lumped together as being insincere, or as having their intellects blinded by moral corruption.

Newman knew that there were many honest skeptics of upright lives. Many of his friends could be placed in this category. Bonomelli, the good Bishop of Cremona in the last generation, has a striking passage which sums up almost perfectly the attitude of Newman: "When I was a young man," writes the Bishop, "I judged men more from books and *a priori,* as the metaphysicians call it, than in themselves. I, too, like many others, was unable to understand how, in the midst of a Christian and Catholic society, with so many strong defences to preserve the Faith and to protect it against the wiles and assaults of falsehood, there could be unbelievers in good faith; it seemed to me to wrong their intelligence and their instruction to suppose them so, and almost to be an offence against good sense. But when, as years passed, I had an opportunity of coming in closer contact with our society and of studying it, not in books and in the abstract (as certain theologians and moralists seem too much to do, who in their convents and in the peace of their cells compose mighty volumes on the subject, creating for themselves an ideal world), I was forced to moderate my judgments and often to change them. I learned then that not only is the phenomenon of a certain good faith in a great number of unbelievers possible, as Monsabré admits, but I handled it and found it *real* and far more frequent than some theologians and rigid, too rigid, moralists believe." [1]

The thoroughness with which Newman realized the skeptic's position is shown in a memorandum he prepared in 1860 on "The Fluctuations of Human Opinion." A confirmed unbeliever could not have put his case better than Newman does:

"(1) We cannot get beyond a judgment such that it denies itself soon and melts away into another—nothing fixed and stable.

"(2) Hence what does Catholicism do but arbitrarily fix what is not fixed, and perpetuate by an unnatural and strained force what else would be transitory? It assumes and wills that this or that should be true which is not true to the mind except for a time or more than something else.

"(3) We cannot get beyond a certain degree of probability about anything, but Catholicism enforces a certainty greater than Mathematics,

"(4) and making it a sin to doubt, artificially prolongs an opinion. It is but an opinion that the Church is infallible, but we commit a man to it and make it a sin to doubt it. If he argued himself into it, why may he not argue himself out of it? If it is a conclusion from premisses at first why not always?

"(5) How can there be a revelation; for the certainty of it must depend on uncertain premisses? Such

[1] *A Doctrine of Hope* (London, 1921), 116.

seems to be the state of human nature. In this state of things what does Catholicism do but unnaturally prolong a particular state of opinion and pretend to a certainty which is impossible?"

Ten years later, after the subject, as he says, had teased his mind "for these twenty or thirty years," Newman finally wrote a book of 487 pages on the subject. Newman called it, modestly enough, as indicating its tentative character, *An Essay in Aid of a Grammar of Assent*. It was dedicated to his friend Serjeant Bellasis, "in memory of a long, equable, and sunny friendship." Ludicrously enough, by a misprint the first proofs read "squabble and funny friendship."

The *Grammar of Assent* was begun in 1866. And one reason for the slowness of Newman's progress, apart from other duties and the inherent difficulties of the subject, was his anticipation of unfriendly criticism from certain Catholics. On August 12, 1868, he wrote to Henry Wilberforce: "I know anyhow, that, however honest are my thoughts, and earnest my endeavors to keep rigidly within the lines of Catholic doctrine, every word I publish will be malevolently scrutinized, and every expression which can possibly be perverted sent straight to Rome—that I shall be fighting *under the lash,* which does not tend to produce vigorous efforts in the battle, or to inspire either courage or presence of mind. And if from those who ought to be friends, I cannot look for sympathy—, if, did I do my work ever so well, they will take no interest in it, or see the use of it, where can I look for that moral aid which carries one through difficulties?"

A year later, August 20, 1869, Newman was still working on the *Grammar,* still hampered by this adverse atmosphere in Catholic circles and in his own mind. He

writes again to the same correspondent, Henry Wilberforce: "What influence should I have with Protestants
and infidels, if a pack of Catholic critics opened at my
back fiercely, saying that this remark was illogical, that
unheard of, a third realistic, a fourth idealistic, a fifth
sceptical, and a sixth temerarious, or shocking to pious
ears? This is the prospect which I begin to fear lies before
me... *Through* a kind friend I come more to see than
I did, what an *irritabile genus* Catholic philosophers are
—they think they do the free Church of God a service
by subjecting it to an etiquette as grievous as that which
led to the King of Spain being burned to cinders."

There was some excuse, perhaps, for Catholics being
especially irritable at such a time, for Newman's work
on the *Grammar* coincided with the fierce discussion of
papal infallibility. Newman's nerves, as well as those of
Manning and Ward, had been frayed by wild assertions
from all directions. Something of this tense atmosphere
is reflected in Newman's contemporary correspondence,
but it is remarkable that the *Grammar* itself pursues its
abstruse question with an unruffled serenity and no hint of
human passions. For all the internal evidence, Newman
might have written this treatise on religious certitude entirely apart from the concrete world of politics.

While working on the *Grammar,* Newman had written to Wilberforce: "*It is a law of our nature,* then, that
we are certain on premises which do not reach demonstration. This seems to me to be undeniable. Then what
is the faculty ... which enables us to be certain, to have
the state of mind called certitude, though the syllogism
before us is not according to the strict rules of Barbara? ..
Paper logic, syllogisms, and states of mind are incommensurables."

To answer these questions was the task Newman set himself in the *Grammar*. But those who wish really to know Newman's answer must read the book for themselves. It is impossible to do justice to Newman in any condensed version, precisely because the whole force of his argument is that "syllogisms and states of mind are incommensurables." A skeleton of the *Grammar* will bear about the same relation to the persuasiveness and charm of Newman's original, that the skeleton of a beautiful woman does to her living allurement. Nevertheless, the attempt must be made to give some idea of Newman's line of argument.

Locke had long ago assumed the position that we have no right to entertain a proposition with greater assurance than the proofs it is built upon will warrant. Whately, from whom Newman had in his youth learned his logic, held the same theory of knowledge, and J. S. Mill was its strongest contemporary prophet. While men who knew nothing of philosophical theories were led on to an essentially similar viewpoint by the brilliant achievements of nineteenth-century physical science, and by the pronunciamentos of its high priests, like Huxley; all around Newman were skeptics and agnostics and liberals professing to withhold religious belief because there was no "scientific evidence" for the dogmas of faith.

Newman pointed out that psychologically such a position is untrue, because it fails to take into account the *fact* that we—skeptics and believers alike—are constantly accepting as true what we cannot "prove," even to our own satisfaction, to be true, but which events justify us in believing. In actual questions, says Newman, we attain certitude in virtue of "a cumulation of probabilities, independent of each other, arising out of the nature and circumstances of the particular case which is under review, probabilities too fine to avail separately, too subtle and circuitous to be convertible into syllogisms, too numerous and varied for such conversion, even where they are convertible."

This does not mean, however, that such certainties are necessarily less certain or convincing than certainties founded on demonstrative evidence, as in physics or mathematics. A man may reasonably remain certain in the face of serious logical difficulties, for, as Newman had said in the *Apologia*, "ten thousand difficulties do not make one doubt." The certitude that we arrive at by these intangible, and perhaps unanalyzable, probabilities, is different from mathematical or scientific certitude, but it is not a lesser certitude. On the contrary, the certitude is all the stronger, because it is the result of our own experience of life. For it is especially life, *our* life, that transmutes mere opinions into convictions. The very essence and nature of certitude are expressed in that word conviction and in the word martyr. As Newman says, there have been many martyrs for religious dogmas, but no one ever died for a proposition in geometry. And perhaps one might add, greater certitude than this no man hath, that he lay down his life for his conviction.

The heart hath its reasons, says Newman following Pascal, that the intelligence wots not of. In fact, the mind reasons spontaneously, and in part unconsciously. And from the nature of its constitution, the mind's power of spontaneous action outruns its reflective power. Many times the mind is unequal to an analysis of the motives that impel it to a conclusion. Hence, certitude as a state of mind may be actually justifiable, although the individual may not be able to draw out the justifying demonstration, as, for instance, in the case of uneducated Christians believing in the Resurrection. The judgment of the mind that it is justified in giving its unqualified assent to a proposition when it is only implicitly conscious of the full reasons therefor, Newman calls the "Illative Sense." It is by virtue of this "Illative Sense," as opposed to "Logical Formulas," this inherent power of right judgment, that a man is justified in coming to absolute decisions, whatever may be the field in which his intelligence moves.

Moreover, the exercise of this "Illative Sense" depends upon starting from certain assumptions and with certain moral dispositions. In the concluding chapters of the *Grammar* Newman considers the evidences for theism and Christianity. But he admits it is not surprising that, although he can prove the truth of Christianity to his own satisfaction, he may be unable to prove it to the satisfaction of one who starts with different underlying assumptions and with different moral dispositions. It is simply in keeping with this viewpoint that Newman passes over very lightly most of the traditional arguments for God's existence, such as that for a First Cause, a Necessary Being, a Prime Mover, and emphasizes conscience as the primeval high priest of God.

Newman wrote his *Grammar of Assent* during the height of Victorian cocksureness that the "scientific method" could eventually solve everything. And although Newman may have had little to do with the change directly, that attitude for some scientists is as dead as Victorian haircloth furniture and antimacassars. In the hands of men like Einstein and Eddington and Jeans, science has become much more metaphysical—one might even say mystical—than in the days of Huxley and Spencer, and the epistemology underlying the new science has come closer to Newman's position. Indeed, in that little book, *Science and the Unseen World,* A. S. Eddington admits a faculty of apprehension in the religious field corresponding somewhat to Newman's "Illative Sense," although he probably never heard of Newman's *Grammar of Assent.*

Newman illustrated the thesis of his *Grammar* with a wealth of examples and pungent aphorisms which put his book in the class of pure literature. The *Essay in Aid of a Grammar of Assent* deals with a deep philosophical subject, and no one would say that it is easy reading. But it is not dull, and it contains some passages of surpassing beauty. And although Newman did not claim to reach finality on the subject—"Of course, I am sensible it may be full of defects, and certainly characterized by incompleteness and crudeness, but it is something to have stated a problem, and mapped in part a country," he wrote to Fr. Coleridge—no student of this problem of how the mind reaches certitude can afford to overlook the *Grammar of Assent.* In spite of the handicaps under which he labored, Newman had produced another great book, one to take its place proudly beside the *Apologia* and the *Development of Doctrine.*

On the other hand, Newman's departure from scholastic and academic treatment of the problem was sure to call down criticism on his head. One can imagine the impatience of that *irritabile genus,* as Newman had called them, who had spent their lives handing out syllogisms, when they came to Newman's statement, "First shoot around corners, and you may not despair of converting by a syllogism"; or, "Life is not long enough for a religion of inferences; we shall never have done beginning, if we determine to begin with proof."

Newman's anticipation of Catholic criticism was not the morbid phobia of a timid soul. Within the year, Fr. Harper, the Jesuit, had written an elaborate attack on the book from the standpoint of a thoroughgoing scholastic. The papers appeared in the Jesuit organ, *The Month*. Newman wrote to Fr. Coleridge, the editor: "I began to read Fr. Harper's papers, but they were (to my ignorance of theology and philosophy) so obscure, and (to my knowledge of my real meaning) so hopelessly misrepresentations of the book, that I soon gave it over. As to my answering, I think I never answered any critique on any writing of mine, in my life. . . . I leave the judgment between Fr. Harper and me to the sure future."

That sure future has only recently given to the world a justification of Newman's philosophy by another scholastic, better-trained, and certainly more open-minded, than Fr. Harper, Sylvester P. Juergens, the Marist. His book *Newman on the Psychology of Faith in the Individual*, is an examination not only of the *Grammar*, but of all Newman's other works touching on this problem of religious certitude.

With the exception of his *Letter to the Duke of Norfolk*, the *Grammar of Assent* was the last important literary work of Newman. He settled into a comfortable routine at the Oratory, which he called "luxurious vegetation." Much of his time was given to writing letters. This was Newman's way of keeping up with old friends, for whom he had a keen and clinging affection. Letters were, too, the vehicle for expressing his thoughts with a greater freedom than he could use in the printed word. And there seems to have been in the back of Newman's mind the idea that some day perhaps his letters would be used to bring out thoughts he had not dared to express publicly during his lifetime. Newman's public attitude towards Manning, for instance, was punctilious, but we have seen what he wrote in some of his letters.

Those who have read only Newman's formal works, would never suspect the humor and the humanness in many of his letters. Who would ever have expected the author of the *Grammar of Assent* or of *Lead, Kindly Light*, to write these verses to J. W. Bowden's niece, Charlotte Bowden, who had sent him some cakes baked by herself?

> "Who is it that moulds and makes
> Round, and crisp, and fragrant cakes?
> Makes them with a kind intent,
> As a welcome compliment,
> And the best that she can send
> To a venerable friend?
> One it is, for whom I pray,
> On St. Philip's natal day,
> With a loving heart, that she
> Perfect as her cakes may be.
> Full and faithful in the round
> Of her duties ever found,
> When a trial comes, between
> Truth and falsehood cutting keen;
> Yet that keenness and completeness
> Tempering with a winning sweetness.
>
> Here's a rhyming letter, Chat,
> Gift for gift, and tit for tat.
> 　　　　　　　　J. H. N."

Despite the multiplicity of his duties and undertakings, no one was too humble to engage Newman's time. Here is a letter written to a domestic servant who had lost her sister. Newman was then seventy-seven.

"My Dear Child,—

"Though my intention was engaged on the 26th, and I could not say Mass for you as you wished, I have not forgotten, and I hope to say Mass for you to-morrow, the 10th. There is always a throng of intentions to be kept at this time. To-day is the anniversary of Mrs. Wootten's death, and now we are in great distress about Fr. Caswall. He cannot live, tho' the time of his death is uncertain. Say a prayer for him.

"I am sorry that you should still be so far from well, but God will bless and keep you in His own good way. We never can trust Him too much. All things turn to good to them who trust Him. I too know what it is to lose a sister. I lost her 49 years ago, and, though many years have past, I still feel the pain.

"God bless and keep you this New Year.

"Yours most truly in Christ,

"John H. Newman."

The same intensity of purpose which Newman exhibited in his literary work and controversial struggles, he showed in his affections. For fifty years and more, as this letter indicates, he had cherished the memory of his dead sister and felt the pain of her loss. During thirty-two years, a good long life of maturity, Newman loved Ambrose St. John with a deepening devotion. If he dropped completely a few friends like Whately, and turned cold to others, such as W. G. Ward—incidentally, Ward is not even mentioned in the *Apologia*—yet to those towards whom he felt drawn in sympathy, Newman was "sweet as summer."

Another attractive phase of Newman's character, brought out in his letters, was his interest in the living things of creation. There are references to "Charlie, the virtuous pony," "thank you for your care of the mulberry," "thank you for the filbert." Newman never forgot the snapdragons in the quadrangle of his Oxford College.

If there was a certain steeliness in Newman's soul in his relations with Manning and others, there was also an abundant tenderness for all the beautiful things of life.

When news came to Newman in 1822 that he had been elected a fellow of Oriel, he was playing the violin. In his later years, music was one of his greatest consolations and the solace of many an hour. Wilfrid Ward says: "We have seen him lay down his fiddle and cry out with joy at the pleasure Beethoven's quartets were giving him." And his love of music and his sense of humor are both illustrated in the incident of his replying to the challenge of an anti-Catholic lecturer to debate: "I am no orator. But if the reverend gentleman is willing, he can give his talk, and I shall play my fiddle. Then the audience can judge which is the better man."

The ear, however, was not the only keen sense possessed by Newman. Sight united with hearing to make the sensible world intensely real to Newman. "This joy of sense, especially in his early youth, had a full measure of the feeling given in Wordsworth's ode to which he was so devoted:

'There was a time when meadow, grove and stream,
The earth and every common sight,
To me did seem
Apparrelled in celestial light,
The glory and the freshness of a dream.' "

There is abundant testimony from his contemporaries that Newman exercised a remarkable personal charm over those who came in contact with him. "The almost unique combination," writes Wilfrid Ward, "of tenderness, brilliancy, refinement, wide sympathy, and holiness doubtless went for much. He had none of the repellent qualities which sometimes make asceticism forbidding. He had an ample allowance of those human sympathies which are popularly contrasted with asceticism. Again, he seemed able to love each friend with a peculiarly close sympathy for the circumstances of his life... His keen sense of humor, his winning sweetness, his occasional wilfulness, his resentments and anger, all showed him intensely alive, and his friends loved his very faults as one may love those of a fascinating woman." [1]

Moreover, Newman was true to his friends. He never sacrificed a friend for the sake of his own advancement, nor because of what those higher up might think. Newman's attitude in regard to Lucas, when Cardinal Cullen frowned upon him, and towards Mrs. Wootten, when the staff of the Oratory school resigned on her account, was typical of his fearlessness in friendship. And at the same time, Newman never hesitated to break with a friend, when that friend had proved unworthy, or when there was no longer sympathy in the great fundamentals.

Newman's sincerity in human relationships was based essentially upon his religious sincerity. Ever since his early Evangelical experiences, Newman's one purpose was to do the will of God, to follow the leading of the "Kindly Light." The path this Light led him, went "o'er moor and fen, o'er crag and torrent," with very considerable discomfort at times to the traveller. But Newman never faltered. And the strength that enabled him to follow the Light, to abandon his friends in the Anglican Church in 1845, to endure the loneliness and misunderstanding and misrepresentation of so many of his Catholic years, to stand so solitary against the "aggressive and insolent faction," came to him from the hours of prayer he spent each day. No one knows Newman who has not read

[1] *Life of Newman,* II, 438.

the posthumous volume of his works called *Meditations and Devotions*. There we get some slight insight into Newman's heart of hearts—*cor ad cor loquitur*.

"The early morning," says Fr. H. I. D. Ryder, "was devoted to meditation, prayers, and ecclesiastical duties." This life of prayer was the great secret of his unfaltering courage. But in his devotions, as in everything else, Newman was simplicity itself. He never took up with what may be called the fads of devotion, as some of the other converts did. The Sacraments themselves, mental prayer, the Stations of the Cross commemorating Christ's dolorous way to Calvary, and other traditional Catholic forms of prayer were sufficient for him. Fr. Neville, one of his companions at the Oratory, has left on record the statement that "his ordinary way was what, under the circumstances, would come naturally to him. . . There would not be anything noteworthy in him to strike an ordinary observer."

Surely, in spite of his own disclaimer, it was from this supernatural life that Newman received the strength to bear his troubles in silence. "What is it to me," he has written, "what people think of me? I lay claim to no supernatural motive; it is the most evident wisdom. I have never defended myself through life.[1] I have been called all manner of names, but those things don't last. Such dirt does not stick. Nor am I allowing scandal to remain, by not speaking; scandal must be somewhere. . . Again, any one who defends himself, puts himself in the wrong. *Si on s'excuse, on s'accuse.* (Excuse my bad French.)"

But although Newman could refrain from any sort

[1] Surely a curious statement for the man who wrote the *Apologia* and who annihilated Kingsley so completely.

of public defence against the accusations in Catholic circles, nevertheless he felt them keenly. As Ward has said, Newman could put his hand in the fire and keep it there, but he could not help flinching with the pain. In 1876, Newman wrote in his journal: "I notice the following lest the subject should turn up after I am gone, and my friends be perplexed how to deal with it.

"I have before now said in writing to Cardinals Wiseman and Barnabó when I considered myself treated with slight and unfairness, 'So this is the return made to me for working for the Catholic cause for so many years,' *i.e.*, to that effect.

"I feel it still, and ever shall,—but it was not a disappointed ambition which I was then expressing in words, but a scorn and wonder at the injustice shown me, and at the demand of toadyism if I was to get their favour, and the favour of Rome. . .

"As to my freedom from ambitious views, I don't know that I need defend myself from the imputation of them. *Qui s'excuse, s'accuse.* But in fact I have from the first presaged that I should get no thanks for what I was doing."

But with the dramatic swiftness that was so frequently an element in Newman's life, all this was about to be changed. Mgr. Talbot was in an insane asylum at Passy, Pius IX was dead, Manning was no longer supreme in Rome. Leo XIII became Pope in 1878, and the contrast between him and his predecessor inspired the friends of Newman with the idea that here was a chance to secure the formal approval of Rome for England's foremost Catholic, the man of whom it had been said in an address in 1867, "every blow that touches you inflicts a wound upon the Catholic Church in this country."

It is noteworthy that the movement to secure the cardinalatial dignity for Newman originated with the laity. But the matter had to be presented to the ecclesiastical primate of England, Newman's long standing adversary, Henry Edward Manning. Abbot Butler has a graphic description of the procedure.

"And so in July, 1878," writes Butler, "the two leaders of the Catholic laity, the Duke of Norfolk and the Marquis of Ripon, took their courage in their hand—and it needed no small courage!—and approached Cardinal Manning, to represent the widespread desire of the Catholic laity of England that Dr. Newman's great services for the Catholic Church should receive the highest reward from the Church by his elevation to the cardinalate. This was perhaps the act of the Duke's life that called forth in the fullest measure that quality of simple straightforward courage that was the secret of the high respect in which he was held and of the great influence he wielded. To Manning the proposal must have come as a shock. If there was genuine conviction in the disapproval and opposition he had shown to Newman during twenty years— and we are bound to give him the credit of sincerity even in the most fanatical of the intellectual judgments so often encountered in these pages—the idea of Newman's life being crowned by the highest and most public act of approval on the part of the Holy See must necessarily have been displeasing to him beyond words. It is related that he bent his head for some moments—at the time it was said he then spoke the words *Fiat Voluntas Tua!*— and then undertook to forward the matter with the Holy See—surely a wonderful act of self-conquest." [1]

[1] Butler, *Life of Ullathorne*, II, 108.

It seems strange that Butler should emphasize to such an extent the courage needed to approach Manning. What could Manning do against the only Catholic duke in England, that he should be afraid of the old man? But Butler's words do serve to bring out the thorough-going opposition of Manning to Newman. Moreover, if Manning sincerely thought that Newman was really a menace to the Church, why did he ever agree to increase that menace by obtaining for him the cardinalate? Manning was scarcely the man to change his view of Newman because a couple of laymen thought Newman should be a cardinal—even if one of the laymen happened to be a duke.

Was Manning's acquiescence merely external, and given with the hope that something somehow might come about to prevent Newman ever getting the honor? Ullathorne certainly thought that Manning tried to block the cardinalate for Newman, and Ullathorne knew more of the ins and outs of the matter than anybody else except Manning. Or was Manning essentially a politician, and realizing that Leo XIII had a very different outlook from Pius IX, did he conform to what he thought would be Leo's mind? The King is dead, long live the King! Or may it be that Manning had actually changed his own mind? Newman had recently done great service in behalf of papal infallibility by inditing his *Letter to the Duke of Norfolk* and he was now a very old man. Manning may have had his fears of Newman's orthodoxy somewhat allayed and may now have felt it was opportune, when he was pressed, to make public recognition of the fact. Subsequent events throw some light on the problem.

Manning wrote to Cardinal Nina, Leo's Secretary of State. In December, five months later, the Duke of Norfolk was in Rome, and taking for granted that the letter to Cardinal Nina had been duly received, he spoke to Leo about the cardinalate for Newman. To the Duke's surprise, Leo had never heard of the suggestion to make Newman a cardinal, and asked: "What does Cardinal Manning think of it?"

"It is unjust and untrue to suggest," thinks Abbot Butler, "as Mr. G. L. Strachey does, but without saying it, that Manning had withheld the letter. It had been entrusted to Cardinal Howard to present to the Holy Father on his return to Rome from England, and he had delayed on the journey, not reaching Rome until after the Duke's audience." [1] However that may be, Newman came very near to missing this supreme honor by the delay or carelessness of a bishop with a letter, just as he had suffered previously through Wiseman's delay about Achilli, and Wiseman's carelessness in not presenting Newman's letter about *The Rambler* affair.

Towards the end of January, 1879, Cardinal Nina wrote to Manning that Leo XIII "had intimated his desire to raise Dr. Newman to the rank of Cardinal." Manning sent this letter to Ullathorne, Newman's bishop.

Newman, of course, was delighted. As he expressed it, "the cloud has been lifted forever." Newman knew that receiving this highest dignity in the Church—short of the papacy itself—would forever silence the cavillers who had plagued his life for so many years. But at the same time, Newman was an old man, with only English readily familiar to him, and he did not wish to settle down in Rome. Consequently, in consultation with Ullathorne, a letter was prepared hinting that Newman, instead of living in Rome, as was usual for those cardinals who were not ordi-

[1] *Life of Ullathorne*, II, 109.

naries, would like the privilege of remaining in England. The letter was addressed to Ullathorne:

"My Right Reverend Father:
    "I trust that His Holiness and the most eminent Cardinal Nina will not think me a thoroughly discourteous and unfeeling old man, who is not touched by the commendation of Superiors, or a sense of gratitude, or splendour of dignity, when I say to you, my Bishop, who know me so well, that I regard as altogether above me the great honour which the Holy Father proposed with wonderful kindness to confer on one so insignificant, an honour quite transcendent and unparalleled, than which His Holiness has none greater to bestow.
    "For I am, indeed, old and distrustful of myself. I have lived now thirty years *in nidulo meo*, in my much-loved Oratory, sheltered and happy, and would therefore entreat His Holiness not to take me from St. Philip, my Father and Patron.
    "By the love and reverence with which a long succession of Popes have regarded and trusted St. Philip, I pray and entreat His Holiness in compassion of my diffidence of mind, in consideration of my feeble health, my nearly eighty years, the retired course of my life from my youth, my ignorance of foreign languages, and my lack of experience in business, to let me die where I have so long lived. Since I know now and henceforth that His Holiness thinks so kindly of me, what more can I desire?
                "Right Rev. Father, your most devoted
                                    "John H. Newman."

On the same day, February 3, 1879, Ullathorne sent this letter to Manning, with one of his own. In his letter Ullathorne wrote:

"Dr. Newman has far too humble and delicate a mind to dream of thinking or saying anything which would look like hinting at any kind of terms with the Sovereign Pontiff. . . As I have already said, Dr. Newman is most profoundly touched and moved by this very great mark of consideration on the part of the Sovereign Pontiff, and I am thoroughly confident that nothing stands in the way of his most grateful acceptance except what he tells me greatly distresses him, namely, the having to leave the Oratory at a critical period of its existence, and when it is just beginning to develop in new members, and the impossibility of his beginning a new life at his advanced age.

"I cannot, however, but think myself that this is not the Holy Father's intention, and that His Holiness would consider his presence in England of importance, where he has been so much in communication with those who are in search of the Truth."

On February 4, 1879, Ullathorne wrote a less official letter to Manning, in which he said:

"Newman who is very much affected by the Pope's kindness, would, I know, like to receive the great honour offered him, but feels the whole difficulty at his age of changing his life, or having to leave the Oratory, which I am sure he could not do. If the Holy Father thinks well to confer on him the dignity, leaving him where he is, I know how immensely he would be gratified."

On February 5, 1879, Newman himself wrote to Manning, what is, perhaps, the clearest statement of his attitude:

"I could not be so ungracious, whether to the Holy Father or to the friends at home who have so interested themselves in this matter, as to decline what was so kindly proposed, provided that it did not involve unfaithfulness to St. Philip."

Nearly fifteen years before, when Manning became Archbishop of Westminster, Newman had written to him:

"A year or two back I heard that you were doing your best to get me made a bishop *in partibus*. . . If so, your feeling towards me is not unlikely to make you attempt the same thing now. I risk the chance of your telling me that you have no such intention, to entreat you not to entertain it. If such an honour were offered me, I should persistently decline it, very positively, and I do not wish to pain the Holy Father who has always been so kind to me, if such pain can be avoided."

It must be admitted that Newman's letters in regard to the cardinalate were not so clear and definite as this letter saying that he would refuse a bishopric. It is very strange that both Newman and Ullathorne wrote in such cryptic language in personal letters to Manning. Whether Manning's recollection of Newman's attitude towards a bishopric made him interpret Newman's letters as indicating the same attitude towards the cardinalate, or whether the wish was father to the thought, Manning did interpret Newman's reply on the cardinalate as being a refusal. Abbot Butler calls this "the most unfortunate and unaccountable mistake of his [Manning's] life." He thinks that Newman's statements to Ullathorne and to Manning himself made perfectly clear that he was not refusing the cardinalate, but merely hinting that he wished to remain in England.

On February 15, 1879, Manning started for Rome. This time he was not going to trust to any other hands the communication to Cardinal Nina that Newman had refused the proffered honor. And three days later, on February 18, 1879, *The Times* published the statement:

"Pope Leo XIII has intimated his desire to raise Dr. Newman to the rank of Cardinal, but with expressions of deep respect for the Holy See Dr. Newman has excused himself from accepting the purple."

Butler thinks that "the leakage of the supposed news could be traced to none other than Manning, and the insertion of the note in *The Times* can only have been, as Newman evidently indicates, the act, direct or indirect, of Manning himself."

If Manning really was responsible for the item in *The Times*, it was here that he over-reached himself. For on February 20, 1879, Newman wrote to the Duke of Norfolk:

". . . As to the statement of my refusing a Cardinal's hat, which is in the papers, you must not believe it, for this reason:

"Of course, it implies that an offer has been made me, and I have sent an answer to it. Now I have ever understood that it is a point of propriety and honour to consider such communications sacred. The statement, therefore, cannot come from me. Nor could it come from Rome, for it was made public before my answer got to Rome.

"It could only come, then, from someone who not only read my letter, but, instead of leaving to the Pope to interpret it, took upon himself to put an interpretation upon it, and published an interpretation to the world.

"A private letter, addressed to the Roman Authorities, is interpreted on its way and published in the English papers. How is it possible that anyone can have done this?"

Certainly, as Newman says, it was a gross breach of etiquette, and he implies as plainly as courtesy allows that Manning was the guilty party. This letter of Newman to the Duke was sent to Manning, and while it is always difficult to make conclusive the argument from silence, it is reasonable to think that if Manning had not been guilty he would have entered some denial, and that the denial would have come down to us. Abbot Butler would seem well within the bounds of prudent inference in saying that "the leakage could be traced to none other than Manning." Such a false step on Manning's part may be taken as a measure of his reluctance to see Newman get the honor.

But Manning had left the Duke of Norfolk out of his calculations. The very day that Newman was writing to the Duke of Norfolk, the Duke had called a special meeting of the "Catholic Union," at which resolutions were passed congratulating Newman upon the honor of the cardinalate. These resolutions were printed in *The Times* on February 21, 1879. And immediately on receipt of Newman's letter, the Duke sent it on to Manning with strong representations of his own. Manning was in an awkward position. He had put his own interpretation—and a false interpretation—on a letter to the Roman authorities. At the worst he had published this interpretation, and at the best he had carelessly allowed it to get out. What was the most graceful way of escape from this situation, and of preventing any embarrassing inquiries at Rome as to the leakage? Naturally, it was to present the letter, and to give its author's authentic interpretation. With that decisiveness of action which was always so marked a characteristic of Manning, he took this course.[1] The outcome of the matter was that Manning promptly saw Nina and Leo, and telegraphed Ullathorne that the cardinalate was secure without the obligation of residence in Rome. The actual reception of the cardinalate was May 12, 1879.

Nearly ten years later Lord Selborne bore a filial

[1] It has been suggested that Manning was perfectly honest in his interpretation of Newman's letter, and that he could still have blocked Newman's cardinalate if he had made representations to Leo. I believe that Manning was honest in his interpretation of Newman's letter. But that leaves his carelessness or his officiousness to be explained, and I think that this latter would have discounted any representations he might have made. Moreover, if Manning had serious enough reasons for opposing Newman after so much publicity had been given the offer of the cardinalate, he would have had to explain why he originally acquiesced in the suggestion of the Duke of Norfolk to recommend Newman for the honor.

message from Newman to Leo XIII. Sophia Palmer, Selborne's daughter, recorded that "His Holiness's face lit
up as he said: 'My Cardinal! it was not easy, it was not
easy. They said he was too liberal; but I had determined
to honor the Church in honoring Newman. I always had a
cult for him. I am proud that I was allowed to honor such
a man.' "[1]

In writing to Pusey, Newman said: "If the common
reports are true, the present Pope in his high place as
Cardinal was in the same ill odour at Rome as I was. Here
then a fellow-feeling and sympathy with him colours to
my mind his act towards me. He seems to say:—

" 'Non ignara mali, miseris succurrere disco.' "[2]

At any rate, it is perfectly clear that Newman was
not made a cardinal on account of the importance or
wealth of some diocese of which he was bishop; nor
because of his special activity on the material side of
religion, such as collecting money for Peter's Pence. Newman's only claim to the honor was the place he had made
for himself through his writings. And so the red hat became a seal of approval on those writings.

Abbot Butler thinks "there is no reason for supposing
that the opposition [to Newman's cardinalate] came from
England; the twenty-year prejudice against Newman in
the Curia amply accounts for it." Perhaps. But it was
English opposition in the first place that created this
prejudice in the Curia. And Manning would have shown
greater consistency if he had fought Newman to the very
end. Such uncompromising opposition would have been a

---

[1] *Memoir of Sophia Palmer, Comtesse de Franqueville,* 190;
quoted by Butler, *Life of Ullathorne,* II, 109.

[2] "Not unknown to misfortune myself, I learn to help the suffering."

better guarantee of previous sincerity. Or if Manning had changed his mind, then he should have admitted frankly that his previous attitude had been a mistake.

On March 1, 1879, when it was still thought in uninformed circles that Newman had declined the cardinalate, *Punch* had the following paragraph:

"CORONATUR, NON PILEATUS.

"The Pope, much to his credit, has respectfully offered to Dr. Newman a Cardinal's hat. The venerable doctor, equally to his credit, has respectfully declined it.

"A Cardinal's hat! Fancy Newman in *that*,
      For the crown o'er his grey temples spread!
'Tis the good and the great head would honour the hat,
      Not the hat that would honour the head.

"There's many a priest craves it: no wonder *he* waives it,
      Or that we, the soiled head-covering scanning,
Exclaim with one breath, *sans* distinction of faith,
      Would they wish Newman ranked with old Manning?"

Others besides *Punch* have publicly expressed the opinion that they would have preferred to have seen Newman remain plain Dr. Newman, without the dignity of cardinal. But the conferring of the cardinalate was not a merely personal matter for Newman, and he did not view it in this light. The cardinalate stamped the seal of the Pope himself upon Newman's orthodoxy. And the opposition of Ward, Manning, *La Civilitá, L'Univers*, and all the others, made the final expression of opinion by the Holy See all the more emphatic. The red hat meant that all those for whom Newman had spoken in his bitter struggles against "an aggressive and insolent faction," could now freely give voice to these same ideas.

There have been cardinals, perhaps, whose orthodoxy was somewhat suspect. The sacred scarlet does not confer infallibility. But in the case of any cardinals who may have been justly frowned upon, their reprehensible opinions were enunciated after they had received the dignity. And so we may rightly regard Leo's act in raising Newman to the cardinalate as a clear expression of his own judgment that Newman's views were essentially sound.

On Newman's return to England, there was naturally a round of dinners, receptions, presentations of addresses. It was all very tiring to the octogenarian Newman, but he went through with it for the same reason that he welcomed the cardinalate itself—because it showed his work had been built on firm foundations.

But the finest thing in Newman's cardinalate—from the standpoint of estimating his character—was the simplicity with which he took it. Newman still liked to be called "Father." The scarlet had not spoiled him. He never reached that childish attitude where the dress of office becomes more important than the substance of things.

For the ten years that remained to him after the cardinalate, Newman settled down to about the same old routine which had been his for some time. He wrote a few articles for the secular journals, such as *The Contemporary Review,* and showed that he was still the old Newman. But for the most part, he led as retired a life as ever. Newman's chief joy seems to have been in receiving the old friends who called upon him, and in writing to the friends he could not see.

Newman died August 11, 1890, and by a somewhat curious irony, Manning preached his funeral sermon. In accordance with his own instructions, Newman was buried in the grave of his beloved Ambrose St. John, that two who were so united in life, might not be separated in death. On the pall was his chosen motto, which so beautifully indicated the friendship between the two men, *Cor ad cor loquitur*. The memorial slab bears the words, chosen by Newman, *Ex umbris et imaginibus in veritatem*.

CONCLUSION

Cor Ad Cor Loquitur
NEWMAN'S COAT OF ARMS AS CARDINAL

ALL that was mortal of John Henry Newman has long ago mouldered into dust in that little burying ground at Rednal. But in the more than forty years that have elapsed since Newman's death, it has become certain that he will live forever in his influence. The publication of various series of his letters, the definitive biography by Wilfrid Ward, studies upon various phases of his work, have brought out into ever clearer relief the true greatness of this Roman convert.

But Newman's position in the hearts of succeeding generations rests not so much upon his literary gifts, the external honors that came to him, his theological disquisitions, as upon his integrity of character. In Newman we have the picture of a man who was absolutely sincere, who was true to himself, and so could not be false to any other man; who gave up possible influence with those in authority rather than desert a friend; who never crooked the pregnant hinges of the knee where thrift might have followed fawning; who never truckled to those in power in order to gain advancement for himself; and who because of his sincerity and courage bore up unyieldingly under such coldness, suspicion, and opposition in high circles as would have crushed many a stronger man.

Cor ad cor loquitur—heart speaketh unto heart. To everyone whose heart responds to staunchness in friendship, dauntless courage, and high adventure, with the romance of final triumph over crushing failure and defeat, John Henry Newman will always be an encouragement and inspiration.

In addition to his fundamental sincerity, his inability to play the part of a politician, Newman added remarkable intellectual gifts. Anthony Froude, Hutton, Shairp, Gladstone, and a host of others, no matter how they differed from Newman in religious outlook, bore generous testimony to his mental power. Assuredly, Newman was one of the most eminent Victorians, and not only—as Lytton Strachey put it—because he was an artist in "the magical spices of words."

Added to his intellectual gifts, Newman had literary powers in prose, at least in certain fields, surpassing any of his contemporaries. As a poet, Newman was fair. His novels, in spite of some brilliant passages, are failures. But fundamentally as a stylist, Newman has never been surpassed—perhaps has never had an equal. His powers of description are shown most vividly in that famous passage in *Callista* on the plague of locusts. But it is rather for his insight into the human heart, and his ability to play upon his readers through the medium of language, that Newman is a supreme stylist.

The great force of Newman's style lies in his choice of words, his delicate sense of rhythm, his touching as accurately as a surgeon exactly the right spot in the hearts of his readers by the words he uses. Lewis J. May has insisted upon Newman's rhythm, and he had this in abundance. But it is rather on the psychological side that Newman's true greatness as a stylist lay, and that we should look for the lasting influence of his writings as literature.

It has been customary to emphasize the perfection of Newman's style from a purely mechanical standpoint. Professor Reilly, for instance, in his book, *Newman as a Man of Letters*, tells us "Newman was a great stylist. Not a single page he wrote failed to be perfect of its kind." "Every clause and phrase has its proper place; there is no jostling, no duty of one forced upon the others." But Newman's writing was not perfect, as Professor Reilly implies, because he always kept the rules of classroom rhetoricians. In fact, Newman seems to have had a careless disregard for such rules.

As a piece of effective devotional writing, Newman's *Stations of the Cross* are about as perfect as can be found. But as a theme in Freshman English they would have come back with innumerable corrections. "His agony in the Garden itself," "Christ who had been made sin for us, who knew no sin," "Simon of Cyrene takes the part assigned to him with joy," "these it was that were," are only a few illustrations of passages that an English teacher would red-pencil. And by searching other writings of Newman, such examples could be multiplied indefinitely. "I only thought of the mercy to myself," where "only" is certainly out of place. In the sentence, "He finds the population as munificent as *it* is pious, and doing greater work out of their poverty," Newman has evidently jumbled up the pronouns of multitude.

No, Newman's style would have shocked some professors of English. Nevertheless, Newman was a supreme stylist in the sense I have pointed out. Anyone who studies the examples of irony in *The Present Position of Catholics in England,* or who reads over carefully the first pamphlet in which he published his correspondence with Kingsley, will see with what wonderful skill he uses English to express his ideas. And after all, is not that the purpose of language? Everybody understands what Newman meant in the sentences I have quoted, and what difference does it make if "only" or "itself" happen to be out of place? Newman showed his bigness by not being too careful of such niceties. Bertram Newman is right in calling the great Cardinal "the most eloquent Christian teacher of the nineteenth century." For Newman "has that in him which is beyond eloquence. There are moments when his simplest words come to us charged with an unearthly import, as straight from out the region where he loved to dwell." [1]

In this sense of style, there must, of course, be content. And Newman had the content. He made at least three important contributions to religious thought. First of all, Newman reconciled creedal life and growth with stability in his essay on *The Development of Christian Doctrine.* This essay was really the stroke of a genius, anticipating the philosophical theory of evolution.

Secondly, Newman outlined and defined the *Idea of a University.* He was not successful in carrying out his idea, but to have put it down on paper was an important achievement.

Thirdly, Newman studied the problem of how the human mind comes to assent to truths or propositions, and thereby did manful spade work in a problem that still confronts all believers. Newman sensed that the battle between religion and infidelity was in the field of epis-

[1] *Cardinal Newman,* 212.

temology, and while not final, his *Grammar of Assent* is certainly an important contribution to the literature of the subject.

Huxley has said that he could compile a skeptic's primer from Newman's works, and J. A. Froude maintained that the leading principles of skepticism were first brought popularly before the English mind by Newman himself. All of which goes to show that Newman understood skepticism as well as the skeptics themselves. And if Newman was not entirely successful in meeting the difficulties raised, certainly any less frank facing of the problem will be less successful.

These three books of Newman—*Development of Doctrine, Idea of a University, Grammar of Assent*—are surely immortal. They perpetuate Newman's influence against the ravages of time. Others of Newman's works, as *The Present Position of Catholics in England,* or even his letter on Vaticanism, may become out of date. But the three outstanding books just mentioned will remain as an intellectual monument to their author.

However, Newman does not live merely in his books. As already pointed out, Newman lives in certain movements persisting to our day, which can easily be traced back to him for their origin.

First, there is the Anglo-Catholic movement. Newman deserted it to become a Catholic, but the movement which he started kept on. And to-day it is stronger than ever.

Secondly, Newman started a movement for conversions to the Catholic Church in the English-speaking world that persists full of vigor in our own time. If Newman had never lived, or had never written, certainly the

Catholic Church would have missed some of her most important recruits during the last seventy-five years.

Thirdly, the conversions to the Catholic Church—including Newman's—gave a somewhat different cast to Catholicism in England from what it would otherwise have had. Newman and his fellow converts opened up activities for the Catholic body that they would never have grasped by themselves, or at least never have grasped so effectively. And Newman has not only made innumerable converts for Catholicism, he has also held many born Catholics who might otherwise have seceded. If the extremists like Ward had prevailed, there is no telling what defections might have occurred.

When Newman came home with the red hat of a cardinal, *Punch* addressed him: "Most venerable Cardinal Newman, your Eminence has well earned your Scarlet Hat. It is to yourself, probably, that the Pope owes the reflecting portion of his British converts. A thoughtful man, if any dogma that you subscribe appears nonsense to him, naturally asks himself, whether it is more likely, that you should credit an absurdity, or that he should be an ass."

Many a truth is spoken in jest, and *Punch* has shrewdly put his finger on the fact that Newman was in himself a living apologetic for the Catholic Church. "For what," Baron Friedrich von Hügel has asked, "is the all-important *apologia* for religion wanted in our days? Nothing more nor less—as one of the chief officials of the Vatican Council was fond of insisting to a close friend of mine—than the demonstration, by a large number of actual realizations, of the possibility within the Catholic Church of the combination of a keen, subtle, open-eyed, historical, critical, and philosophical spirit with a child-like claimlessness and devoted faith."

Newman was one such actual realization. But it must be confessed that for many years he got very little encouragement. Manning and his group did everything possible to keep him from being "open-eyed, historical, critical." And no one can estimate what the Church lost by this policy of suppression. In 1854, Ullathorne knew that Newman wanted to write against the infidelity of the age, but "that nothing short of a request from the Pope himself would give him confidence to do so, after the way he was denounced for heterodoxy." [1]

Because of this hesitation on Newman's part, there are those who "speak of Newman as hypersensitive, a *souffre-douleur*. But when count is taken of the nature of the persistent campaign carried on against him in England and in Rome by Ward, Talbot, Coffin, Herbert Vaughan, and with Manning's assent; how such charges as unorthodoxy, unsoundness, disloyalty, worldliness, lowness of view, evil influence, Gallicanism were freely levelled against him during a period of ten years and more; and further when it is remembered that he knew quite well all the time all that was being spoken and whispered against him, so that he felt the cloud he was under: when all this is taken into consideration, it will be recognized that to possess his soul in peace and not to mind, he must needs have been not merely uncommonly thick-skinned, but even rhinoceros-hided."

But Newman's supreme distinction, his greatest right to immortality, lies in the fact that he is a symbol of that perpetual struggle between the reactionary and the developing, between the separatist and the progressive forces

[1] Butler, *Life of Ullathorne*, II, 128.

in Catholicism. One can trace this struggle back to Apostolic times—and even before. For the Pharisees were separatists. St. Paul had Newman's spirit when he was willing to give up the non-essential of circumcision for the sake of getting the Gentiles to accept the essential of Christ's divinity. Cyprian had the reactionary spirit when he insisted that baptism conferred by heretics was invalid; and Tertullian when he would not grant the possibility of forgiveness for certain sins.

Newman stood bravely against the reactionary forces, at the cost of having his own orthodoxy questioned and impugned. Newman fought the good fight, and he won his crown of a cardinalate—and, we may hope, his eternal weight of glory. Moreover, Newman won the fight for others, in the sense that anyone may now without fear preach the principles of development of doctrine, the limitation of papal infallibility, and everything else for which Newman specifically stood.

But Newman did not win the fight in the sense that men of his spirit to-day can without similar opposition do for the twentieth century what Newman did for the last half of the nineteenth century. Anyone to-day who would make as important and new a contribution to contemporary religious thought as Newman made in his essay on development, would meet with the same unthinking opposition Newman met. But, then, neither did St. Paul win the fight in this sense. There will always be reactionaries to oppose the men who think. If St. Paul had won a complete and permanent victory over the forces of reaction, Newman's path would have been smoother.

Our Lord has told us that "every scribe instructed in the kingdom of Heaven is like to a householder, who bringeth forth out of his treasure *new* and old things," *nova et vetera.* True to his name, Newman was such an instructed scribe, and did bring forth new things. But what seems to be true, although Our Lord did not add it, is that those who have been accustomed to the old, will resent the new. The "instructed scribe" will be accused of innovation, of adding to the deposit of faith, of contradicting tradition. And he will have to bear up under a persecution such as Newman suffered. For the reactionaries put their emphasis upon the "old," and they forget that Christ said the instructed scribe would bring forth "new" things as well as old.

And so, at the end of this little life of Newman, one may think of those words of John Ball: "Men fight and lose the battle, and the thing they fought for comes about in spite of their defeat. And when it comes, it turns out to be not what they meant, and other men have to fight for what they meant under another name." Newman in the nineteenth century fought for, under a different name, essentially what Paul fought for in the first century. "Every scribe instructed in the kingdom of Heaven is like to a householder, who bringeth forth out of his treasure *new* and old things."

CHRONOLOGY

1801, Feb. 21: Birth of John Henry Newman.

1817, June: Newman begins residence at Oxford.

1822, Apr. 12: Newman elected Fellow of Oriel College, Oxford.

1824, May: Newman takes Orders and becomes Curate of St. Clement's, Oxford.

1826, Newman becomes Tutor of Oriel.

1828, Newman appointed Vicar of St. Mary's.

1829, Apr. 13: Catholic Emancipation Act passed.

1832, June 7: Reform Bill passed.

1832, Dec.: Newman begins travels on Continent, visiting Rome for first time.

1833, June 16: Newman writes *Lead, Kindly Light*.

July 14: Keble preaches sermon, *The National Apostacy*, marking beginning of Oxford Movement.

Sept.: *Tracts for the Times* begin to appear.

1837, Nov. 13: First Parliament of Queen Victoria.

1838, Aug.: Chartist Riots.

1841, Feb.: *Tract 90* published.

1842, Apr. 19: Newman retires to Littlemore.

1843, Oct. 3: Newman resigns his Fellowship.

1845, Oct. 9: Newman received into the Catholic Church.

1846, English translation of Strauss' *Das Leben Jesu* (Original published 1835).

1847, May 30: Newman ordained priest.

1850, May 9: Lectures on *Difficulties of Anglicans* begin in London.

Oct. 7: Wiseman's pastoral *From Out the Flaminian Gate;* Catholic hierarchy re-established; anti-Catholic riots.

1851, Apr. 6: Manning becomes a Catholic.

June 30: Newman's lectures on *Present Position of Catholics in England* begin.

1852, May: Newman, as rector-elect of the proposed Catholic University, begins his lectures in Dublin on *The Idea of a University*.

June 25: Newman convicted of libelling Achilli.

1856, Apr.: Newman resigns as rector.

1857, Newman asked to edit new translation of Bible. Work soon abandoned.

1859, Darwin publishes his *Origin of Species*.

1860, Apr.: Newman becomes editor of *The Rambler*.

July: Newman's article, *Consulting the Faithful in Matters of Doctrine*, delated to Rome. Newman resigns as editor.

1864, Apr. 21: First part of *Apologia* appears.

1865, Feb.: Wiseman dies and is succeeded by Manning.

1866, Apr.: Newman makes arrangements for house at Oxford; plan blocked by Propaganda; address of laity: "Every blow that touches you inflicts a wound upon the Catholic Church."

1868, Dec. 9: Gladstone becomes premier.

1870, June: Vatican Council passes decree of papal infallibility.

Sept. 20: Italian troops enter Rome.

1873, July: May Laws in Prussia.

1874, Feb. 21: Gladstone resigns as premier, and shortly after publishes his *Vatican Decrees and Their Bearing on Civil Allegiance*. Newman answers with his *Letter to the Duke of Norfolk*.

1878, Feb. 7: Pius IX dies and is succeeded by Leo XIII.

1879, May 12: Newman created Cardinal.

1890, Aug. 11: Death of Newman.

A SHORT BIBLIOGRAPHY

I. NEWMAN'S WORKS

A COMPLETE and uniform edition of Newman's works, as revised by himself during the '70's, is published by Longmans, Green and Co., in 30 volumes. This edition includes a posthumous volume of *Meditations and Devotions*, edited by the Oratorians, and an *Index to the Works of John Henry Cardinal Newman*, by Joseph Rickaby, S.J. In the following list, the date indicates the year in which the book was first published.

Apologia pro Vita Sua, 1864. This is also published in Everyman's edition, and various others. The Oxford University Press has issued an edition with an introduction by Wilfrid Ward, showing the various readings of different editions.

The Arians, 1833.

St. Athanasius, 2 volumes, 1841-4.

Callista, 1855.

Development of Doctrine, 1845.

Difficulties of Anglicans; volume I, 1850, contains Newman's King William Street lectures; volume II, 1865-1875, contains Newman's letter to Pusey replying to Pusey's *Eirenicon;* and Newman's *Letter to the Duke of Norfolk* replying to Gladstone's pamphlet on Vaticanism.

Discussions and Arguments, 1836.

An Essay in Aid of a Grammar of Assent, 1870.

Essays Critical and Historical: volume I, 1840; volume II, 1846.

Historical Sketches: volume I, 1824, 1853; volume II, 1833; volume III, 1834.

Idea of a University, 1852.

Lectures on Justification, 1838.

Loss and Gain, 1848.

Meditations and Devotions (posthumous), 1914.

Essays on Miracles, 1825, 1843.
Discourses to Mixed Congregations, 1849.
Sermons Preached on Various Occasions, 1850.
Parochial and Plain Sermons: I, 1834; II, 1835; III, 1836;
IV, 1839; V, 1840; VI, 1842; VII, 1843; VIII, 1843.
Present Position of Catholics in England, 1851.
Sermons on Subjects of the Day, 1843.
Sermon Notes, 1849-1878.
Tracts Theological and Ecclesiastical, 1871.
Oxford University Sermons, 1843.
Via Media: I, 1837; II, 1841.
Verses on Various Occasions, 1867.

PRIMARY SOURCES

Correspondence of John Henry Newman with Keble and Others,
1839-1845, edited at the Birmingham Oratory: Longmans,
Green and Co., 1917.
  Letters and Correspondence of J. H. Newman, 2 volumes,
edited by Anne Mozley, Longmans, Green and Co., 1890.
  Notes on My Campaign in Ireland, by J. H. Newman
(printed privately, but may be found in several libraries in
the United States as well as in England).

BOOKS ABOUT NEWMAN

The Life of John Henry Cardinal Newman, by Wilfrid Ward,
2 volumes, Longmans, Green and Co., 1913. This is the defini-
tive biography, and contains many extracts from unpublished
letters and journals. For this reason, perhaps, it should be
classed as a primary source.
  Cardinal Newman, by Richard Holt Hutton, Methuen,
1905.
  Cardinal Newman, by J. Lewis May, Dial Press, 1930.
  Index to the Works of J. H. Newman, by Joseph Rickaby,
Longmans, Green and Co., 1914.
  The Anglican Career of Cardinal Newman, by Edwin A.
Abbott, 2 volumes, Macmillan, 1892.
  The Mystery of Newman, by Henri Brémond, Williams
and Newgate, 1907.

Newman on the Psychology of Faith in the Individual, by Sylvester P. Juergens, S.M., Macmillan, 1928.

Newman as a Man of Letters, by Joseph J. Reilly, Macmillan, 1925.

Newman's Apologetic, by J. D. Folghera, O. P., Herder, 1930.

Cardinal Newman and His Influence on Religious Life and Thought, by Charles Sarolea, Edinburgh, T. & T. Clark, 1908.

Cardinal Newman, a Biographical and Literary Study, by Bertram Newman, London, Bell, 1925.

Six Oxford Thinkers, by Algernon Cecil, London, Murray, 1909.

Three Religious Leaders of Oxford and Their Movements, by S. Parkes Cadman, Macmillan, 1916.

Great Oxford Leaders, by Aug. B. Donaldson, Rivington, 1900.

Cardinal Newman, by William Barry, Scribner's, 1905.

WORKS IN WHICH NEWMAN MATERIAL MAY BE FOUND

The English Catholic Revival in the Nineteenth Century, by Paul Thureau-Dangin, Dutton.

The Dawn of the Catholic Revival; The Sequel to Catholic Emancipation, by Bernard Ward. Longmans, Green and Co., 1915.

The Life and Times of Bishop Ullathorne, by Dom Cuthbert Butler, 2 volumes, Benziger, 1926.

William George Ward and the Oxford Movement, by Wilfrid Ward, Macmillan, 1889.

William George Ward and the Catholic Revival, by Wilfrid Ward, Longmans, Green and Co., 1912.

Life of Henry Edward Cardinal Manning, by E. D. Purcell, 2 volumes, Macmillan, 1896.

Cardinal Manning, by Shane Leslie, Kennedy, 1921.

Thomas William Allies, by Mary Allies, Burns, Oates and Washbourne, 1924.

Reminiscences, Chiefly of Oriel College and the Oxford Movement, by T. Mozley, 2 volumes, 1882.

Catholicism: Roman and Anglican, by Principal Fairbairn, 1889.

The Oxford Movement, by R. W. Church, Macmillan, 1904.

John Henry Newman Portraits: 18 reproductions of portraits and photographs selected as being amongst the best and most characteristic in the judgment of those Fathers of the Birmingham Oratory who knew him intimately, Burns, Oates and Washbourne, 1924.

INDEX

Abbott, Edwin A., on Newman, 25, 49
Academic freedom, 98 ff.
Achilli trial, 68 ff.
Acton, Lord, 127
Alfonso, St., 157
Allies, T. W., 94
Anglican Church, ix, 2 ff.
Anglicans, Lectures on Difficulties of, 52 ff.
Arians of the Fourth Century, 11
Armonia, 193
Authority in religion, 180 ff.

Bellarmine, Cardinal, 203
Benedictine Centuries, The, 124
Bible, translation of, 117 ff.
Bonomelli, Bishop, 212
Brémond, Henri, on Newman, 49
Broadhurst, Henry, 46
Brownson, Orestes A., 43
Butler's, Bp., *Analogy*, 15

Cadman, S. Parkes, on *Apologia*, 165
on Newman, xx
Capecelatro, Card., on Manning, 47
Carlyle, Thos., 46
Catholic Church, viii ff.
Catholic Congress at Malines, 177

Catholic Emancipation, 13
Catholic University in Dublin, 76 ff.
Catholics, "old," 36
Catholics and university education, 73 ff., 104 ff.
Catholics in England, xviii, 39 ff.
Cecil, Algernon, on *Apologia*, 166
Certitude in religion, 211 ff.
Church and Democracy, 172 ff.
Church and State, 137 ff., 171, 201 ff.
Civil Allegiance, 200 ff.
Civiltá, La, 193
Conscience, 199 ff.
Controversy in religion, 189 ff., 198 ff.
Conversions, 144 ff.
Coulton, G. G., 162 note
Cullen, Cardinal, xx

Darwin, Chas., xx, 126
Darwinism, xiv
Deism, viii
De Lisle, A. P., on Newman, 80
Development of Christian Doctrine, 30 ff., 43 ff.
De Vere, Aubrey, on Newman, 17
Difficulties of Anglicans, 197 ff.
Disraeli, Benj., on *Tract 90*, 34
Doellinger, J. J. I., on Newman, 51